T0334002

·ing the Asian
·cture Investment Bank

Studying the Asian Infrastructure Investment Bank (AIIB) through the lens of international relations (IR) theory, Chen argues that it is inappropriate to treat the AIIB as either a revisionist or a complementary institution.

Instead, the bank is still evolving and the interaction of power, interests and status that will determine whether the bank will go wild. Theoretically, the current shape of the AIIB will influence global strategic conditions and global perceptions of the bank itself, consequently affecting China's level of dissatisfaction with its power and status in the international financial system and maneuvering in the AIIB. To empirically show that, this book presents the evolution of the AIIB, compares the bank with its main competitors in the Asia-Pacific region, and conducts ten comparative case studies to show how countries around the world have positioned themselves in response to the emergence of the AIIB.

This book presents critical insights for scholars and foreign-policy practitioners to understand China's surging influence in international organizations and how China can shape the world order. It should prove of interest to students and scholars of IR, strategic studies, China studies, Asian studies, developmental studies, economics and global finance.

Ian Tsung-yen Chen is Associate Professor in the Institute of Political Science at National Sun Yat-sen University, Taiwan.

Rethinking Asia and International Relations

Series Editor: Emilian Kavalski

*Li Dak Sum Chair Professor in China-Eurasia Relations
and International Studies, University of Nottingham, Ningbo, China*

This series seeks to provide thoughtful consideration both of the growing prominence of Asian actors on the global stage and the changes in the study and practice of world affairs that they provoke. It intends to offer a comprehensive parallel assessment of the full spectrum of Asian states, organisations, and regions and their impact on the dynamics of global politics.

The series seeks to encourage conversation on:

- what rules, norms, and strategic cultures are likely to dominate international life in the 'Asian Century';
- how will global problems be reframed and addressed by a 'rising Asia';
- which institutions, actors, and states are likely to provide leadership during such 'shifts to the East';
- whether there is something distinctly 'Asian' about the emerging patterns of global politics.

Such comprehensive engagement not only aims to offer a critical assessment of the actual and prospective roles of Asian actors, but also seeks to rethink the concepts, practices, and frameworks of analysis of world politics.

This series invites proposals for interdisciplinary research monographs undertaking comparative studies of Asian actors and their impact on the current patterns and likely future trajectories of international relations. Furthermore, it offers a platform for pioneering explorations of the ongoing transformations in global politics as a result of Asia's increasing centrality to the patterns and practices of world affairs.

Recent titles

Maritime and Territorial Disputes in the South China Sea
Faces of Power and Law in the Age of China's Rise
Edited by Yih-Jye Hwang and Edmund Frettingham

For more information about this series, please visit: https://www.routledge.com/Rethinking-Asia-and-International-Relations/book-series/ASHSER1384

Configuring the Asian Infrastructure Investment Bank

Power, Interests and Status

Ian Tsung-yen Chen

LONDON AND NEW YORK

First published 2021
by Routledge
2 Park Square, Milton Park, Abingdon, Oxon OX14 4RN

and by Routledge
52 Vanderbilt Avenue, New York, NY 10017

Routledge is an imprint of the Taylor & Francis Group, an informa business

© 2021 Ian Tsung-yen Chen

British Library Cataloguing-in-Publication Data
A catalogue record for this book is available from the British Library

Library of Congress Cataloging-in-Publication Data
Names: Chen, Ian Tsung-yen, author.
Title: Configuring the Asian Infrastructure Investment Bank : power,
    interests and status / Ian Tsung-yen Chen.
Description: Abingdon, Oxon ; New York, NY : Routledge, 2021. | Series:
    Rethinking Asia and international relations | Includes bibliographical
    references and index.
Identifiers: LCCN 2020031079 (print) | LCCN 2020031080 (ebook) |
    ISBN 9781138350359 (hardback) | ISBN 9780429435942 (ebook)
Subjects: LCSH: Asian Infrastructure Investment Bank. | Development
    banks—Asia. | Banks and banking, International—Asia. |
    China—Foreign economic relations.
Classification: LCC HG1976.C6 C44 2021 (print) | LCC HG1976.C6
    (ebook) | DDC 332.1/53095—dc23
LC record available at https://lccn.loc.gov/2020031079
LC ebook record available at https://lccn.loc.gov/2020031080

ISBN: 978-1-138-35035-9 (hbk)
ISBN: 978-0-429-43594-2 (ebk)

Typeset in Times New Roman
by Apex CoVantage, LLC

For my wife Jennifer, who is always by my side

Contents

About the author

Ian Tsung-yen Chen is Associate Professor in the Institute of Political Science at National Sun Yat-sen University, Taiwan. His research interests include international relations, international political economy, international organizations and financial politics with a focus on the Asia-Pacific region. His recent research projects focus on political economy of the Asian Infrastructure Investment Bank and the Belt and Road Initiative. His research is published in *Asia Europe Journal*, *International Relations of the Asia-Pacific*, *Issues & Studies*, *The Pacific Review* and *Mainland China Studies*.

Figures

Tables

Abbreviations

ADB	Asian Development Bank
ADF	Asian Development Fund
AfDB	African Development Bank
AIFFP	Australian Infrastructure Financing Facility for the Pacific
AIIB	Asian Infrastructure Investment Bank
AOA	Articles of Agreement
ASEAN	Association of Southeast Asian Nations
BRI	Belt and Road Initiative
BRICS	Brazil, Russia, India, China and South Africa
CDB	Caribbean Development Bank
CGIT	China Global Investment Tracker
CIS	Commonwealth of Independent States
CNPC	China National Petroleum Corporation
CPC	Communist Party of China
DiD	Difference-in-Differences
DPP	Democratic Progressive Party
EBRD	European Bank for Reconstruction and Development
ESEL	Environmental and Social Exclusion List
EU	European Union
FDI	Foreign Direct Investment
FRG	Federal Republic of Germany
GNI	Gross National Income
HHI	Herfindahl-Hirschman Index
IADB	Inter-American Development Bank
ICT	Information and Communications Technology
IFC	International Finance Corporation
IFI	International Financial Institution
IMF	International Monetary Fund
IO	International Organization
ISIS	Islamic State of Iraq and Syria
KMT	Kuomintang
MAC	Mainland Affairs Council
MDB	Multilateral Development Bank

MNC	Multinational Corporation
MOU	Memorandum of Understanding
NDB	New Development Bank
OBOR	One Belt One Road
ODA	Official Development Assistance
OECD	Organisation for Economic Co-operation and Development
OLS	Ordinary Least Square
PRC	People's Republic of China
ROC	Republic of China
SDR	Special Drawing Right
SIT	Social Identity Theory
SOE	State-Owned Enterprise
UN	United Nations
UNGA	United Nations General Assembly
UNSC	United Nations Security Council
UNSG	United Nations Small Group
YPP	Young Professionals Program

Preface and acknowledgments

My kids are big fans of giant pandas, or pandas as most people call them. Although pandas are as big as bears, their adorable appearance makes them look gentle, friendly and harmless. Most of them reside in the mountain ranges of central China, and the Chinese regard pandas as a national treasure. Although physiologically they are carnivores, giant pandas have become adapted to an exclusively vegetarian diet of bamboo. As China's national symbol, giant pandas have long been presented as diplomatic gifts to other countries. "Panda diplomacy" can be traced back to AD 685, during the Tang Dynasty, when the Empress Consort Wu presented two pandas to the Japanese Emperor Tenmu. When China revived its panda diplomacy in the 1950s, zoos in many countries competed to obtain a young giant panda from China. In February 1972, Premier Zhou Enlai of the People's Republic of China (PRC) gave two giant pandas, Ling-Ling and Hsing-Hsing, to the United States during Richard Nixon's trip to China. After the two pandas arrived at the National Zoo in Washington, DC, in April that year, panda-mania swept the US, with the *Washington Post* reporting their arrival under the headline, "Awwwwwwww, They're Cute." First Lady Pat Nixon welcomed the arrival of the pandas in an official ceremony, remarking that "pandamonium is going to break out right here at the zoo." Prior to this, most of the PRC's panda gifts went to other communist countries. From 1957 to 1982, the PRC presented 23 giant pandas to 9 different countries as part of its effort to improve China's diplomatic relations. Eventually, destruction brought about a decline in the number of pandas, forcing the PRC to stop giving pandas as gifts; instead, they were "rented out" or sent abroad for research purposes only. Panda diplomacy epitomizes China's efforts to adopt a seemingly harmless approach in its engagement with the rest of the world.

There is no doubt about it, pandas are superstars in their zoos. They receive plentiful supplies of food and the resources necessary to live a comfortable life. But you have them wrong if you think pandas can be messed with, especially in the wild. Their gentle appearance is deceptive. They have massive chewing muscles – allowing the animal to crack through the tough sheath of a bamboo stem – that can deliver a stronger bite than most carnivores. Unlike captive pandas that are bad at sex, their wild counterparts are aggressive and competitive in courting their mates, and courtship can end up in a group fight. There is a reason why the giant panda is part of the family of *Ursidae*. In the wild, when they are infuriated or frightened, they will spare no effort to crush their opponent.

To some extent, the panda is a metaphor for China's self-proclaimed peaceful rise. Beijing is reassuring the world that its growing military and economic power will not pose a threat to global peace and stability. The Western media also like to caricature a rising China as a gentle-looking panda. Responding to the China phobias and paranoia from the international society, the Chinese government likes to depict China as a giant panda, which is big, but its size has nothing to do with threat, as well as likening China to the animated film character "Kung Fu Panda" who is a loyal and amicable companion and a defender of justice. Indeed, as this book shows, since its emergence into the international financial system, China appears to be behaving like an adorable and benign captive panda, nurtured by the other great powers. When China began to reach out to the world in the late 1970s, it was too weak to inspire fear. The sheer size of the Chinese market made China attractive to many countries. Everyone wanted to get close to China and play a part in the country's development. In this atmosphere of goodwill, China benefited enormously from foreign assistance that fueled its rapid growth. But in international politics, it is quite normal for a country to become more unwilling to accept external constraints as it grows stronger. Its sponsors may begin to see it as a potential rival and may occasionally provoke it. As a result, having once been the darling of the international community, it may suddenly turn into a wild panda that must learn to survive in its own way. Captive pandas with their gentle temperaments cannot survive in an anarchic jungle.

The focus of this book, the Asian Infrastructure Investment Bank (AIIB), is a China-led international financial institution (IFI) that, at present, is behaving like a lovable and docile panda. Countries across all continents are embracing this initiative. In just a few years, it has become the world's second largest IFI in terms of its membership. Most countries seem to love this idea. Even those countries that have refused to join have refrained from criticizing it too harshly. The AIIB does indeed look charming to me as a researcher. China appears to be harmless as it enters the world of international development finance. But is there any possibility that the world is being misled? As the bank evolves, will it and its sponsor, China, continue to behave benignly, or will it execute a U-turn? How will the world react to this possible transformation? This book will respond to these questions in a variety of ways.

The AIIB is young and green and certain to face challenges ahead. I am under no illusion that this book will provide definitive answers to the above questions. My modest goal is to collect and analyze as much data and information as possible so that I can give readers a better understanding of the current configuration of the AIIB four years on from its creation as well as to gauge its likely influence on the world. As the book will show, it is the interaction of power, interests and status that help configure the bank's present and its future. These are the factors that will determine whether this giant panda will go rogue.

My interest in the AIIB has its roots in late 2015 when I was invited to participate in the 44th Taiwan-American Conference on Contemporary China hosted by the Institute of International Relations (IIR), National Chengchi University, Taiwan. This was around the time when the AIIB was beginning to emerge. So, I would like to express my gratitude to Arthur Ding, the Director of IIR, who invited me to present my perspective on the AIIB and encouraged me to delve further into this subject. Later, I was lucky enough to meet Emilian Kavalski, who enthusiastically encouraged me to publish a book on the subject in the "Rethinking Asia and International Relations" series that he edits at Routledge. This book would not have seen the light of day without his recognition and support. I would also like to express my gratitude to Rob Sorsby and his professional team at Routledge who have patiently and tirelessly guided me through the whole publishing process.

My work for this book has benefited from the academic meetings I have attended. They include the 2016 and 2018 NSYSU-UCSD Bilateral Research Symposiums, the 2016 International Jean Monnet Conference Taipei, the 75th Annual MPSA Conference, the NSYSU-CCKF Conference on Xi Jinping's China, the 25th IPSA World Congress of Political Science, and the 2019 Pacific International Politics Conference. I am immensely grateful to organizers and participants who were kind enough to provide me with opportunities to present my AIIB research and also to offer valuable comments and encouragement, among them Mark Beeson, Chang Chia-chien, Chang Tai-lin, Chang Teng-chi, Chang-Liao Nien-Chung, Cosette Creamer, Fang Songying, Sabrina Habich-Sobiegalla, He Kai, Ho Szu-yin, Ayse Kaya, Soo Yeon Kim, Konstantinos Kourtikakis, Dries Lesage, Li Xiaojun, Jessica Liao, Lim Guanie, Lin Wei-hsiu, Ng Kwai, Ngeow Chow-Bing, Aliya Peleo, T. J. Pempel, Pu Xiaoyu, Alexey Semenov, Victor Shih, Shin Chuei-Ling, Sun Guo-xiang, Tan See Seng, Alex Tan, Dennis Trinidad, Joel Voss, Wang Jenn-hwan and Ray Wang. The anonymous reviewers for this book project and for my previous work on the AIIB also gave me valuable advice and insights that helped me refine my ideas.

I started to write this book when I was a postdoctoral researcher at IIR, and by the time I completed the manuscript, I was an Associate Professor at the Institute of Political Science, National Sun Yat-sen University. Those institutions provided me with friendly and supportive environments in which I could concentrate on this book. I enjoyed stimulating interaction and/or administrative support from mentors, colleagues and students during the writing process. I owe an enormous debt of gratitude to Chen Mei-chun, Titus Chen, Daniel Davies, Alice Duan, Dzeng Yi-Ren, Hsieh Chung-ying, Huang Yu-ching, Dachi Liao, April Lin, Frank Liu, Sherry Liu, Lu Shiau-yun, Samuel Ku, Barry Tang, Teng Hsiao-jung, Roy Tseng, Poe Yu-ze Wan, Wen Zhi-hong, Judy Wu, Yang Shang-ju and Nina Yen. I also received outstanding research assistance from Cheng An-chin, Jaylene Fu, Huang Huei-hua, Hsu Chih-hsuan and Lin Ya-ting.

As a student in this field, I was exposed to classic and cutting-edge research in the field of international relations, China studies and methodology during my graduate studies in the United States and Taiwan. Without this, I could not have had the knowledge and tools necessary to bring this book project to fruition. Here, I would like to express my gratitude to Evan Berman, James Fearon, Kou Chien-wen, Kuan Ping-yin, Li Ming-juinn, Lin Jih-wen, Phillip Lipscy, Liu Fu-kuo, Lo Chih-cheng, Alice Miller, Jean Oi, Poong Hwei-luan, Douglas Rivers, Mike Tomz, Tsai Chung-min and Tung Chen-yuan. The support of friends has also kept me motivated to advance my academic career. My immense gratitude in this regard goes to Alan Hao Yang, who has been around to support me on countless occasions. I am also grateful for the constant support and encouragement of Chang Chun-yen, Chen Tsung-Yuan, Eric Chiu, Alex Hsueh, Wu Wen-chin and Yen Yung-ming. I also sincerely thank Judith Fletcher for her constructive suggestions on the manuscript at a time when her home country was under attack by COVID-19.

This book was also made possible thanks to financial support from the Ministry of Science and Technology, Taiwan. Portions of the book have previously appeared as papers in academic journals. The material in Chapters 3 and 4 has been expanded with permission from a 2016 article published in *Mainland China Studies* entitled, "Is China a Challenger? The Predicament of China's Reformist Initiatives in the Asian Infrastructure Investment Bank," and a 2020 article published in *The Pacific Review* entitled, "China's Status Deficit and the Debut of the Asian Infrastructure Investment Bank." Chapter 6 is adapted and slightly expanded from a 2018 article published in *Asia Europe Journal* entitled, "European Participation in the Asian Infrastructure Investment Bank: Making Strategic Choice and Seeking Economic Opportunities." Permission to reuse this material from IIR, Springer Nature and Taylor & Francis is greatly appreciated.

Last on the list, but first in my heart, my deepest gratitude goes to my family, without whom my academic journey – let alone this book – would not even have begun in the first place. I am very grateful to my grandmother, Lin-Hsiao Hua, who devoted her entire life to making sure our lives were better than hers. I deeply regret that she passed away in 2018 before seeing my book in print. I am immensely grateful to my parents, Lin Tsai-yun and Chen Mi-ching; my father-in-law, Tseng En-tan; my sister, Chen Tsung-ying; and my brother-in-law, Wang Tso-lin for the loving and selfless support they have given me in my academic career. My thoughtful daughter Chen Pei-ching accompanied me to my office on many occasions when I was preparing the manuscript. She always asked when the book would be completed. Now I can finally tell her the good news. My son, Chen Yuan-an, became a part of our family during this project and is growing up with my writing. I am indebted to my children's patience, tolerance, laughter and love. I hope someday, when they are old enough to read this book, they will find something useful in it and have a better understanding of the world in which they are growing up and that they will evolve together with the AIIB.

This book is dedicated to my dear wife, Jennifer Tseng, who has been my best companion for two decades, supporting and encouraging me every step of the way in this book project. I am immeasurably grateful to her for tolerating my incessant disappearances into my office. She has a big heart that is always full of trust, supports me in various ways and deals with all the anxiety and stress that has accompanied this undertaking. Nobody has been more important to me than Jennifer in the pursuit of this project.

Ian Chen
April 2020
Kaohsiung, Taiwan

1   Introduction

With the arrival on the scene of the Asian Infrastructure Investment Bank (AIIB) in January 2016, the three international financial institutions (IFIs) most important to Asian development were all headed by people of Asian descent. Jim Yong Kim, the president of the World Bank from 2012 to 2019, emigrated from South Korea with his family at the age of five. He grew up in the United States and dreamed of becoming an NBA player. He was valedictorian of his class and played quarterback for the football team and point guard for the basketball team. After high school, he went to the University of Iowa and then Brown University, where he graduated magna cum laude with a bachelor's degree. Kim obtained his MD at Harvard Medical School and a PhD in anthropology. He was a successful graduate of Ivy League universities who grew up in the most powerful capitalist democracy in the world (Falkenberg, 2011). When he was president of Dartmouth College, Kim was named by US President Barack Obama to head the World Bank. He was an ideal candidate to lead the Bank, whose functions and policy orientation fit well with Kim's educational, professional and ideological background.

Takehiko Nakao, the president of the Asian Development Bank (ADB) from 2013 to 2020, is a Japanese national. He graduated from the elite Tokyo University with a bachelor's degree in economics. He later enrolled in the University of California, Berkeley, where he earned his MBA. Nakao was a career civil servant in Japan's Finance Ministry and was serving as vice minister of finance for international affairs when, in March 2013, he was nominated to head the ADB by the Shinzo Abe government. At that time, both the US and Japan were advanced economies with high living standards. Moreover, both governments and IFIs they headed were leading donors and investors in the Asia-Pacific region. In 2015, the total value of development loans committed by the World Bank and the ADB accounted for about 84% of total investment commitments by all IFIs in the Asia-Pacific region. Moreover, both banks uphold the standards embedded in the neoliberal Bretton Woods system and therefore collaborate closely with each other.

At the time when Kim and Nakao were in charge of these two major IFIs and working hand in hand, Jin Liqun (金立群) was about to be appointed by Beijing as the first president of the AIIB. Unlike Kim and Nakao, who grew up in democratic, capitalist and developed societies, Jin's high school career was interrupted when he was 17 by the outbreak of the Cultural Revolution. While Kim was dreaming of playing in the NBA, Jin was joining Mao Zedong's Red Guards. Later, he was sent to the countryside to work long hours with the peasants in the rice paddies. He would volunteer to work night shifts so that he could get a free supply of kerosene, and he would read a copy of Shakespeare, given to him by a former teacher, by the light of an oil lamp. Two years after the end of the Cultural Revolution, in 1978, the Beijing Foreign Studies University reopened, and Jin was admitted at the age of 29. Although his university planned to hire him as professor of English literature after graduation, he joined China's Ministry of Finance and moved to Washington, DC, in 1981 to start his career as an apprentice representative of China at the World Bank (Anderlini, 2016). By then, the People's Republic of China (PRC or China hereafter) had replaced the Republic of China (ROC or Taiwan hereafter) as the only legitimate representative of China, and the communist regime was transforming from a planned to a market economy. Having grown up under a planned economy, Jin encountered an enormous ideological shock when he started work in an institution practicing neoliberal policies. Instead of shunning the new thinking, he lapped up Western liberal economic theories (Liu, 2007). After two years at the World Bank, in 1983, Jin accompanied China's vice minister of finance to a meeting in the Philippines which marked a new chapter in China's association with the Bretton Woods institutions. That trip involved secret talks with the president of the ADB, Masao Fujioka, regarding the PRC replacing the ROC in that institution. That was Jin's first contact with the ADB. Throughout the 1980s, Jin was responsible for external affairs in the Ministry of Finance. In 1988, he was appointed alternative executive director for China at the World Bank.

After years of working with IFIs on behalf of the PRC, Jin was promoted to the position of director-general of the World Bank Department at the Ministry of Finance and served as vice minister of finance from 1998 to 2003. This was a time when China was becoming actively engaged with the international financial system. The Chinese were given a warm welcome and received some hefty development loans. Chinese nationals started to work in senior positions within international organizations. Sometimes, however, things did not go as expected. When he was a vice minister, Jin accused the World Bank of being politically manipulated to impose Western standards on China's loan projects, one of which had been denounced as involving resettlement plans that would jeopardize the Tibetan people (Blustein, 1999). In particular, he accused the Western media of spreading rumors and deliberately defaming China (China Central Television, 2000).

Twenty years after his first encounter with the ADB, Jin became the first Chinese national to serve as the bank's first vice president, taking over from his Korean predecessor. He ascribed his success to the rise of China. His first big challenge was to work in harmony with Japanese and American executive directors at the ADB. Moreover, he sought to effectively manage the bank's relations with developing countries. He was of the opinion that those countries were always asking for things that the bank could not offer and that their governments were sometimes too corrupt to be allowed to implement the ADB's development projects (Zi, 2009). As Jin worked to improve the bank, he came to the conclusion that it was the time for China to compete with the West in effectively financing developing countries not only in Asia but throughout the world (Perlez, 2006). The Bretton Woods system did not always work well in these areas.

During his career at the ADB, Jin was an active advocate of shortening the project cycle, devising reasonable loan projects that better met borrowers' needs and relaxing stringent loan conditions. While recognizing the need to bail developing countries out of poverty, he also emphasized the importance of encouraging good governance by establishing effective legal and monitoring frameworks in the borrowing countries. He did not believe in overly strict enforcement, however, preferring gradual progress instead. Although Jin spent most of his life working with institutions that upheld liberal ideas, he remained a firm supporter of China's authoritarian communist regime. For example, he recognized that those engaged in research should be allowed to follow their own interests and form their own opinions, but believed they should guard against becoming over-confident and deviating from the central position of the communist party. He encouraged people to extend the scope of their knowledge but, at the same time, thought they should adhere to Marxism, just like Mao Zedong (Jin, 1997).

Although Jin was a member of the Communist Party of China (CPC), he appeared to distance himself from politics. When Beijing first mooted the idea of an Asian Infrastructure Investment Bank, Jin was appointed secretary-general of the Multilateral Interim Secretariat set up to establish the bank. He probably expended most effort on convincing countries that the AIIB was not a Chinese Trojan horse designed to replace the Bretton Woods institutions. Jin stayed low-profile; rather than acting like an aggressive politician, he adopted more of the demeanor of a kindly professor of English literature. His background in Bretton Woods institutions and his self-effacing and apolitical manner helped to persuade the AIIB's prospective members that the bank would pursue a peaceful and cooperative global agenda. He always emphasized the strong track record of the existing institutions and reassured people that he was looking forward to further cooperation. Moreover, he promised that the AIIB would be a good global citizen and adhere to the principles of transparency, openness, independence and accountability. To Jin, the bank is not owned, managed or operated by China; instead, it intends to follow universally accepted practices without bias (Watts, 2015).

By the end of 2019, the AIIB under Jin's leadership had attracted more than one hundred members. But it still has a lot to prove. As this book will show, so far, the AIIB has been happy to comply with the established order, although Beijing retains a firm hold on the reins. The question is, if the CPC wants to lead the bank in a new direction, does Jin have the power to resist and keep it on its original path? Will the AIIB have to make room for China's distinct strategic objectives? Even if Jin himself never has to confront such a dilemma, his successors will have to carry out the adjustments needed to lead the bank in an era of rapidly changing global politics; this could deal them an ideological shock similar to that encountered by Jin when he first joined the World Bank. Back then, Jin was able to accustom himself to the Bretton Woods system. This time, he is the leader of an institution that ostensibly espouses the spirit and practices of Bretton Woods while at the same time following the directives and foreign policy objectives of the CPC. It could be difficult for the AIIB and the Bretton Woods institutions to coexist peacefully for long.

The objective of this book is to understand the possible motivation behind the creation of the AIIB and to gauge the bank's impact on the international financial system. The AIIB is still a rookie in the league, and it is too early to draw any definitive conclusions. Rather than trying to accurately predict and explain the bank's behavior, this book will focus on sorting out the various conjectures about the AIIB and investigating which kinds of these can best help readers understand the bank. Another main concern is how the AIIB is likely to develop in the long term. The evidence provided in this book suggests that although the bank is still on the same page as the other IFIs, Beijing has a considerable amount of power to direct it onto a different course. The bank's future trajectory will depend on how satisfied China is with the world's perception of Beijing's global financial status. If China becomes more discontented with its perceived status and believes that it is not receiving the respect it deserves, Beijing will be more likely to manipulate the AIIB to serve its geo-strategic goals. If that happens, other countries will likely become more suspicious of the AIIB, which will further fuel China's dissatisfaction. This kind of vicious cycle seems very likely. However, if things go in another direction, the AIIB may continue to act as a good global citizen, just as Jin envisages.

In the remainder of this chapter, I will summarize the history of China's engagement with the international financial system since the CPC came to power in mainland China in 1949. This will be followed by an outline of the book's structure and a brief introduction to each chapter.

China's participation in the global financial system

This section offers a brief history of China's engagement with international financial institutions. The first period of engagement was from 1949 to 1980 when China was for the most part isolated from the rest of the world, although, towards the end of the period, it was beginning to engage. The second period covers 1980 to 2000, when China was starting to accommodate and integrate itself into the world. Although there was some conflict at times, China was generally welcomed into the IFIs. Finally, I will look at the period since 2000, when Beijing felt able to express its dissatisfaction with the status quo. Having previously been vulnerable, China was now confident and competent enough to make some noise on the world stage.

Before 1980: prepared for engagement

After the CPC achieved victory in the Chinese Civil War in 1949, it took control of the whole of mainland China. Under Mao Zedong, the country developed into a socialist state with the party in direct control of the economy and society.

However, it was not uncommon to see sharp turns in economic policy, which served the interests and followed the ideology of whichever political faction was in power at the time. Although a series of economic reforms were attempted, they were often accompanied by famine, violence and factional struggle. The economic, political and social turmoil that afflicted China during this period seriously hindered it from starting the engine of economic development. The CPC was forced to look inwards in order to provide the country's basic needs, as it had limited resources or capability to look outwards (Naughton, 2007, pp. 55–84). Internationally, Maoist China did not adopt the cosmopolitan outlook of its predecessor, the Chinese Nationalist Party under Chiang Kai-shek, which cooperated with the Allies during World War II. Memories of the Chinese Civil War and past foreign aggression, combined with domestic political intrigue, made the CPC regime hostile to foreign countries. As a result, during this period, China did not perceive engagement in international economic affairs as a priority.

The PRC could not have participated in international organizations during this period even if it had wanted to. This was because its nationalist rivals, now ensconced in Taiwan, were recognized as representing China in the United Nations (UN) and other key international organizations. Beijing had put a great deal of effort into seeking global recognition as the legitimate government of China with the sole right to represent China in international organizations, thus supplanting Taiwan. Without first securing membership in the UN, China could not apply for membership in UN-affiliated bodies or specialized agencies, such as the International Monetary Fund (IMF) and the World Bank. In most cases, only UN members qualify to join the IMF, and to be a member of the World Bank a country must first join the IMF.

The history of Beijing's attempts to engage with the Bretton Woods system dates back as far as 1950. In February of that year, Bohumil Sucharda, the IMF's director representing both Czechoslovakia and Poland, challenged the legitimacy of the Taiwan government's membership of that organization. The IMF Board of Directors passed responsibility for that issue to the Board of Governors. In August 1950, Premier Zhou Enlai sent a cable to Camille Gutt, the IMF's managing director, claiming that the PRC was the only legal representative of the Chinese people and asking for the ROC representative to be excluded from participation in both the Board of Governors' annual meeting and the World Bank. This request later took the form of a resolution at the annual meeting, proposed by Czechoslovakia and supported by the governors from India and Yugoslavia. The governor from the Philippines said that the resolution was out of order because it was a purely political issue, and it was rejected on a show of hands (Horsefield & De Vries, 1969, p. 258). From 1951 to 1954, the Czechoslovak governor repeatedly proposed the same resolution, but it failed on every occasion when met with opposition from the representatives of the ROC, the Philippines, the United Kingdom and the United States. After Czechoslovakia was expelled from the IMF and the World Bank, the issue was dropped. While the PRC and its ideological allies were on the offensive, the ROC adopted a passive stance. It lost the right to appoint an executive director in 1960 because of the decline in the relative size of its quota and subscription. Consequently, Taiwan was no longer a part of the constituency of any elected executive director of the IMF and the World Bank (Jacobson & Oksenberg, 1990, pp. 60–63).

Having failed to gain entry to the IFIs, China opened another front by courting countries in similar circumstances, in particular, developing countries that were anti-Western and had chosen a socialist path of development. These countries later aligned with Beijing to seize China's seat at the UN. Despite being embroiled in the Cultural Revolution, Beijing signed an agreement with Tanzania and Zambia in September 1967, agreeing to bankroll the construction of the Tanzam Railway. This was a project that the World Bank had rejected as being impracticable and uneconomic (Ashford, 1976). At that time, it was Beijing's largest aid project in the Third World and the third most expensive infrastructure project in Africa. Beijing expected that it would enhance its prestige and influence on that continent. The railway was financed by a generous US$406 million interest-free loan with a grace period of five years. The project would employ between seven and eight thousand Chinese engineers and technicians (New York Times, 1971). The railway was important as it would be the only route for transporting goods from Zambia's copper belt to the Indian Ocean without the need to pass through white-ruled territories (Bailey, 1975). This was the beginning of the PRC's use of its financial clout to enhance its influence.

In October 1971, after years of diplomatic effort by Beijing, the UN General Assembly adopted Resolution 2758 recognizing the PRC as the only legitimate representative of China to the United Nations and ousting the ROC from its seat. The resolution was supported by 76 countries and opposed by 35. The PRC thus became a member of the UN and was set to replace the ROC in all the major international organizations. However, China waited awhile to commence its assault on the Bretton Woods system. Trapped in the Cultural Revolution, and with all of its competent bureaucrats laboring in the countryside, China was in no position to engage with specialized international organizations. Plus, Beijing had not expected to acquire UN membership quite so soon (Jacobson & Oksenberg, 1990, p. 61). In general, the ticket to international organizations had come too fast and China was not ready to respond. This lack of experience prompted the Bank of China to set up a United Nations Small Group (UNSG) in 1972, under the bank's Institute of International Finance. The UNSG was responsible for analyzing issues related to China's prospective membership of the UN's financial agencies, such as the IMF and the World Bank, and it began to observe these institutions closely. While the Cultural Revolution was still in progress, members of the UNSG risked being suspected of harboring pro-Western, capitalist ideas. Thus, an unfavorable domestic political situation delayed China's advance into the Bretton Woods system.

While China was lying low, the president of the World Bank, Robert McNamara, said that he would welcome China's application to join the organization after he received a cable endorsed by Mao himself requesting that the Bank expel Taiwan. McNamara's strong interest in admitting China was based on two concerns. First, the main function of the World Bank was to provide development assistance and it was not appropriate to deprive such a huge country of the chance to access its funds. Second, the Bank's resources and influence would be increased by China's participation. However, McNamara could not get his way immediately because of opposition from the White House. Although President Richard Nixon had broken the ice with Beijing in February 1972 and proposed a Marshall Plan-like financial aid program involving the World Bank (McDonald, 1972), the administration remained cautious about embarking on a political adventure that would damage Taiwan, thus provoking Taiwan's supporters in Congress. Another obstacle to China's entry stemmed from its concern that it would have an insufficient quota of votes. It would only be entitled to a vote share of 1.68% in the IMF and 2.83% in the World Bank. Moreover, Beijing considered the IMF Charter to be hostile to its socialist monetary system. China feared losing control of its foreign exchange policy, which was designed to keep the country self-reliant and insulate the Chinese economy from the influence of external market forces. Finally, China's fiscal policy was opposed to external borrowing (Jacobson & Oksenberg, 1990, pp. 63–65).

To summarize, China's domestic situation in this period was too fragile and the country was too isolated to link up with the global system. The domestic political turmoil generated by Mao's Cultural Revolution deprived the country of a generation of bureaucrats competent enough to engage in international economic affairs. Moreover, powerful member states of major international organizations still supported Taiwan as the official representative of China and were hostile toward Beijing's socialist regime. The PRC and the IFIs appeared to be incompatible. During this period of its history, the PRC could only prepare itself for the next step. In 1978, after Mao's death and the purging of the pro-Cultural Revolution factions, Deng Xiaoping was able to consolidate his leadership and embark on economic reforms that emphasized modernization and development. As the reforms progressed, China became more able to participate in international economic affairs and to take advantage of the benefits of membership of the IFIs.

1980–2000: a rising star

In 1979, the People's Bank of China and the Ministries of Finance and Foreign Affairs delivered a report to the PRC State Council containing the conclusions reached over the past seven years of deliberations by the UNSG and specialists from the Bretton Woods institutions. The report concluded that the overall situation favored an immediate Chinese application to join the IMF. At the same time, the US broke with Taiwan, which had already been expelled from many UN-affiliated bodies, and established formal diplomatic relations with China. Third World countries were also looking forward to China joining major international organizations. For China's top leaders, joining the IMF would be a clear demonstration of the PRC's diplomatic victory over the ROC and provide China with timely knowledge and resources to facilitate its economic development. One downside, however, would be that China would have to disclose economic and financial data deemed confidential by its leadership. The CPC regime was also wary of allowing frequent fact-finding visits by IMF and World Bank officials, and it was reluctant to take on the financial burden of the quota subscription to the IMF and the Bank (Jacobson & Oksenberg, 1990, pp. 69–71).

After weighing up the pros and cons, China decided to take a big step forward. In 1980, the Chinese ambassador to Washington, Chai Zemin, approached McNamara and revealed China's intention to join the World Bank in the coming months. In response, McNamara ordered a small working group to be set up in anticipation of China's membership. Without much controversy, on April 17, 1980, the IMF Executive Board decided that the PRC should represent China in the organization (acquiring membership in the IMF was a prerequisite for joining the World Bank). After this initial approach, negotiations began between China and both institutions. The main issues were China's quota and the disposition of gold reserves. Although the ROC's initial subscription had been the IMF's third largest, Taipei had been economically and financially too weak to increase its subscription as the IMF expanded its shares. Also, Taipei was blocked from participating in important IMF and World Bank gatherings after Taiwan was expelled from the UN in 1971. As a result, China's quota relative to that of other members fell, which not only led to a decline in its voting power and access to funds but also deprived the ROC of the right to appoint an executive director. The PRC was dissatisfied with its disadvantageous position in the IMF when it took over the ROC's seat. After a series of meetings and negotiations, the IMF agreed to allow an increase in China's quota from Special Drawing Right (SDR) 1.2 billion to 2.39 billion in 1983; thus China as represented by the PRC secured the ninth largest number of shares, giving it 24,159 votes, or 2.58% of the total. That qualified China to constitute a single constituency that could elect its own executive director. The gold reserves dispute concerned whether the PRC could inherit the gold and other obligations left by the ROC. At Washington's insistence, Taipei was allowed to purchase the gold at the official price. Taiwan was also permitted to repurchase SDR 124.1 million using US dollars to restore China's reserve tranche position. This gave the PRC a clear credit position upon joining the IMF. Unlike the happy ending of the quota issue, the problem of the gold reserves disposition infuriated PRC officials (Jacobson & Oksenberg, 1990, pp. 75–77).

Right after the PRC secured its membership in the IMF, on May 17, 1980, the World Bank's Board of Governors decided to expel the ROC and admit the PRC as the sole representative of China. The decision met with opposition from the US government under President Jimmy Carter, which anticipated a furious reaction from Congress. At that time, the White House was seeking congressional support for its Seventh International Development Association Replenishment proposal for the World Bank. Nevertheless, the PRC's entry into the World Bank and the associated negotiations went more smoothly than they had done for the IMF, thanks to McNamara's persistence and rising US enthusiasm for entry into the Chinese market. Beijing was given 12,250 votes, or a 2.84% share, which allowed China to constitute a single-state constituency (Jacobson & Oksenberg, 1990, pp. 77–78). Of the two flagship Bretton Woods institutions, the World Bank interested China more than the IMF; membership in the latter involved having its economic and financial policies monitored, while the former could provide much needed financial support for China's ongoing economic reforms (Vogl, 1980a).

After settling down in the IMF and the World Bank, the PRC turned its attention to another important IFI, the Asian Development Bank. Beijing first indicated its intention to join the ADB in 1983 when Minister of Foreign Affairs Wu Xueqian approached the ADB president, Masao Fujioka. Beijing wanted to see the ROC expelled at the same time, but Fujioka considered that to be against the rules laid down in the bank's charter. The ensuing deliberations ended in stalemate. In response, Beijing indicated that it was willing to accept a compromise solution, including an option that would allow Taipei to remain a member providing it did so under a title that the Chinese found satisfactory. In 1985, the PRC confirmed its intention to join the ADB and sent a working group to the bank's 18th annual meeting in Bangkok in order to urge delegates to advance the PRC's admission. On February 17, 1986, on the recommendation of the ADB Board of Directors, the ADB Board of Governors approved the PRC's membership, allowing the ROC to remain under the title "Taipei, China" (McCawley, 2017, pp. 144–146). China's subscribed 114,000 shares, about 7% of the total, which allows it to elect an executive director. Only the US and Japan had more votes than Beijing. Membership in the ADB not only provided China with financial assistance but also offered investment opportunities for Chinese companies. The ADB charter restricts procurement in non-member countries.

In addition to participating in regional institutions, China sought, during this period, to extend its financial influence to other continents. For example, the People's Bank of China began investigating the African Development Bank (AfDB) and, in September 1984, dispatched a mission to its headquarters in Abidjan, Côte d'Ivoire. The following year, after China had subscribed the required number of shares, the AfDB accepted China as a non-regional member. China's initial share subscription amounted to US$60.32 million. Although, as a non-regional member, China could not apply for financial assistance from the AfDB, Chinese companies would now be eligible to bid for the bank's projects. In 2018, China's voting power in the AfDB accounted for 1.083% of the votes. China approached the Inter-American Development Bank (IADB) in March 1993, sending a People's Bank of China delegate to Hamburg, Germany, to participate in the IADB's 34th annual meeting as an observer. Another delegate was dispatched as an observer to the 23rd annual meeting of the Board of Governors of the Caribbean Development Bank (CDB), held in Barbados in May 1993. In August and September 1993, respectively, China formally submitted applications to join the IADB and CDB. China's membership of the CDB was approved in May 1997; Beijing subscribed to 5.45% of the shares, making it eligible to elect its own executive director. Admission to the IADB came somewhat later, on January 12, 2009. It only subscribed to 184 shares, a trivial 0.004% of the total. Rather than economic benefits, Beijing saw engagement with these regional financial institutions as a way of enhancing its political and diplomatic influence in Africa, Latin America and the Caribbean, where many of Taiwan's diplomatic allies were located. Beijing realized that it could use financial incentives to sabotage Taiwan's international relations.

After settling the membership issue, China actively participated in and interacted with the IFIs, especially the IMF and the World Bank. China seized the opportunity to host academic and professional workshops, conferences and other activities, and to gain the advice, techniques and knowledge necessary for its reform and development schemes (Sutter, 2008, p. 117). Chinese bureaucrats began to be exposed to Western ways of financial management. Moreover, in order to fulfill its reporting responsibilities, Beijing took the opportunity to learn statistical data collecting methods that were compatible with those of the Bretton Woods institutions. China was also keen to invite fact-finding delegations from the IFIs to China. This was useful for the World Bank, as when China joined, the Bank itself had little knowledge of China's economic and financial system, and the question of which kinds of projects and levels of commitment would be appropriate to sustain a country with a population of one billion was still a mystery (Vogl, 1980b).

Aside from capitalizing on the benefits of membership in the IFIs, the Chinese delegations raised a number of concerns during the annual meetings of the IMF and the World Bank. They complained about the developing countries' large exchange rate fluctuations, which they thought arose from weak macroeconomic coordination among the major industrial countries. Moreover, Beijing urged the IMF and the Bank to boost their financial commitments to developing countries, which suffered from unfavorable trade terms resulting from growing trade protectionism. China also called on the industrial countries to shoulder greater responsibility for relieving the developing world's huge burden of debt. After the Asian financial crisis of 1997, Beijing called for a coordinated international bailout of the region. Aside from global economic issues, China started to turn its attention to institutional matters within the Bretton Woods system. On the issue of quota distribution, China drew attention to the decline in the proportion of shares subscribed by developing countries and urged the institutions to improve the principles and methods of share allocation so that the power of the developing countries was enhanced, rather than diluted. Beijing was also concerned about its own representation in the IFIs. The Chinese delegation to the annual meeting of the IMF Board of Governors in 1995 expressed grave concern that it had dropped to 16th place in terms of share of the votes, despite the country's gross domestic product (GDP) having grown by an average of 9% over the previous 16 years.

During the 1980s, US President Ronald Reagan appointed A. W. Clausen to succeed McNamara as the World Bank's president. The Bank's relationship with its largest shareholder was strained under the Reagan administration which was skeptical of the institution and saw its poverty alleviation projects as a welfare giveaway. It was, therefore, unwilling to take on further international financial responsibilities. This was the time when China had just joined the World Bank and was seeking financial assistance. China criticized Reagan's policies toward the Bank and worried that Clausen, as a former president of a commercial bank, Bank of America, would run the World Bank along more commercial lines and might significantly reduce the Bank's financial commitments to the Third World. To counteract the Reagan administration's passivity, China even issued a procurement order that barred American companies from bidding for a rubber development project in southern China that was to be financed by a World Bank affiliate (Farnsworth, 1983).

Aside from Beijing's dispute with Washington, China's participation was also a new source of stress to the World Bank and to other developing countries. The latter feared that the entry into the Bank of a country as big and populous as China would result in a reduction of fund allocations to other members. India, the largest borrower, and other major loan recipients would have suffered the most from this (Francis, 1982). During the 1980s, India, on average, obtained US$2.4 billion per year from the World Bank, while China received US$966 million. The change in their relative shares occurred in the 1990s (see Figure 1.1). On average, during that decade, China obtained about US$2.6 billion annually while India received US$1.8 billion. The same pattern may be observed in relation to Brazil, which was another major borrower. In 1984, the Bank even set a ceiling for the combined borrowings of China and India at 40% of the commitments allocated to the poorest countries for the next three years (Wall Street Journal, 1984).

Although China managed to cultivate good relations with the West through most of the 1980s, it encountered a major setback in the World Bank in June 1989 as a result of its military crackdown on the student-led demonstrations in Beijing's Tiananmen Square. Fang Lizhi, the respected dissident astrophysicist whose liberal ideas inspired the students on the street, urged Western societies to gradually divest from China and the World Bank to suspend its loans and credits. Fang also criticized the fact that only 10% of World Bank commitments to China were earmarked for education (Cuomo, 1989). In response to Fang and other critics of Beijing, the ADB and the World Bank postponed new loans to China. The ADB's scheduled loan package that was put on hold amounted to US$5.59 billion, one of its biggest project loans ever (Brauchli, Guenther, &

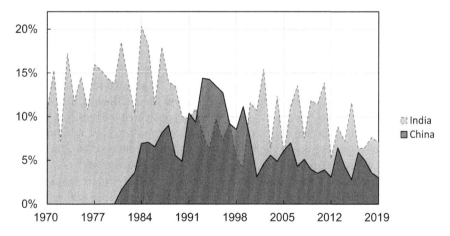

Figure 1.1 Percentage of World Bank loans received by China and India
Source: Projects & Operations, The World Bank

Hunt, 1989). The US under the George H. W. Bush administration used its influence as the largest shareholder in the World Bank to force the Bank to delay US$780.2 million in loans to China indefinitely, but it did not block the US$8 billion in loans that had been granted earlier (Wechsler, 1989). Even though China tried to persuade the Bank to resume its financial assistance during the 1989 annual meeting, the US, Japan and other industrial countries decided to continue the sanctions (New York Times News Service, 1989). The cut in funds can be observed in Figure 1.1. The total commitments received by China in 1989 were down 28% from the previous year, and this was followed by another drop of 16% in 1990.

As foreign governments were pulling out of China, the Bank's bureaucrats responsible for Chinese affairs went in the opposite direction and fought to sustain normal relations. Shahid Javed Burki, the head of the World Bank's China Department at the time of the Tiananmen Incident, recommended to the Bank's president that he should resist political pressure from the G7 countries to suspend loans because China remained creditworthy. Moreover, China was still pursuing macroeconomic policies that aligned with those of the Bank and continued to implement projects effectively (Gill & Pugatch, 2005, pp. 126–127). Thanks to support from the Bank's senior management and the efforts of the Bush administration to improve relations with China, a US$30 million loan for earthquake relief was approved in 1990 (Farnsworth, 1990). From Figure 1.1, we can see that after that date, the Bank accelerated its loans to China to such an extent that, in 1991, China surpassed India as the Bank's largest borrower. This advantage was sustained throughout the rest of the 1990s.

On June 22, 1999, China suffered another setback in the World Bank when a loan for its "Western Poverty Reduction Project," in the provinces of Gansu and Qinghai, was postponed by the World Bank Board of Directors. Because the project was to involve the resettlement of 58,000 farmers from an ethnic Tibetan area, it was considered to constitute a threat to Tibetan cultural identity. Those opposing the resettlement program feared that it would dilute the population of ethnic Tibetans in western Qinghai province (Sanger, 1999). These fears were echoed by advocates for Tibetan independence and several members of the board. The postponement of the loan came around the same time as the NATO bombing of the Chinese Embassy in Belgrade, which further heightened tension between China and its Western fellow-members of the World Bank (Blustein, 1999). In a subsequent meeting held two days later, the board considered the president's loan recommendation again and this time approved a sum of US$160 million. The chairman noted that the board appreciated the assurance conveyed by Zhu Xian, the Chinese executive director, that China would fully cooperate with and facilitate any investigation of the project authorized by the board (International Bank for Reconstruction and Development, 2019). Although this episode did not cause too much trouble for China, heightening awareness of environmental issues and the need for sustainable development during the 1990s put increasing pressure on China's authoritarian government to address such impacts as early as possible (Zweig, 2002, pp. 235–236).

Despite experiencing some setbacks after it embarked on its adventure with the Bretton Woods institutions, China did not walk away. Instead, Beijing institutionally accommodated itself to the World Bank's operations. First, China established a special division in the Ministry of Finance charged with coordination with the World Bank. Second, it set up the China Investment Bank to allocate project funds issued by the World Bank and the ADB. Third, China eventually compromised on the Bank's requirement for international competitive bidding. Beijing initially opposed competitive bidding, especially for road and dam projects, which required a huge labor force, because it believed it should be allowed to favor domestic companies. The Chinese were eventually forced to give in when faced with the Bank's insistence on this practice. After that, Chinese industries changed their mentality and improved their skills and knowledge in the face of global competition. As a result, China became more capable of bidding successfully for large-scale construction projects around the world (Lardy, 1999, pp. 211–212).

In sum, during the 1980s and 1990s, the world came to realize that it was inappropriate to exclude the world's most populous country, China, from participating in the international financial system. After the PRC replaced the ROC in the major IFIs, the government in Beijing began to interact in earnest with those institutions, thereby gaining not only knowledge and technical experience but also the financial assistance critical to the advancement of its domestic economic reforms and development. Although its authoritarian methods occasionally provoked opposition from the international community, enthusiasm for engaging with China among foreign governments and the IFIs eclipsed their concerns about the communist regime. China seized this opportunity to accommodate and integrate itself further with the international financial system. As a result, China was able to maintain its popularity and become the largest beneficiary of the Bretton Woods institutions. By the end of this period, it was ready to embark on the next stage.

After 2000: confident but unhappy

As the world entered the twenty-first century, China's impressive economic growth was fueled by domestic reforms, integration into the IFIs and trade liberalization. Not only did China rise in terms of its national macroeconomic indicators, it utilized its accumulated wealth in its interactions with the rest of the world. This wealth mainly came from China's massive trade surplus during the period as well as the vast amounts of inward foreign investment and development assistance it received. During the first decade of the century, China became a major global buyer of primary goods and achieved a dominant position in the region. Its geo-economic power grew more salient year after year (Chen, 2014). Moreover, China started to spend and invest its capital around the world. As we can see from Figure 1.2, China's overseas investments and foreign aid increased enormously. By 2017, the value of China's outward investments hit a plateau at around US$175.6 billion. The massive increase in outward investment was part of Beijing's "go out policy," or "going global strategy," initiated in 1999. These initiatives were driven by the need to use China's huge foreign reserves, to address

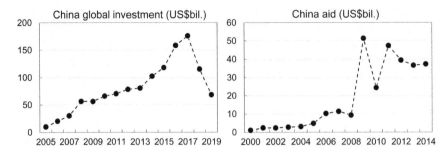

Figure 1.2 China's global aid and investment since 2000

Source: Data comes from Scissors (2020) and Dreher et al. (2017).

the upward pressure on the value of the renminbi, to seek external financial opportunities and to support China's then shaky state-owned industrial sector.

In addition to investments, China also increased its foreign aid. Although it is difficult to obtain clear and consistent official data on China's foreign aid, scholars estimate that China's official development assistance (ODA) rose from US$2.4 billion in 2001 to US$37.3 billion in 2014. This rise coincided with the decline in its share of World Bank financial commitments. China was no longer receiving the largest share; that position was reclaimed by India, while countries like Brazil, Indonesia, Mexico, Pakistan and Turkey also inherited some of China's lost share. As well as being a debtor, China became a major global creditor, conducting government-to-government lending and expanding its global investments through state policy banks, state-owned enterprises and official agencies. Its state-led creditor status consequently enhanced its financial, as well as its political, influence over the countries to which it was lending (Chin & Helleiner, 2008). While commercial considerations remained important to the state's finance department, the way that aid could be used to serve China's diplomatic objectives was no less important to Chinese leaders (Varrall, 2016). At this stage, China was no longer satisfied with waiting passively for capital to flow in from outside. It had become a wealthy and confident nation that sought to engage the outside world in its own way.

The gap was narrowed between China and other powers in the region. In macroeconomic terms, China had already outperformed Japan in exports of goods and services by 2005, and by 2010, it had a higher GDP. The gap in economic performance between China and India had begun to widen in the 1990s. China was also trying to catch up with the US, the most powerful country in the world. Quantitatively, China has surpassed the US on several macroeconomic indicators. Figure 1.3 shows that, in terms of global share, China is the largest trading country, has the greatest reserves and has the most resources important to national capability. In addition, China's GDP, outward investments and military expenditure are approaching those of the US, although it is not likely to catch up soon. These impressive economic results boosted China's confidence still further as it developed its engagement in international financial affairs. The Chinese felt comfortable contributing a larger share of their wealth to developing countries through government-to-government or private channels. But more than just money was needed if Beijing were to assume a greater role in the system; it had to receive recognition and approval from the system's dominant players.

China's predicament is apparent in Figure 1.3(i) which shows that its voting power in the World Bank was not commensurate with its economic strength. It manifests that the Western-dominated global economic system did not feel ready to allow China more space to accommodate its rise. As a result, Beijing started to show its dissatisfaction with its global status. China's main complaints were that, first of all, the Western-dominated IFIs had refused to bail out China's neighbors during the Asian financial crisis of the late 1990s unless they accepted the IMF's neoliberal cure. China condemned these neoliberal conditionalities for threatening the recipients' economic, political and social stability (Rosser & Tubilewicz, 2016). Second, China criticized the West for making their foreign aid conditional on recipients' domestic factors, such as the style of governance and human rights performance. Vivid examples of how this affected China in relation to the World Bank were discussed earlier. Third, major donors had shifted their aid budgets from the production and physical infrastructure sectors to social infrastructure, such as education and health (Dreher, Fuchs, & Nunnenkamp, 2013). China considered the needs of the former sectors to be more urgent. Besides, Western-led

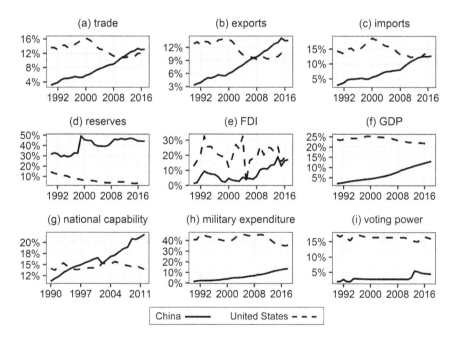

Figure 1.3 The change in Sino-US relative power since the 1990s

Sources: Data for (a), (b), (c) come from United Nations Conference on Trade and Development; data for (d), (e), (f), (i) come from the World Bank; data for (g) come from National Material Capabilities (v5.0) in Singer, Bremer, and Stuckey (1972); data for (h) come from SIPRI Military Expenditure Database.

investment in social infrastructure might undermine a communist society. Fourth, China was unhappy with the international financial system's underappreciation of its financial status, manifested in particular by China's lack of voting power in the Bretton Woods system, underrated sovereign credit and lack of appreciation for the renminbi's international status (Chen, 2020).

China's confidence was growing during this period due to its increasing power and active participation in many important international organizations. It was also seeking to mobilize other emerging countries to join it in managing global affairs in a way that provoked hostility in the West. Yet, China was dissatisfied with how it was perceived in the world. Beijing was unhappy that the current system was not able to adjust itself to embrace a rising China and other emerging economies, but it did not abandon the established IFIs. Instead, Beijing spent a great deal of effort establishing an IFI of its own, the AIIB. This new bank can be seen as China's hedge against the possibility that the Western-dominated institutions would dismiss China's complaints (Feigenbaum, 2017). For some people, the arrival on the scene of the AIIB demonstrates China's position as the world's second largest economy and as such deserving of more respect and a higher status. It could help to shape new global institutional arrangements (Ren, 2016).

The emergence of the AIIB was a reflection of China's situation in the world. China was isolated from the global financial system before 1980 as the ROC represented China in the UN and the PRC was not ready to rise. During the following two decades, economic reform provided Beijing with the resources and opportunities it needed to participate in the international financial system. China was welcomed into the Bretton Woods system despite its autocratic regime. Western countries expected that their financial assistance would not only facilitate economic reform in China but might also trigger political reform. As China stood up economically and started buying up the world, it became a confident but unhappy great power. Political reform has not ensued. There is still a huge gap between China and the Western powers regarding views on how the world should be managed. Unable to get what it wants from the current system, China now has the ability to create a system of its own. We need to give serious attention to how this new system will interact with China and the rest of the world. The emergence of the AIIB is not a purely economic matter. The bank will have a no less important role in shaping global politics.

Structure of the book

The story behind China's entry into the international financial system helps us to understand how it has reached the point of being able to create its own IFI, the AIIB, just 35 years after it entered the Bretton Woods system. This book focuses on two major topics. The first is the probable motivations for China's creation of the AIIB and whether the AIIB's actual behavior corresponds to those motives. The second is the world's reaction to the AIIB. China's motivations are dealt with in the first part of this book. I present the current debates about the AIIB, discuss the evolution of the bank and how it compares with its main competitors in the Asia-Pacific region – the ADB and the World Bank. The second part focuses on how countries around the world have positioned themselves in response to the emergence of the AIIB. Analyses in this part show that each country's reaction depends on its strategic and economic concerns. Methodologically, this book employs both quantitative and comparative case studies to test the main arguments. The book is grounded in theories of international relations, international political economy and international organizations.

In Part I, Chapter 2 establishes the theoretical foundations for the book. It presents a survey of scholarly works concerning the AIIB and tries to gauge China's motivations accordingly. In general, these scholars either suspect China's geopolitical and geo-economic ambitions or welcome the AIIB as an effort by China to coordinate financial resources and use them to improve regional infrastructure. There is also a less discussed theory that the AIIB is configured to have a reputational effect, and rather than merely being a material instrument, it is a diplomatic tool for reassuring the international community that China's rise is peaceful and that it is simply seeking international recognition for its status as a great power. These different perspectives thus yield different propositions as to how other countries perceive and interact with the China-led AIIB. These discussions are accompanied by corresponding scenarios concerning the AIIB that can be adopted to test which perspectives may be most useful for understanding the bank. This chapter seeks to integrate those contending perspectives in order to provide a systematic framework to explain the underlying logic of the configuration of the AIIB.

Chapter 3 follows the theoretical foundation of the previous chapter and tracks the configuration of the AIIB from its inception to the end of 2019. We see that, when China first conceived the idea of creating the AIIB, it is likely to have seen the AIIB as a potential competitor for the other IFIs. However, the bank has evolved to become more cooperative and inclusive since then, and China's geopolitical considerations are taking a back seat. This transformation may be the result of a reduction in China's status deficit – the gap between the world's perception and China's perception of its financial power. This argument is tested by comparing the external circumstances China was in before and after 2014 as well as quantitative analyses of whether the AIIB was configured to promote China's geopolitical interests and whether the bank's loans were distributed in such a way as to promote those interests. The findings in this chapter suggest that, as long as China retains tight control over the AIIB, the dynamic of its status deficit may influence the future trajectory of the bank.

After investigating the longitudinal evolution of the AIIB, Chapter 4 presents cross-sectional analyses that compare the AIIB with the ADB and the World Bank. The results suggest that the AIIB shares the other IFIs' often-criticized power concentration problem. The only difference is that China is the boss. When we compare the institutional design of the AIIB with that of the ADB and the World Bank, the AIIB does not appear to be a norm challenger. However, comparing the three banks' concerns for the environmental and social impacts of loan projects, the AIIB deviates slightly from best practice both legally and in practice. Nevertheless, no crystal-clear evidence can be found to suggest that a serious problem of a race to the bottom will emerge anytime soon. As for the issue of loan competition, research findings show that the ADB has boosted its financial commitments in several respects, while the World Bank behaves ambiguously. Although the AIIB certainly has the potential to challenge the status quo while it is under China's control, such ambition may be thwarted by its current configuration.

Having examined the AIIB itself, I switch focus to other countries' responses to it. In Chapter 5, I investigate the interaction between the AIIB and the countries of Asia and Oceania. My findings indicate that these countries, in general, have a positive and optimistic view of the emergence of the AIIB. But different levels of geopolitical and geo-economic concern have led each country to take a distinct approach to their engagement. This chapter deals with India, Indonesia, Kazakhstan and the Pacific island countries as one case. Although the bank is considered complementary in the region, India is the most alert to the trajectory of the AIIB and seeks a stronger role in restraining it. Medium-sized powers like Indonesia and Kazakhstan, on the contrary, are much less interested in the bank's politics and care more about getting their hands on funds. The influence of the Pacific island countries in the bank is trivial. But their unique strategic position enhances their popularity with the IFIs. There is rivalry among the great powers over loans or grants to the countries of Oceania.

Chapter 6 explains why some European countries decided to join the AIIB as founding members at a time when their powerful strategic ally, the United States, asked them to walk away. An explanatory framework shows that each European country's decision depended on the configuration of its strategic triangle with Beijing and Washington, as well as its level of economic dependence on and perception of opportunities in Asia. A quantitative analysis and three comparative case studies of Germany, Belgium and Romania are employed in this chapter. The findings suggest that countries that have already established a strategic partnership with China and are more extensively engaged in Asian markets are the biggest enthusiasts for the AIIB. Germany was the most likely to join the AIIB because of its strategic partnership with China and its eye for business opportunities in Asian markets. Belgium has remained lukewarm due to its low level of dependence on Asia, weak infrastructure investment momentum and dire financial difficulties. Romania did not participate in the bank at the beginning due to its need for a close strategic partnership with Washington and relatively low dependence on Asian markets.

In Chapter 7, I look at countries that had, by the end of 2019, refused to join the AIIB. This group of countries sees the potential benefits as being ambiguous. At the same time, they carry a high level of strategic concern about a rising China. Concern is highest among China's traditional power rivals in the region, including the US and Japan, as well as Taiwan, which is under military threat from China. Washington and Tokyo fear that their endorsement of the AIIB would further boost China's comprehensive power capability in the region and jeopardize their power and influence in the global and regional financial system. For Taiwan, joining the bank would involve the risk of a gradual degradation of sovereignty. These countries' apprehension concerning the strategic threat posed by China tops any prospect of economic benefit. As a result, they keep the AIIB under extreme scrutiny.

Chapter 8 concludes the book with the main findings. First, the book demonstrates how the AIIB internally reflects the power transition phenomenon and may potentially become a revisionist instrument. Second, it shows that in practice, the AIIB is behaving itself in its relations with the rest of the world. In the final part of this chapter, I make an initial comparison between the AIIB and China's Belt and Road Initiative (BRI). The results indicate that BRI projects are more likely than those of the AIIB to go to countries that are on the same wavelength as China. Readers may not find enough empirical support for the argument that the AIIB is revisionist. However, this book wants to remind readers that, although the AIIB is continuing to display self-restraint, it may be depicted as a hidden dragon that has the potential to allow China to expand its influence. Its future path may depend on how China perceives and situates itself in the world as it interacts with its main global competitors. This will be a dynamic process. Thus, countries around the world should be paying close attention to the AIIB and adjusting themselves as their strategic positions change. This book records the history of the AIIB up to the point of its fourth anniversary. More changes can be anticipated in future decades.

Part I

Evolution of the AIIB

2 An integrative framework

Power, interests, status and global responses

This chapter will discuss the literature dealing with China's motivations for creating the AIIB. Probably the most relevant literature examines whether IFIs, such as the World Bank, ADB, or AIIB, serve the interests of one or another of the great powers or the international community as a whole. For realist scholars, international organizations (IOs) are epiphenomenal to state power and interests. They cannot change the nature of the anarchic world that leads to concerns about anarchy, uncertainty, self-interest and relative gain. The IOs are created to serve the interests of the great powers rather than to provide public goods that can be evenly shared and enjoyed by all in an unselfish and unbiased way. According to this school of thought, one should not expect that the emergence of IOs will result in peace and stability (Mearsheimer, 1994). Indeed, existing IO literature finds that the operation of IFIs is associated with the interests of the great powers. They can use their institutional power to influence the weaker member states politically and strategically. For example, Kilby (2006) argues that the ADB's loan decisions reflect the interests of the major donors (i.e., Japan and the US). One cannot deny the hidden political agenda within the ADB. A similar situation may exist in the Bretton Woods institutions. Research suggests that developing countries more closely aligned with the US have a higher chance of receiving loans or receiving loans with lower levels of conditionality (Kilby, 2009; Thacker, 1999). Scholars working from this perspective see the IFIs as instruments of the great powers, used to fulfill their political or strategic agendas. Even though the IFIs are not directly related to security issues, they cannot escape the great powers' strategic maneuvering.

In contrast to this realist pessimism, neoliberal institutionalists see the emergence of IOs as a solution to the self-interest dilemma. Although not denying that international society is anarchic, they consider states' refusal to cooperate as a problem of coordination. If the level of concern about relative gain is low, IOs can provide solutions to help states coordinate. By reducing transaction costs and uncertainty, providing needed information and forming stable mutual expectations about members' behaviors, IOs can encourage international cooperation (Keohane, 1984). For a rational, far-sighted country that values stable strategic interaction with its counterparts in the future, collaboration through the creation of a multilateral organization can be more efficient than resorting to the prerogatives of power (Martin, 1992). Different strategic circumstances will result in different institutional designs, including membership rules, scope of issues covered, centralization of tasks, rules for controlling the institution and flexibility of arrangements (Abbott & Snidal, 1998; Koremenos, Lipson, & Snidal, 2001). A group of countries in similar strategic circumstances can furnish an IO with an appropriate institutional design to solve their own coordination problems. Rather than treating the IOs as marginal, neoliberal institutionalism thinks highly of IO's coordination function. The areas of global or regional development finance may be particularly relevant in this respect since they require a high degree of efficiency in channeling financial resources to needy countries. In a diverse world, IOs remain relevant.

A brief review of the literature of international political economy and international organizations provides a theoretical basis for examining the AIIB's possible behavior. Most of the recent political economy-related research on the AIIB is based on such literature. The fact that the bank is too young for scholars to reach a conclusive judgement about it means that most of the literature is quite open-minded in its evaluation of the AIIB. In general, the literature can be divided into four groups, each one emphasizing a different perspective. First, some see the bank as an instrument for boosting China's power in the international financial system. By interaction within the AIIB, China may be able to change other countries' perceptions of and behavior toward itself. At the extreme, the AIIB has the potential to become the predominant IFI. There is a risk that the current governance structure of the international financial system may be replaced by the Chinese governance model. This kind of pessimistic view of the AIIB is found in many parts of the world, and was especially prevalent around the time when Xi Jinping first brought up the idea.

Second, rather than seeing the AIIB as a realist tool, there are quite a few observers who see it as a complementary institution designed to promote infrastructure development in Asia. They would argue that the bank is not a tool for maximizing relative power; instead, it will fill a gap in the existing international financial system. Furthermore, the AIIB could avoid the shortcomings for which the World Bank and the ADB are criticized. The creation of the AIIB may be a timely force for reform of the international financial system. If the AIIB can function properly, it will benefit not only China but also other members of the bank and the whole system.

Third, some consider the AIIB to be neither Beijing's tool in a power struggle nor a way for the Chinese to obtain mutual benefits. Instead, they believe that it is an institution that will enable China to boost its international status and reputation, allowing it to achieve positive recognition from other countries and be included among the financial great powers. From this point of view, the creation of the bank was not motivated by considerations of power or interests, but by China's concern for its international status, reputation and image. China has always claimed that its rise will be peaceful; how it manages the bank will show whether that claim is sincere. The AIIB's future will, in the opinion of these scholars, depend on China's status in the international community.

The fourth and final group of studies consists of discussions of how countries around the world perceive and react to the AIIB. It appears that reactions depend on strategic circumstances. After discussing these four kinds of studies below, I will present an integrative framework that seeks to link them all. This framework will shape the empirical analysis of this entire book.

A revisionist instrument of power

Observers who follow the realist tradition argue that the emergence of the AIIB may be the result of changes in the changing structure of power distribution. The US and its Asian allies once dominated the region militarily, economically and financially. Since the rise of China, the power gap between the US and China has narrowed. China is catching up with the US, and this changing power structure is likely to create a Thucydides Trap – circumstances in which fear generated by the rise of a state makes war inevitable (in Thucydides' case, the rising state was Athens and the fearful one was Sparta). A rising power will expect international arrangements to be adjusted to reflect the changing power structure while the established dominant power, being accustomed to its high status, will try to dismiss this expectation. The growing pride and confidence of the rising power will cause it to demand further rearrangement of the international order, but it will not receive a satisfactory response from the dominant power. As a consequence, the rising power will take the initiative in forging a new world order that it finds more satisfactory. In this sense, the creation of the AIIB is a footnote to the ongoing Thucydides Trap involving the dominant US and a rising China. Considering that the arrangements within IFIs do not realistically reflect China's pride, expectations or national interests, this school of thought holds that a dissatisfied China has created the AIIB to be more in line with its current power status and to satisfy its strategic interests (Allison, 2018). The bank will eventually seek to replace the US-led IFIs and write its own rules in such a way as to maximize China's power and interests.

This perspective echoes the literature of power transition theory, which focuses on the results of differential growth rates among powerful states. Rapid industrialization and modernization in China over the past few decades has led to an increase in China's power. Beijing may already have been transformed from a potential power into a transitional power. The growth in its power has outpaced that of the other major powers, and as a result, its relative power has increased at the expense of other countries. China's huge, longstanding trade surplus with the US has helped narrow the economic power gap between Beijing and Washington. If a slightly less powerful China can accept Washington's leadership of the international financial order, then China will be satisfied and more likely to become a good partner; thus the power transition period will be more peaceful.

However, if the rapidly rising country does not participate in the establishment of the dominant international order and the established power has no intention of granting the newcomer more privileges or room to participate, the rising power may become a challenger and seek to create a new institution for itself. According to this scenario, a rise in relative power will be accompanied by dissatisfaction, which may turn into aggression (Organski, 1968, pp. 338–376). Eventually, China, as a rapidly rising power, will likely become a revisionist state that challenges the existing international order (Kastner & Saunders, 2012). Rationally, if a dissatisfied power calculates that the expected benefits of challenging the international system exceed the costs, the rising power will attempt to change the system (Gilpin, 1981). Rather than simply considering the rivals' internal capabilities, scholars have found that externally decided capabilities made possible by alliances should be included in the dynamic of power transition analysis. In other words, during the power transition period, rival states play this game by factoring in their external strategic partnerships with other states (Kim, 1991). As China becomes more dissatisfied, it may seek more strategic partners with which it can collaborate to change the international arrangements.

From the perspective of power transition theory, the establishment of the AIIB reflects China's dissatisfaction with the current international financial system and its rejection of the international financial arrangements made by the US and its allies. Under these circumstances, international conflicts are likely to break out, and China's determination to challenge Washington will increase.

The preceding discussion suggests that China's creation of the AIIB stems from a combination of a perceived change in the distribution of power in Asia, dissatisfaction with the existing international order and a determination to change it and a desire to continue increasing its relative power. In these circumstances, China would have positive expectations of the political, strategic and economic advantages the bank could bring. Discussion of these factors follows.

A result of power transition

Among those who consider China to be a revisionist state that is dissatisfied with the US-led international order, the creation of the AIIB is seen as evidence that China will treat the bank as an instrument for acquiring global wealth and that will ultimately allow China to acquire more control of the global financial system. Ikenberry and Lim (2017) argue that China's rapid growth in relative power gives it five possible institutional choices: those of a status-quo stakeholder, an authority-seeking stakeholder, an institutional obstruction, an external innovator or (outright) opponent. They hold that it is not obvious that the AIIB is being manipulated by China to avoid the rules that govern existing international arrangements. Instead, they suggest that the AIIB is more like a type of external innovation. This choice of institutional statecraft comes either from an intention to offer a new form of international cooperation within the existing system and a new instrument for enhancing China's bilateral or multilateral influence or, at the other extreme, from a wish to challenge and replace prevailing substantive rules and norms. Although the level of disagreement or dispute is not as high as power transition theory would predict, the level of dissatisfaction was high enough for Beijing to configure a new bank that serves its national interests in a way that the existing system does not and reflects Beijing's own perception of its relative power. If it is operating from this perspective, China believes that the power distribution in the Bretton Woods system during the early 2010s did not accurately reflect its growing power. China became more dissatisfied as the major Western stakeholders blocked it from subscribing more shares. Confronted with this obstruction, Beijing established the AIIB which has at least the potential to replace the Bretton Woods system.

China became more daring in its pursuit of its geostrategic interests in the region. The current regional equilibrium which favors the US and Japan is no longer acceptable to Beijing. China overtook Japan in terms of volume of merchandise exports in 2004 and in terms of GDP five years later. China's outward foreign direct investment caught up with that of Japan in 2010, and by 2015, Beijing was providing a larger volume of global direct investment than the Japanese. Despite having become a regional and then a global economic and financial powerhouse, however, Beijing was blocked from further participation in the Bretton Woods system. An ideal option was to create an alternative regional institution that it could control and that would reflect the increase in China's relative power at the expense of other regional great powers. For example, the ADB is the dominant financial institution in Asia in terms of total loans issued. Tokyo, together with Washington, controls the ADB, and China has only been allowed to play a marginal role. It is understandable that, before its rise, China was a recipient of ADB loans and was too weak to take the helm. During this period of regional power transition, Beijing no longer deems such a marginal role to be acceptable, but the ADB does not appear to welcome China's active engagement. Beijing's creation of the AIIB signaled its dissatisfaction with the ADB and its intention to replace Japan as the leading player in regional financial institutions. The distribution of voting power in the AIIB represents a shift away from the US and Japan toward China, which has the largest number of subscribed shares and the power to veto agenda items that require a supermajority (Hecan, 2016). Besides, the institutional design of the AIIB limits non-regional members to 25% of voting shares. Compared with the ADB, the participation of the Western powers is thus minimal (Ito, 2015). No country will be able to challenge China's commanding position in the AIIB in the near future.

Although power transition theory tends to see the world as a ruthless place, some would argue that transition does not necessary lead to conflicts. Foot (2017) argues that while the rise of China is significant and comprehensive and Beijing has, in many respects, replaced Washington as the dominant player in the region, under the Obama administration at least, Beijing and Washington accepted a logic of coexistence due to the constraints of interdependence. In addition, the US has allowed China more power in the Bretton Woods system, thus reducing China's level of dissatisfaction. He and Feng (2019) have developed a leadership transition framework that borrows insights from institutional balancing theory and role theory (He, 2008). They argue that since the US remains the leading power, it is more likely to adopt an exclusive institutional balancing strategy in the international financial system. At the same time, China's role as a challenger will encourage it to recruit more dissatisfied followers to join the new institution it has created in order to boost the AIIB's strength and legitimacy. Therefore, an inclusive institutional balancing strategy is more likely to appear initially, one that focuses on providing benefits as public goods to attract more followers. Institutional competition for legitimacy – rather than power alone – between China and the US will reduce confrontation to a level lower than traditional power transition theory would suggest.

If the power transition arguments hold, one should observe at least three phenomena: (1) when the AIIB was established the relative power of the US and China would have undergone a significant change; (2) China was blocked from greater involvement in the existing system and was therefore more dissatisfied before it created the AIIB; (3) the AIIB is an inclusive institution that seeks to attract dissatisfied followers.

Challenging the current international financial system

If the AIIB emerged at a time of change in relative power and if China was indeed dissatisfied with the existing international financial system, how China intends to act is an important question. Intuitively, we might believe that China will act more aggressively and seek to challenge the international financial system by setting up an institution within which it can call the shots. When President Xi Jinping first brought up the idea of the AIIB, many commentators saw it as a product of strategic collaboration between China and the other four BRICS countries (Brazil, Russia, India and South Africa) that would challenge the Bretton Woods system and become an alternative to the World Bank. It was thought that the bank, under China's leadership, would spend billions of dollars supporting the One Belt One Road initiative (OBOR), now the Belt and Road Initiative (BRI), which is aimed at replacing rather than bolstering the existing international system (Zakaria, 2014).

Ikenberry and Lim (2017) suggest that the new AIIB might follow the "the logic of counter-hegemonic institutionalism" and may "achieve reform of certain rules, practices, and norms of the existing system of institutions and the issue areas they regulate; increase [China's] influence and authority within the existing system of institutions and liberal international order, and accordingly reduce that of the US; and/or . . . propagate rules, principles, and norms that could form the basis of a rival international order." The AIIB can thus become a powerful institution that will enable China to carry out its threat to exit the Bretton Woods system and provide an alternative space for other countries that share China's perceptions. However, these authors consider that the AIIB is unlikely to become a real counter-hegemonic institution unless it can get other like-minded states to participate and build up enough power to mount a challenge. But China and other like-minded states are not completely barred from participation in the existing multilateral system, and to some extent, they need and can still benefit from it. However, if China one day requires other countries to choose between the existing IFIs and the AIIB, it might "create conditions for a new kind of Cold War in Asia. Such development will help to destroy the current international order featuring peace and prosperity" (Zakaria, 2014).

Chen (2016) takes a less optimistic view and suggests that "China set up the AIIB because it was dissatisfied with global power politics in existing IFIs and was seeking a revolution." From this perspective, China is troubled by who is at the helm of the current system and is thus likely to join in the competition and try to weaken the US-dominated international financial system. China's predicament is reflected in the unfair distribution of voting power within the Bretton Woods system, which affords China a disproportionately low level of influence over policy and loan decisions. Current international arrangements make it difficult for China to influence the way the existing organizations operate or to expand its geo-economic influence (Beeson & Xu, 2019, p. 352). Therefore, creating a new multilateral development bank under its own control is a rational strategy for China (Xing, 2016, p. 31). China's dissatisfaction is reflected in the configuration of the AIIB. The power structure of the bank is more concentrated than that of the World Bank or the ADB. Furthermore, most of the power is in Beijing's hands, as it has slightly over 25% of the voting power and can also single-handedly veto crucial proposals. The institutional design of the AIIB reveals that China is not only seeking to attract more followers but also wants to ensure that it can fulfill its ambition to challenge the current international system.

As part of China's effort to recruit more followers, Hecan (2016) argues that the AIIB is designed to allow developing countries more representation than they have in the mainstream IFIs. Given the fact that global economic power has shifted away from the West toward the emerging economies, the AIIB gives those countries an opportunity to pool their financial resources in opposition to other institutions. Ito (2015) believes that the relationship between the AIIB and other IFIs, such as the World Bank and the ADB, will become a problem for China. It will be difficult for China to carry on enjoying low-interest loans to develop its domestic infrastructure while at the same time guiding the AIIB toward financing the infrastructure needs of the rest of Asia. This kind of contradiction may lead to disputes or conflicts between institutions.

If such conflicts emerge, Wan expects the AIIB to weaken the liberal international order, because its lead country is not a liberal democracy. The operation of the AIIB may not be compatible with the Bretton Woods system because it is likely to mirror China's style of governance. Wan even worries that participation in the AIIB will cause democratic countries to pick up non-liberal governance habits which will weaken their democracies. He fears that non-Western democracies, like India and Japan, are the most susceptible to this because they are under particular pressure to accommodate themselves to the changing international environment (Wan, 2016, pp. 102–103). Should the Bretton Woods system weaken, those countries may be more likely to link up with China as the AIIB grows stronger. And because President Xi Jinping's reputation is at stake, he has every reason to make sure that the AIIB becomes a powerful player in international development finance. Interestingly, Wan actually envisages the AIIB as more of a status quo institution that will participate in the established arrangements. However, despite his optimistic viewpoint, he cannot rule out conflict altogether.

Instead of coming to a snap judgment concerning China's motivations for establishing the AIIB, He and Feng (2019) argue that the bank's behavior will depend on China's perception of its role in the international community and how that will shape Beijing's foreign policy. Rather than shaping the AIIB as an exclusive institution configured to challenge the existing order, as a country that identities itself as a challenger might be expected to do, they suggest that it is the country that identifies itself as the leader in an area of global governance that will endeavor to undermine the influence and value of the new institution. The country that identifies itself as a challenger is more likely to develop an inclusive, peaceful and tolerant institutional balancing strategy in order to secure the support of other states. Such a strategy can better ensure the success of the new institution. In their research, He and Feng claim that the AIIB's behavior in its early days supports the argument that China perceives itself as a challenger and therefore created the AIIB as part of an inclusive institutional balancing strategy. But once the AIIB becomes a leading institution, and once China perceives itself to be a leader of the international financial system, the bank may seek to undermine the declining Bretton Woods institutions and prevent them from becoming predominant once again.

If the AIIB appears to be challenging the established international financial system, it is likely to meet strong opposition from the leaders of the Bretton Woods institutions, such as the Western countries and developed countries elsewhere in the world. Chow (2016) argues that the US would be the country most affected by the advent of the AIIB because Washington has been the underwriter of the world's financial system for decades. The stronger the AIIB becomes, the greater the chance that Beijing will replace Washington as the final arbiter of the rules of international trade and finance. Wan (2016, p. 99) contends that the creation of the AIIB has influenced the trilateral relationship between the US, Japan and China. The former two financial powers have moved closer together in their alliance against China which has the potential to become stronger on account of the AIIB. During a visit to the US before the AIIB was established, Japanese Prime Minister Shinzo Abe was encouraged by the Americans to act assertively to counter Beijing. By the end of 2019, four years after the AIIB began operations, neither country had applied for membership.

However, not all the developed countries followed Washington's lead with regard to the AIIB. Wu (2017, p. 35) argues that "since the 2008 financial crisis . . . the results of the voice, voting and governance reforms [of the Bretton Woods institutions] have actually compounded the impact of initial disparities and have perpetuated developed countries' sway over the development agenda." It is possible that developed countries could move away from the Bretton Woods system and search for new sources of finance and models. Despite strong pressure from Washington, half of the countries of the European Union (EU) became founding members of the AIIB (Chen, 2018). Although there is a divergence in perceptions of the AIIB on the two sides of the Atlantic, this might be because the bank has not yet acted as a challenger (Chen, 2020). Once the bank becomes more powerful, and thus more ambitious and "disobedient," it is possible that the West might unite more strongly behind the Bretton Woods system and against the AIIB.

If the argument that the AIIB is an ambitious challenger holds, one should observe at least three phenomena: (1) the institutional design of the AIIB should deviate sharply from that of the established IFIs; (2) the rise of the AIIB should be at the expense of the established IFIs; and (3) the lead countries of the established IFIs should be uniting against the AIIB.

Securing strategic and diplomatic allies

In the above discussion, we mentioned that the success of the AIIB depends on increasing its membership. Increased membership, however, will augment the power not only of the AIIB but also of China itself. If they receive financial assistance from a China-led IFI, members of the AIIB may be more willing to cooperate with China diplomatically and strategically. More allies among its neighbors, which China currently lacks, would put Beijing in a more comfortable strategic position for its competition with the other major powers.

Ikenberry and Lim (2017) observe that the financial relationship between loan and grant recipients and the AIIB can lead to asymmetric interdependence. Financially weaker states can be more easily influenced by a growth in cross-border economic transactions with a major funding state, which in the case of the AIIB, is China. A large volume of economic exchanges can result in a strong bilateral relationship. In addition, financial investments through an IFI like the AIIB can appear more credible, clean and legitimate than funds coming directly from the Chinese government. Investments made by the Chinese government or its state-owned enterprises may lead to anti-China sentiment in recipient countries due to problems of lack of transparency, corruption and worries about neo-colonialism. Funds channeled through the AIIB can enhance China's bilateral relations with the recipient while minimizing anti-China feeling.

China sees the AIIB as an important instrument of the BRI, as it is a multinational institution acceptable to other countries in the region. One key to the success of this initiative is getting China's neighbors to accept its leadership and its regional integration plans and models (Xing, 2016, p. 29). The establishment of the AIIB is crucial for implementing Xi Jinping's plans for the BRI, which are to strengthen economic cooperation and diplomatic relations with neighboring countries. Xi Jinping believes that China needs a multinational institution accepted by most Asian countries to exercise its leadership and influence the direction of regional economic integration and that the AIIB is that institution. It can help China enhance its diplomatic standing as it demonstrates Beijing's growing economic and political power. Other countries are more likely to follow China's lead in the AIIB if they think they can benefit from it (Hecan, 2016). Rather than joining the US in its efforts to balance the rise of China, it appears that Asian countries, given that their understanding of "sovereignty" differs from that of the West, may join ranks with China because of the financial benefits, stability and legitimacy they may gain from it. This tendency will be greater if China is strong enough and rich enough to preserve the hierarchical order in Asia (Kang, 2003). If the development of the AIIB does not cause alarm within the region concerning China's strategic ambitions, China may attract more diplomatic allies willing to dance to its tune.

Aside from the effect on China's diplomatic standing, countries may choose to join the AIIB out of expectations of the economic and financial advantages provided by the bank's loan policies. Countries that are diplomatically, strategically or politically important to China may be more likely to receive loans with less stringent conditions attached. Countries that cannot secure loans from other IFIs may go to the AIIB, which may become Beijing's instrument for attracting more allies. The AIIB may also become China's own treasury, pooling global financial resources for China's own infrastructure projects (Ito, 2015). As a consequence, the bank will become a diplomatic, political and strategic tool of the Chinese. Beijing can thus acquire more close regional partners at the expense of the US and become more powerful.

If the argument that the AIIB will help China buy more allies holds, one should observe at least three phenomena: (1) when a country joins the AIIB its relations with China will improve; (2) the AIIB's loan policy will favor those countries which have friendlier diplomatic and political relations with China; (3) the AIIB's loan conditions will be less stringent than those of other IFIs, especially for countries with friendlier diplomatic and political relations with China.

Targeting strategic locations and sectors

It will be interesting to discover whether the AIIB will become a critical financial arm of China's grand strategic plan, the BRI. Beijing's geopolitical strategy where the BRI is concerned is to bind the countries of the region closer to China through economic and financial investment. As Beeson and Xu (2019) have written, "If we understand geo-economics as applying economic instruments to advance geopolitical ends, then China has the potential to exert a growing influence on international affairs." They suggest that an examination of the behavior of the AIIB and the closely associated BRI will show whether China is adapting both of them to achieve its strategic ambitions. If such an adaptation is taking place, it should be possible to observe that both of these initiatives are involved in places and sectors that are strategically important to China.

Scholars also worry that the BRI may facilitate China's "debt-book diplomacy," in that Beijing will leverage its accumulated debt to achieve its strategic aims. China's debt-for-equity swap investment contracts can plunge loan recipients into serious debt problems, and they eventually have no choice but to cede control of their strategic assets to China. For example, locations in seven South Asian countries may become Beijing's targets for debt-book diplomacy in order to allow the Chinese navy freer access into the Indian Ocean via the Malacca Straits. The Sri Lankan port of Hambantota is an oft-cited example of this. The port is too unprofitable to allow Colombo to service the large amount of debt it owes to Beijing for its construction, so the two countries agreed to allow China to take over control of the port (Parker & Chefitz, 2018).

In addition to strategically sensitive locations, financing specific economic sectors can help China achieve its goal. BRI projects funded by the AIIB can also result in debt traps for developing countries that are rich in natural resources. This may involve acquiring key technology and intellectual property through state-backed, technology-seeking Chinese investments (White House Office of Trade and Manufacturing Policy, 2018). So far, it appears that the BRI has emerged as the cornerstone of Beijing's economic statecraft aimed at realizing its geopolitical ambitions (Kliman et al., 2019). Complementing China's national banks, the AIIB provides an additional source of financing for BRI-related infrastructure projects. It adds a veneer of legitimacy, since the AIIB is an international institution. As a consequence, the bank can help China augment its power in a low-profile manner.

If the preceding strategic arguments hold, one should observe at least three phenomena: (1) instead of operating independently, the AIIB will become closely associated with and supportive of the BRI; (2) AIIB loans will go to strategically important places and sectors; (3) the AIIB loans will involve debt-for-equity swaps.

Reinvigorating China's sluggish domestic economy

Since China opened its markets and launched its economic reforms in the late 1970s, its domestic economy has maintained astonishing growth. This has resulted in huge amounts of wealth being transferred from overseas. forming the economic and financial basis for the expansion of China's power. According to the Lowy Institute's Asia Power Index (Lowy Institute, 2019), China and the US are the only two superpowers in Asia in terms of economic performance alone, and in 2019, China's score (93.0) was higher than that of the US (92.5), although the US was still number one in terms of overall power. However, China's growth rate has appeared to slow down since the beginning of the 2010s – declining from 10.6% in 2010 to 6.6% in 2018. Although there is room for further growth, domestic production has outpaced demand. While China is seeking to stimulate domestic demand, looking for foreign outlets for its products is another policy option (Wang, 2020). An excessive capital surplus resulting from China's huge foreign exchange reserves is another side-effect of China's economic rise which may fuel inflation. In addition, China has come under strong international pressure to float the renminbi which is widely considered to be undervalued. Transferring wealth out of China by means of overseas investment can alleviate this pressure. Finally, projects financed by the AIIB can help reverse the decline in demand for Chinese exports from markets in Asian countries, as these infrastructure projects may encourage the procurement of Chinese manufactures (Xing, 2016). Given its trade war with Washington, Beijing has become more anxious to find alternative export destinations.

Financing infrastructure projects through Chinese national banks, policy banks or the AIIB can channel excess Chinese wealth to Asian countries in order not only to defend against pressure to allow the renminbi to appreciate but also to advance the internationalization of the currency. Countries that are recipients of AIIB funding can use those funds to purchase goods from Chinese multinationals, allowing those enterprises to secure markets that will ease their overcapacity problems and increase their profitability. Furthermore, channeling funds through the AIIB lowers the risks involved in such investments since the bank has adopted international best practice in its allocation of loans. Co-financing with other IFIs ensures that these projects are sound and that any risks involved are shared. At the same time, China can still influence the destination of its investments (Ikenberry & Lim, 2017).

In addition to macroeconomic factors, the financial flows made possible by the AIIB are also of interest to Chinese corporations in specific sectors. Although the AIIB will not become as profit orientated as a commercial bank, it may be wrong to assume that its intentions are entirely benign. Sectors of the Chinese economy, such as construction, natural resources or renewable energy, may be the biggest winners from participation in AIIB projects outside China (Hecan, 2016). Many of these companies have benefited from China's economic expansion and become large conglomerates. Most of them are state-owned enterprises (SOEs) that are controlled by the communist party-state system. Beijing expects them to grow into national champions capable of competing with the largest multinational companies in the world (Chow, 2016). The party will need these SOEs to survive in order to preserve its ruling legitimacy. If many of the SOEs go bankrupt, the resulting unemployment would likely provoke a political crisis damaging to the party's reputation. The emergence of the AIIB will therefore not only allow China to escape from an economic quagmire but also ensure the legitimacy of the regime. These enterprises are key elements in China's continuing rise.

If the preceding arguments concerning the role of the AIIB in China's domestic economy hold, we should observe at least four phenomena: (1) the emergence of the AIIB will boost China's exports and overseas direct investments; (2) AIIB loans will go to sectors in which China is experiencing over-production; (3) the emergence of the AIIB will lead to growth of China's SOEs in specific sectors; (4) Chinese SOEs will have a strong presence in infrastructure projects funded by the AIIB.

A race to the bottom

If the AIIB is configured to be a revisionist instrument, it would have to outcompete the other major IFIs. The main challenge for a new institution like the AIIB is attracting more international clients and encouraging them to apply for loans. One way to compete with other IFIs is to lend to projects that other banks would reject out of concerns such as adverse environmental impacts or violations of best practices. To attract those kinds of applications, the AIIB would have to impose less stringent loan conditions. Such a race to the bottom would damage existing global financial arrangements.

In practice, developing countries are too financially weak to take into consideration negative environmental and social ramifications of their infrastructure projects. For example, rather than investing in renewable energy, developing countries might favor the development of cheaper coal-fired power plants. However, IFIs such as the ADB and the World Bank show little interest in coal-fired projects (Chin, 2016; Otto, 2015). At the outset, the AIIB did not place any restrictions on financing coal-fired plants (Kynge, 2017), meaning that member states, such as India and Indonesia, that needed cheap fixes for their energy shortages would prefer to go to the AIIB for financial assistance (Chen, 2020).

Another complaint frequently heard among the developing countries is that the major established IFIs place too many conditions on their loans based on the neoliberal Washington Consensus. Sometimes, these conditions involve introducing reform programs that developing countries consider to be premature (Stiglitz, 2002). Studies have even found that loans from the Bretton Woods institutions were coupled with the political and strategic interests of the major shareholding powers (Dreher, Sturm, & Vreeland, 2015). In order to attract the attention of developing countries, the AIIB issues loans without any strings attached.

In addition to competitive pressure, the institutional design of the AIIB itself may also further the race to the bottom. Ito (2015) argues that the AIIB's non-resident board of directors could result in the bank's financial operations strongly favoring the preferences of its president and its executives who are mostly Chinese. With China dominating the board and the senior management team, even a resident board design would be unlikely to curb Beijing's ambitions if the Chinese decided to steer the bank away from international best practice. For the AIIB to comply with best practice, China's consent is necessary. Even though the bank has so far not shown any signs of leaving the current system, there is no guarantee that it will not happen in the future. The institutional design of the AIIB makes it easier for China to start a race to the bottom if it wants to.

If the preceding concerns are justified, one should observe at least three phenomena: (1) the emergence of the AIIB should lead to a decline in loans from major international financial institutions; (2) the loan policies of the AIIB will deviate from international best practice; (3) the AIIB will finance more environmentally and socially detrimental infrastructure projects than other IFIs.

Satisfying the Chinese communist party

The creation of the AIIB may simply be the result of the Chinese Communist Party needing an IFI that it can control in order to fulfill the realist objectives mentioned above. So far, the underrepresentation of China in the Bretton Woods system has hindered Beijing's global financial maneuvering. The AIIB's first president, Jin Liqun, is a former Chinese finance minister and a senior party member. He is likely to have been handpicked by China's party-state system to make sure that the bank operates in the interests of the party (Chow, 2016, p. 1287).

Chow (2016) suggests that, according to the AIIB's current organizational arrangements, its daily operations are conducted by its president, his management team and their staff. They work daily at the headquarters in Beijing without much interference from the board of directors. According to the Articles of Agreement of the AIIB, the president's term is limited to five years and he or she can only be re-elected once. The president's nationality is not specified, but given that the election of a president requires a supermajority vote from the board of governors, China could single-handedly veto a non-Chinese candidate. This suggests that the

Chinese Communist Party can easily control the president and direct the bank's operations in its favor. This kind of autonomy is not enjoyed by the heads of the World Bank or the IMF, who answer to their respective resident boards of directors living and working in Washington, DC.

If the preceding arguments hold, one should observe at least three phenomena which would keep the AIIB under China's tight control: (1) for a long period of time, the president of the AIIB will continue to be a Chinese national; (2) there will be more Chinese nationals among the AIIB's top management; (3) there will be only a low level of interference from the board.

These discussions support our conjecture that, in the ongoing power transition period, the AIIB will turn into an instrument of Chinese power. If this argument holds, many of the phenomena presented should occur.

A complementary institution supporting the status quo

Undeniably, the AIIB could not have come into being without a power transition between the US and China, but it is not a foregone conclusion that the bank will become an instrument of Chinese power, used to achieve Beijing's revisionist ambitions. If China only needed to maximize its power, it could have done this by means of its mega national banks, which have more assets than the AIIB and are more susceptible to manipulation by the Chinese state in the service of its national strategic plan. These banks have been channeling funds to overseas infrastructure projects for quite a long time. If this were the sole motivation, why would China bother to create a relatively weak IFI that is not under China's exclusive control? Some scholars argue that in order to better understand why China would invest so much effort and resources into the AIIB, we need to adopt a functional approach. Maximization of power is not the only answer.

The advent of the AIIB should not be considered as a zero-sum game for the Bretton Woods system. If it is run properly, the AIIB can contribute to the development of a better and more efficient international financial system. Rationally speaking, international institutions like the AIIB can solve the problems of market failure that afflict China and its Asian neighbors. China has an abundance of financial resources and developing countries are in need of funds to develop their infrastructure. The AIIB can further lower the transaction costs involved in this exchange. China needs international participation in the bank so that it can gain experience in managing an IFI and the ways to minimize potential risks from others. Other members of the bank can also have access to information about loan recipients which have a closer political relationship with China. Major shareholders can therefore learn from China's more extensive knowledge of the Asian region. Increased competition, made possible by the arrival on the scene of the AIIB, will facilitate the development of a more transparent international financial system. All these factors reduce transaction costs and investment risks. In addition, if the AIIB follows best practice, cases involving irresponsible investment or moral hazard in the developing countries of Asia will become less frequent. Since loans issued by Chinese national banks are considered problematic, the growth in the relative importance of the AIIB can help build a healthier and more efficient development finance system in the region. From the perspective of neoliberal institutionalism, the AIIB can be functionally useful in facilitating a stable international financial system.

In addition, financing through an IFI like the AIIB has positive centralization and independence effects. A centralized and independent organization provides consistent support for states to interact according to a constitution and to pool resources and share burdens collectively. It enhances the legitimacy of the operation and implementation of projects; behaves as a neutral, trustworthy information provider; serves as an honest arbiter and broker; and engages in norm elaboration and coordination to enhance cooperation (Abbott & Snidal, 1998). Although the AIIB may not be perfect in all respects, these properties help alleviate states' suspicions of interacting with each other. If the AIIB can be established properly and deliver positive centralization and independence effects, more states will join. It will also facilitate the development of common norms and practices in international development finance.

Another issue is the distributional effects of the creation of the AIIB – does the AIIB provide China with relative gains that it cannot reject? Or will the AIIB provide resources that complement those provided by the established system and increase absolute economic gains for the major powers that dominate that system? From a liberal perspective, the aforementioned functional benefits can mitigate fears of cheating and distributional conflicts. If the AIIB functions properly, institutionalized reciprocity can be made possible. Furthermore, infrastructure financing is a less politically and strategically sensitive issue area than security, so realist concerns about relative gains may be eased (Keohane & Martin, 1995). As a result, the power considerations inspired by the power transition theory may not be applicable in the case of the AIIB. If the AIIB can magnify absolute benefits for as many concerned parties as possible, then, far from being an instrument of Chinese power, it will become a status quo bank.

Following the institutional arguments, one should not try to understand China's establishment of the AIIB solely from a realist perspective. If the AIIB functions properly, the benefits it produces will help mitigate realist suspicions among the international community. The bank will institutionally constrain China's financial power, pooling and allocating resources more effectively and efficiently, bridging the North and the South, and facilitating reforms in the current system. In the end, the bank can create mutual benefits for all members. China and the AIIB will act as a responsible stakeholder providing international public goods for investment in infrastructure. Below, I discuss several commonly seen dimensions of the institutional perspective.

Integrating into the international financial system

Rather than seeing the AIIB as an exclusive, China-led instrument, optimists expect it to become an inclusive bank. They believe it will embrace prospective members from the developed world rich in funds, knowledge and experience.

Together, they will configure the AIIB into an obedient multilateral bank that promotes greater connectivity and further development in Asia. Knoerich and Urdinez (2019) argue that the involvement of advanced Western countries will prevent the bank from developing into a small homogenous grouping of Asian debtor countries. Instead, it is more likely to develop into a heterogeneous global organization of both debtor and creditor states. Persuaded by China, many Western countries agreed to join the AIIB and were "granted agency in the process of determining the AIIB's organizational design" (Knoerich & Urdinez, 2019, p. 336). These members were well placed to prevent the initial institutional design of the AIIB from departing from that of the established multilateral development banks. The bank has thus been able to integrate into the current system. These authors provide evidence that most of the AIIB's founding members see it as complementing the existing multilateral development banks and increasing the number of available financing options (Knoerich & Urdinez, 2019).

Some scholars hold that the more Western members the AIIB can recruit, the more pressure there will be on China to run the bank in line with Western expectations (Wan, 2016, p. 43). They argue that instead of rejecting the AIIB, Washington and Tokyo should consider joining it. In fact, the bank will be nested to IFIs like the World Bank and the ADB, as the AIIB's behavior does not drastically differ from theirs. There is no need for Washington to be afraid of the AIIB. On the one hand, China will be constrained by the other members, and on the other, the liberal pacifying effects of US participation will lead to greater economic interdependence, international institutions and norms and probably democratic governance, which will allow both superpowers to further cooperate within the existing system (Lipscy, 2015b). Judging from the current global representation within the bank, China may exercise strategic restraint to attract more great power involvement.

Some observers argue that China decided to forgo veto power in the AIIB in order to attract more members from among non-regional, advanced economies. This would allow Beijing to acquire the funds, knowledge and experience necessary to run the AIIB (Weaver, 2015). Recruiting these countries also serves to demonstrate that Beijing did not intend to treat the bank as its power instrument or to replace existing institutions. It may show that China's preference for learning and acquiring resources from the existing system outweighs its ambition for greater material and ideological influence (Wilson, 2017). However, one should not ignore the fact that, even though China gave up veto power over all loan decisions, Beijing remains the largest shareholder with more than 25% of the voting power. This allows China to veto any important proposals that require a supermajority vote.

If the preceding arguments hold, one should observe at least three phenomena: (1) the AIIB will develop into an inclusive international financial institution that welcomes non-regional members; (2) the institutional design of the AIIB will basically conform to that of the established IFIs; (3) Beijing will be restrained from using its veto power.

Pooling additional resources

Rather than becoming a competitor, the AIIB may simply seek to fill the gap in funding for infrastructure development in Asia. An ADB report published in 2009 predicted that Asia would need an investment of US$8 trillion in over-all national infrastructure in the period 2010–2020 (Asian Development Bank Institute, 2009). This works out to an average of US$800 billion per year. Yet, in 2013, the ADB could only contribute US$21 billion (Chen, 2016). Similarly, the Chinese estimated that the amount needed for this purpose was US$730 billion per year (Weaver, 2015). So, there is a need for additional sources of funding to plug this shortfall if the region is to develop the infrastructure nec-essary to sustain economic development (Calderón & Servén, 2004). As Xi Jinping has acknowledged, "China cannot develop in isolation from the Asia-Pacific, and the Asia-Pacific cannot prosper without China." He also recog-nized the difficulties in the global economic situation (Perlez & Cochrane, 2013). China's outside options of creating another financial vehicle are poor, which means that China has more to lose if the region falls short of finan-cial resources to improve the connectivity necessary for prosperity. In order to address this problem, the Chinese had to invest in creating a new institution, the AIIB. It was no good waiting for the established powers to increase their aid and fix the problems (Kastner, Pearson, & Rector, 2018). A multilateral investment bank will help China configure itself as a credible and responsible stakeholder that can contribute to economic connectivity and growth in the region (Dai & Li, 2015).

In addition to plugging a financial gap, the AIIB may help remedy the Asian development finance system's lack of specialization, which does not properly reflect a growing number of complex global issues. While the ADB's main mis-sion is to cover a wide variety of issues pertaining to poverty reduction, the AIIB focuses on infrastructure financing (Wihtol, 2014). If the two Asia-specific IFIs can collaborate properly, the resulting division of labor can bring about a more efficient and accurate allocation of resources. Scholars also argue that the AIIB is a complementary institution that recognizes the central role of the US-led liberal financial system as well as focusing on the provision of additional public goods in a way that is not adequately addressed by existing institutions. As a result, many US allies in the region have ignored political pressure from Washington and sup-ported the AIIB (Kim, 2020). Therefore, rather than being a threat, the AIIB could be a valuable regional asset in that it will not only make available more funds but also cooperate with other institutions (Lam, 2014, p. 135). Other institutions, such as the ADB, the World Bank and the IMF, publicly welcomed the idea of the AIIB when China first mooted it in early 2014. Those organizations appear to be optimistic about further collaboration with the AIIB.

If the preceding arguments hold, one should observe at least three phenomena: (1) an increase in AIIB loans will not lead to a decline in loans offered by other IFIs; (2) the AIIB will focus on investment in infrastructure projects; (3) the addi-tional funds coming from the AIIB will be welcomed by other institutions.

Connecting the developed and the developing worlds

Another theory concerning China's motive for creating the AIIB is that it is aimed at bridging the gap between the developed and the developing economies. While the former possess the abundance of cash, skills and knowledge necessary to undertake large-scale overseas investment in, for example, infrastructure, the latter are short of all of these resources. The AIIB is an ideal platform for facilitating the supply and demand of finances for infrastructure projects in Asia. Instead of investing in Asia independently, developed countries can reduce costs and risks by working with China through a China-led IFI; China may have more information about its neighbors and can thus match developed countries with the right destinations for their investment. The AIIB also provides developing countries with alternative sources of financial assistance. In some cases, developed countries cannot channel funds to the developing world due to legal restrictions, such as the prohibited investment lists of the World Bank and the ADB. Developed members of the AIIB now have a new platform through which they can invest in projects that are barred by other institutions.

The benefits for the developed countries come not only from returns on investments per se but also from the business opportunities resulting from their previous economic engagement, such as continuing investment opportunities and increased trade. Overseas markets for their merchandise may be especially attractive to developed countries that are experiencing a slowdown in economic growth. Those that are currently reliant on, or are becoming more dependent on, Asian markets should certainly welcome the AIIB. Chen (2018) finds that the potential material benefits provided by the AIIB were important incentives for European countries to join. Specifically, European countries that have invested more in the AIIB's potential borrowers in Asia, China, Southeast Asia and South Asia, as well as those which export more to China, are more likely to join the AIIB. This finding, at least, shows that developed countries may see the AIIB as a bridge that can aid their engagement in Asian markets.

If the preceding arguments hold, one should observe at least three phenomena: (1) the developed economies are keen to participate in the AIIB; (2) the developed economies take into consideration the trade and investment benefits of the AIIB when deciding whether to join; (3) the developed economies' trade and investment with Asia will increase after they join the AIIB.

Improving efficiency through competition

The emergence of the AIIB has increased the level of competition in the international development finance system. Greater competition, in theory, can facilitate greater efficiency and effectiveness of fund allocation. Xing (2016, p. 36) considers that direct or indirect financial resources provided by the AIIB not only enhance regional connectivity through investment in such sectors as energy and transport infrastructure but also improve the efficiency of resource allocation through an increase in competition. All the IFIs will have to work more closely with national governments and design better loan and development solutions in order to sell their financial products. From the consumers' point of view, national governments will have more options to choose from and are more likely to obtain better deals.

International development requires a proactive and effective financial system. Wu (2017) suggests the idea of "co-progressive development," which "entails a normative principle that puts self-initiation and external inducement as a means of promoting self-initiated action at the center of international development agendas and programs." He recommends that the AIIB and the Bretton Woods institutions should engage in friendly competition to achieve a common goal. What the AIIB can contribute is its knowledge of the development experiences of the emerging economies. Their success stories give them the legitimacy to compete in the international development market and attract the attention of other developing countries. Therefore, competition should result in a more advanced and effective global development agenda.

If the competition arguments hold, one should observe at least three phenomena: (1) AIIB loans will be more competitive than loans from other IFIs; (2) other institutions will offer infrastructure loans on better terms as a result of competition with the AIIB; (3) the AIIB's share of loans to developing countries will increase.

Stimulating a reform agenda in the international financial system

Competition not only affects the quality of loans; it also leads to institutional change in the international financial organizations. When there is increased competition in a certain policy area, this creates more options for member states as they can threaten to exit a particular organization if their demands for change are not answered. Lipscy (2015a) finds that, although the World Bank and the International Monetary Fund (IMF) are quite similar in terms of their institutional design, the former faces more extensive competition in its policy area of development aid than the latter does in its area of balance of payments. He shows that this competition gives World Bank members more outside options and has thus resulted in institutional changes that better reflect members' underlying capabilities.

The Bretton Woods system has been criticized for not reflecting the underlying global power distribution. Although emerging countries account for a large share of economic power globally, they consider themselves to be underrepresented in the system – this is particularly the case for China (Chen, 2016). We can link the establishment of the AIIB to the need for reform in the international financial system. There are at least five areas in need of reform: (1) the unfair distribution of voting powers; (2) inefficient management and redundant procedure; (3) Western monopolization of the presidency; (4) loan conditionality; and (5) a lack of experts from a variety of disciplines (Chen, 2019; Chin, 2016; Chow, 2016; Malkin & Momani, 2016; Ong, 2017; Zedillo, 2009). If the AIIB's institutional design avoids these problems, the bank can push for further reforms to the Bretton Woods institutions.

Investigating the AIIB in its first three years of operation, Chen (2020) finds that the bank has made the most significant progress in the area of efficiency. The AIIB appears to be leaner than its counterparts. However, it still has a power distribution problem. Lichtenstein (2019) also finds that the AIIB has some innovative features, such as its non-resident board, streamlined decision making and uniquely detailed oversight arrangements. However, both of these authors admit that the institutional structure of the AIIB remains uncertain on account of the geopolitical and geo-economic shifts that are occurring in the region. It remains to be seen how the AIIB will carry out reforms that can reflect regional and global interests rather than the interests of the emerging countries alone.

If the reform argument holds, one should observe at least three phenomena: (1) the AIIB's institutional design should reflect the underlying national power of its members; (2) the presidency will not always be held by a Chinese national; (3) the operation and management of the AIIB will be more efficient.

Independent from the Belt and Road Initiative

Beijing's grand strategy of "One Belt One Road," which subsequently became the Belt and Road Initiative (BRI), was first announced in September 2013 by President Xi Jinping. Just a month later, Xi proposed the creation of the AIIB. Although Xi made no mention of the AIIB becoming a source of funds for the BRI, it is hard not to see a strong connection between the two when they were both proposed almost simultaneously. In contrast to the AIIB, the BRI is obviously under Beijing's firm control and is configured to further China's geopolitical and geo-economic interests. Thus, the greater the association between the BRI and the AIIB, the more the international community will suspect China's motivations and intentions in setting up the AIIB.

When the idea of the AIIB was first mooted in November 2013, Xi said that the purpose of the bank was to facilitate regional communication, connectivity and integration and that it would work with other regional banks to promote continued stable development in Asia. Looking at the AIIB from the point of view of its governance structure, Sanders (2017) does not believe the AIIB and the BRI are linked, as China is not the dominant power in the former. In addition, the AIIB Charter, signed by 57 members in 2015, does not mention the BRI, nor do the institutional rules or operational policies. From a strictly legal point of view, the AIIB's loan decisions should not be influenced by the BRI. From an operational standpoint, at least between 2016 and 2018, the distribution of loans by the BRI and the AIIB were quite different. While the former appears to be more strategically beneficial to China, the latter does not (Chen, 2020). Unlike the BRI, the AIIB seems to be more concerned with creating regional benefits rather than serving China's narrow interests.

If the preceding arguments hold, one should observe at least two phenomena: (1) there should be few official mentions of the association between the AIIB and BRI; (2) the AIIB's distribution of loans should be different from that of the BRI and less politically and strategically sensitive.

These discussions have identified six dimensions in which the AIIB is not exclusively linked to China's power ambitions. Instead, it is suggested that there are a variety of ways in which the AIIB can contribute to the international community. The bank is still too young and green to be a challenger. If it engages properly, the AIIB has the potential to become a status quo bank that complements the existing global financial system.

Pursuing status and reputation

If one sees the AIIB as a means for China to maximize its power, we can expect the bank to become more ambitious and to prioritize China's interests at the expense of other countries. However, if one adopts a functional perspective, we may expect it to complement the current system and contribute to the international community. These two different points of view are to be found in most of the debates in the literature. There is another strand of argument that seeks to reconcile these different perspectives, suggesting that both scenarios are equally plausible and whether they come about depends on such factors as image, perception, identity, reputation and status. In other words, the configuration and trajectory of the AIIB depend on China's perceptions.

Applying social identity theory (SIT) to international politics, Larson and Shevchenko (2014) argue that the behavior of a country in a lower-status group depends on its opportunities for social mobility. If the status hierarchy is considered improper or illegitimate and if social mobility opportunities are lacking, countries in an inferior group may turn to social competition with the superior group in order to win higher status. The competing country may become a spoiler, trying to sabotage the established system of global governance. On the other hand, if the status hierarchy is perceived as acceptable and stable, countries in an inferior group may become socially creative and advocate new international norms, regimes, institutions or development models. From the point of view of SIT, the AIIB can be seen as part of China's strategy for enhancing its international status. Depending on where China sees itself in the status hierarchy of the international financial system and how proper and permeable it perceives that hierarchy to be, China will direct the bank toward becoming either competitive or complementary. Rather than power, it is the pursuit of status that matters more in the AIIB case.

Yang (2016) also applies SIT to the case of the AIIB, arguing that in its search for great power identity and status, China neither completely accepted the existing rules nor sought to engage in geopolitical rivalry when it formulated the institutional design of the AIIB. The identity management strategy chosen by China seems to be one of social creativity, emphasizing institutional innovation that promotes alternative models, norms and institutions of global governance. This may reassure the international community and enhance the bank's legitimacy. China's primary concern here may be to simultaneously improve its global status and its international image. Chen (2020) argues that the management of status is dynamic rather than static. The AIIB should be seen as a dynamic institution that will evolve in line with the gap between China's recognized international financial status and its own perception of its financial power – what is called China's status deficit. If the deficit is large, China will tend to use the AIIB as an instrument of global competition; if the deficit is small, the bank is more likely to behave cooperatively.

In addition to concerns about status, Hecan (2016) argues that the AIIB was devised by China as a multilateral institution which will help China build a cooperative international image. Supporting multilateralism in the AIIB can highlight the problem of arbitrary unilateralism often associated with the US government. The creation of the AIIB as a multilateral financial aid platform can be seen as concrete evidence that China aspires to a peaceful rise and a harmonious world. Peng and Tok (2016) hold that with the endorsement of the 57 founding members and in collaboration with other IFIs, the AIIB will enhance China's normative power and improve the regional and Western perceptions of China.

According to this line of argument, rather than becoming a power instrument or a resource allocator, the AIIB is associated with how China perceives itself and how it wants to be perceived by the rest of the world. When China feels more comfortable with the status hierarchy, the AIIB should look more like a diplomatic tool which will promote positive recognition of China's great power status while alleviating international concerns about its rapid rise. Therefore, China will seek to build a responsible and unselfish AIIB which will in turn elevate China's global status and reputation. But whether this optimistic view is correct remains to be seen. If China remains dissatisfied with the status hierarchy and how it is perceived internationally, there is a greater chance that the AIIB will deviate from its current path and become an instrument of China's efforts to displace those powers that currently dominate the international order. These arguments indicate that Beijing is playing a dynamic game.

If this status argument holds, one should expect the institutional design of the AIIB and the bank's operations to be related to China's perception of its global status and whether it is satisfied with how it is perceived by others. The bank's future will depend on this. Rather than a debate between the revisionist and the complementary camps, the focus should be on China's perception of itself and its status in international development finance.

Global responses to the AIIB

The literature discussed so far seeks to elucidate the past, present and future of the AIIB. Now, we will focus on how countries around the world have responded to the bank. In general, response to the AIIB depends on how concerned a country is about China's power, its perception of China's reputation, and whether it thinks the bank offers any potential benefits.

Those countries which were most concerned about the strategic ramifications of the rise of China, such as the US and Japan, were inclined to block the establishment of the bank. The theories of power transition that have been discussed thus far suggest that the establishment of the AIIB was aimed at replacing the US-led international financial system, so it is hardly surprising that Washington refused to participate and sought to persuade its allies around the globe to do likewise. Xing (2016) believes that the birth of the AIIB presented Japan with a dilemma, as Tokyo relies on its leadership of the ADB to exercise its influence through supporting regional development projects. The ADB helps nurture Tokyo's regional soft power and build up its international reputation as an advanced, peaceful and democratic country. All of these advantages are threatened by competition from the AIIB. The more successful the AIIB becomes, the more strategic advantages Japan, as the leader of the ADB, will lose. Although Japanese public opinion was divided on the question of whether Japan should join the AIIB, the Abe administration refused to join and raised concerns about the AIIB's governance and operations. Vieira (2018) finds that early members of the AIIB tend to be more politically distant from the U.S, while countries that are politically and strategically closer to Washington or which share Washington's security concerns were more likely to say no to the AIIB. However, this research also finds that with the passage of time, more countries that were aligned with the US as well as more ADB members joined the AIIB.

Setting power concerns aside, Knoerich and Urdinez (2019) find that many countries joined the AIIB because of the public goods that it could provide and how it could finance their national infrastructure projects. Besides this, broader economic and development considerations also came into play when countries made their decisions on membership. They recognized that investment in infrastructure would result in more economic growth and development. Non-regional members may have been less concerned about strategic issues since, to them, China is geographically remote. Although Mendez (2019) criticizes the countries of Latin America and the Caribbean for being slow to join, he ascribes this inertia to domestic political rivalry. In his view, those countries should have acted faster in order to grasp the economic and financial opportunities provided by the AIIB. African countries may have shared the same economic concerns. Prinsloo (2019) argues that the AIIB can provide attractive low-cost financial assistance to African economies. The bank would win more advocates on that continent if it could provide more support for technical capacity-building and financial instruments for low-income countries.

European countries also value the potential economic opportunities opened up by the AIIB, as, despite being staunch military allies of Washington, they are not as concerned about power transition as the US. Chen (2018) finds that European countries that were getting increasingly friendly with China and becoming more dependent on the potentially gigantic Asian market were the most likely to join the AIIB. European states that are not so geared toward China or Asia were least likely to join. Where only one of these factors is present, the country will remain hesitant. He and Feng (2019) also suggest that if potential member states are aware of specific and concrete benefits provided by the challenger's international institutions, such as the AIIB, the attraction of these benefits will make them choose to support the new institution established by the challenger state. However, if the country does not see such benefits, it will be more likely to join with the leader of the existing institutions in order to stabilize the status quo. This could explain why the United Kingdom changed its mind and became a founding member of the AIIB, while Japan rejected the bank because of security concerns and concerns about economic statecraft generated by the rise of China. Similarly, many East Asian countries came to their decisions on membership by weighing up pressure from Washington against the lucrative opportunities offered by China. If they consider that the latter outweigh the former, East Asian countries will become more enthusiastic about the AIIB and vice versa (Lam, 2014).

High-income countries and those with a sound institutional foundation are more likely to join if they think they can exert influence within the AIIB. This is another important incentive for membership, as only by joining can countries ensure that the bank adheres to high governance and lending standards. Membership will also give a say in shaping the AIIB's structure, rules, politics and loan decisions from within (Knoerich & Urdinez, 2019).

Aside from strategic or economic concerns, regime type, past experience and level of representation in the Bretton Woods system may influence whether a state decides to join the AIIB. Wang (2018) argues that less democratic countries are more likely to apply for AIIB membership. He contends that autocracies face fewer political constraints when considering whether to join an international organization led by a communist regime. Strong pressure from the US government constitutes another factor, particularly for Western democracies. In addition, these countries took into consideration the behavior of their neighbors as well as their experience of previous interaction with China in international organizations. Countries whose neighbors had already joined the AIIB, who had already been a member of a China-led international organization and who were underrepresented in the existing international financial system were more likely to join the AIIB.

An integrative framework

Based on this discussion, this book proposes an integrative analytical framework through which to understand the creation and the configuration of the AIIB, its possible trajectory and how it is perceived by the international community (see Figure 2.1). According to this framework, when China first proposed the establishment of the AIIB, it was dissatisfied with its power and status in the international financial system. There was a huge gap between China's externally recognized international financial status and its own perception of its financial power, which led, in China's eyes, to a huge status deficit (more theoretical and empirical analysis of this can be found in Chapter 3). At that time, however, China remained open as to the shape and design of the AIIB. Beijing wanted to see how the international community responded to its cry of dissatisfaction before making the next move. Once the AIIB was created, countries with different strategic concerns and economic interests reacted differently to it, with reactions being colored by the comments of powerful countries as well as the number of founding members recruited.

If the global reaction to the idea of the AIIB is mostly negative, it will result in an increase in China's status deficit. If this is the case, the AIIB will become

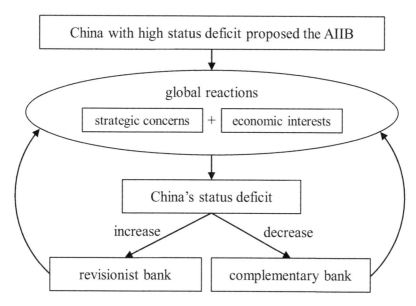

Figure 2.1 A theoretical framework for the book

a revisionist bank used by China to challenge the current international financial system, secure strategic and diplomatic allies, control strategic locations and facilities, reinvigorate China's sluggish domestic economy, and satisfy the political interests of the Chinese Communist Party. If the global reactions are mostly positive and appreciative, China's status deficit will shrink. The AIIB will then become a complementary bank that will focus on integrating itself into the international financial system, pooling additional resources, connecting the developed and developing worlds, improving the bank's operational efficiency, stimulating reform of the international financial system and keeping its distance from the Belt and Road Initiative.

The future development of the bank will in turn influence future global reactions to the AIIB, which will then start another round of cause and effect. This should be seen as a dynamic circle influenced by the changing strategic conditions experienced by countries around the world, by China's status deficit and by the development of the AIIB. It is clear that this analytical framework does not seek to predict whether the AIIB will follow the realist or the neo-functionalist path. Instead, it suggests that the AIIB is likely to veer between both paths in the future. The empirical analysis in the following chapters will emphasize this dynamic process.

Conclusion

In this chapter, I have examined a variety of scholarly works on the AIIB from which I have suggested possible future scenarios for the bank. Those who suspect

China's underlying geopolitical and geo-economic motivations for establishing the AIIB see the bank as an instrument of power for Beijing that will serve China's own interests during the power transition period. Eventually, China will run this bank strategically in order to realize relative gains at the expense of its major global and regional rivals. Many other studies take a more optimistic view of the AIIB, believing that it can improve the functional coordination of the financial resources necessary to improve regional infrastructure. The participation of Western countries can also ensure the bank's compliance with global best practice. From a status or reputational perspective, the AIIB is more than just a power tool or a multilateral platform for coordination. It serves as a diplomatic instrument that China can use to persuade the international community that its rise will be peaceful and that it is willing to become a responsible stakeholder. At the same time, China is using the bank to gain recognition of its status as a great power in the international financial system. As a result, the bank's trajectory may depend on how China identifies itself and how it wants to be perceived. Each country will respond to the AIIB in a different way according to circumstances. Suspicious countries will be alarmed and thus refuse to participate, while countries that take a more optimistic view will be eager to join and will expect direct and indirect benefits from the bank. Instead of considering these arguments independently, this book provides an analytical framework to integrate all of them. This framework embraces the evolution of the AIIB and global responses to it and how these two interact.

It would be premature at present to make any conclusive judgment about the AIIB. The bank is still young and institutionally incomplete. It is subject to institutional changes, and there is insufficient data to draw any conclusions. It is also too soon to gauge the international community's reaction to the bank – a dynamic process that will be affected by many strategic and economic factors. As the trajectory of the AIIB remains undecided, so does the strategic and economic situation shaped by the bank and thus the perceptions and behavior of each individual state. Through the lenses of these divergent perspectives and assisted by the integrative framework presented above, the following chapters will analyze the AIIB four years into its existence to see whether the reality fits the proposed theory.

3 China and the evolution of the AIIB

The Asian Infrastructure Investment Bank (AIIB) has drawn attention and heated debates globally since the institution was first proposed by China's President Xi Jinping in October 2013. The US Treasury Department during the Obama administration criticized the creation of the AIIB as a deliberate effort to undercut the international financial institutions established after World War II and a political tool for China to court neighboring countries that have quarrels with Beijing (Perlez, 2014). Rebutting such criticism, China described the bank as an open and inclusive IFI committed to regional development rather than as a tool for China to compete with established rules (*Global Times*, 2014). In the beginning, when China pondered the configuration of the bank, several options were considered. The bank could be developed as a China-dominant exclusive development aid agency that would respond to China's geopolitical interests and its grand strategy, the Belt and Road Initiative (BRI), or as an inclusive and multilateral investment vehicle with an emphasis on commercial purposes and seeking collaborations with other relevant parties in bankrolling regional infrastructure development (Sun, 2015). This chapter finds that the constitution and behaviors of the AIIB so far suggest that the AIIB has become more cooperative, inclusive and focused on mutual benefits and reform of the international financial system while playing down China's geopolitical considerations.

To explain, this chapter argues that the AIIB is a dynamic institution that will evolve according to the gap between China's recognized international financial status and its own perception of its financial power – what is called here China's status deficit. If the deficit is large, China tends to use the AIIB as an instrument of global competition; if the deficit is small, the bank is more likely to behave cooperatively. The AIIB's future development will depend on whether China is accorded a position in the international financial system commensurate with its own perception of its power.

The next section consists of a discussion of studies on the AIIB. It will be followed by six empirical sections. The first empirical section identifies the source of China's status deficit as a combination of its disproportionate voting power in the Bretton Woods system, underrated sovereign credit and lack of appreciation for the renminbi's international status. The second empirical section analyzes China's ambitions to compete for power prior to the signing of the Articles of

Agreement (AOA) and the corresponding idea of the bank's configuration. The third section presents quantitative results of the analysis of the political and economic factors that may have influenced countries' decisions on joining the AIIB as founding members. The fourth empirical section also uses quantitative analysis to test whether there is any political/strategic basis for the AIIB's loans. In the fifth section, I investigate whether the AIIB has become a cooperative and complementary multilateral agency. The last empirical section compares the distribution of funds by the AIIB and the Belt and Road Initiative (BRI) and considers their possible divergent trajectories. The final section draws some conclusions and discusses the bank's future.

Power, interests and status

Based on the discussions in Chapter 2, most of the existing literature on the AIIB focuses on China's purpose in creating the bank. Those studies that adopt a more pessimistic perspective see the AIIB as being a revisionist instrument wielded by a rising and dissatisfied China and downplay the bright sides of the coming of the AIIB. With little regard for negative political, economic, social or environmental impacts, the bank aims to surpass other major IFIs dominated by the West and seeks to redefine the international financial system. Thus, these works suggest that the bank is more likely to finance projects that serve China's geopolitical interests (Chen, 2016; Chow, 2016; Cook, 2015; Etzioni, 2016; Hecan, 2016; Ikenberry & Lim, 2017; Ito, 2015; Lam, 2014; Reisen, 2015; Wan, 2016; Xing, 2016). In contrast, another line of argument considers that, rather than challenging the existing international financial order, China intends to use the AIIB to coordinate and supplement the resources required for Asia's continued economic development, thereby benefitting all parties in the region. By admitting members from outside the region, China is practicing multilateralism, which will effectively restrain its power ambitions. China will then act as a responsible status quo power that it has always claimed to want to be. Those works tend to appreciate the potential benefits of the AIIB and have played down the role of China's geopolitical ambitions. From this perspective, the purpose of the AIIB is to realize shared sustainable development objectives, foster regional connectivity and cooperation with other IFIs, promote transparency and accountability, and accept and improve current global governance. (Chin, 2016; De Jonge, 2017; Gabusi, 2017; Liao, 2015; Lipscy, 2015b; Ren, 2016; Weaver, 2015; Wu, 2018).

With a few exceptions, these two lines of argument, although informative, have two problems. First, some analyses in those works came from theoretical deduction without enough empirical support while others were based on facts extant before the AIIB started to operate; therefore, empirical findings were not sufficiently supported by the actual behaviors of the AIIB. Second, while debating the two opposite scenarios of the AIIB, those works downplay the possibility that both pessimistic and optimistic considerations can exist. A more pertinent question is to explore the wax and wane of both pessimistic and optimistic dynamics and the possibility of changes in their relative weight. A more satisfying explanation should be a dynamic one. This is especially the case when I traced the development of the AIIB since its inception at the end of 2013 until the end of 2018; China in fact had multiple options in shaping the AIIB initially. As China started to lobby more countries to participate and negotiated with potential founding members for the bank's constitution, the AIIB became a multilateral development bank that played down revisionist intentions and, more concerned with mutual interests, sought to conform to established international practice. Therefore, a more satisfying explanation should address the possible factors that caused China to lead the AIIB into a more complementary and cooperative IFI.

A possible factor that influenced the AIIB's trajectory is China's international status, which is considered as one of the main drivers for China's foreign policies (Deng, 2008; Scobell, 2012). Volgy et al. (2011) consider China to be an overachiever state – states that are given great power status but fall short of commensurate capability – in its quest for status, which has led it to bypass high-risk foreign policy for fear of losing status. In the international financial system, this book argues that China, in fact, resembles an underachiever state – one that possesses significant financial power but which has yet to be dully recognized by other great powers. Situated in such a circumstance, an underachiever is more likely to attempt to resolve its status by competing more aggressively and enlarging its role in international society. Rather than resorting to power competition for greater status, Suzuki (2008) argues that a "frustrated great power," which is dissatisfied with its internationally recognized status, can gain "legitimate great power" status by persuading and convincing its peers of its due qualification. He found that its participation in the United Nations Peacekeeping Operation, which featured upholding core norms of international society, has afforded China the recognized image of a responsible great power. Regarding the AIIB, Yang (2016) argues that the establishment of the bank was part of a social creativity strategy aimed at improving China's international status. Callaghan and Hubbard (2016) claim that if the AIIB can depoliticize loan decisions, it can boost China's image in the region. Although these studies have ascribed China's approach toward international participation as status seeking, they remain inconsistent as to the nature and level of China's international status and the means by which Beijing seeks to improve its status. In addition, these studies focus on a static analysis, thereby lacking any emphasis on the possibility of change in China's status and how Beijing might react to the dynamic situation.

In its contribution to the status hypothesis, this chapter argues that China's choice of either revisionist or cooperative policies depends on whether the state experiences a status deficit, that is, a gap between the status it is accorded by others and its own perceived power level. Renshon (2017) finds that when states experience status deficits, it will lead to status dissatisfaction, which will trigger a state's heightened status concerns. Consequently, the dissatisfied state will likely initiate status-altering events to defend or change their relative status by changing or updating international community's belief of its status in the international society. Those status-altering events can be either conflictual – featuring power-struggle – or cooperative. Renshon (2017) not only links a state's status to its sequential behavior but also allows the former to be dynamic. This chapter thus follows his proposition and argues that when China first came up with the idea of the AIIB, it was experiencing a disjunction between the status it was accorded in the international financial hierarchy and its own perception of its global financial power. With several options in hands, China was more prone to make the AIIB more revisionist-oriented. When it was clear that China's international financial status received positive recognition and the AIIB was well received by developed countries, China's status deficit was reduced and Beijing therefore switched to a more cooperative strategy in creating this new IFI.

The AIIB and China's status deficit

From the preceding discussion, it is imperative to identify the sources of China's status deficit in place prior to the conception of the AIIB. China has experienced impressive economic growth since the beginning of the century; but that did not automatically result in China's achieving equivalent status in the international financial system. In 1990, China's GDP and outward FDI was small compared with the top two economic powers, Japan and the US. However, China's voting power in the World Bank and the ADB outweighed its economic power. Since 2000, however, China has surpassed Japan and is catching up with the US. From the Composite Index of National Capability in the National Material Capabilities (v5.0) dataset (Singer, Bremer, & Stuckey, 1972), we can see that China's aggregate power has surged even more significantly in relation to the US and Japan. However, it is obvious that greater economic power does not necessarily lead to a higher status in the two IFIs. Many in the US claim that the US Congress's repeated rejection of IMF reform is responsible for China's dissatisfaction with the current order and its decision to establish the AIIB (Donnan, 2015).

Table 3.1 China's GDP, OFDI, ODA and voting power as a percentage of those of the US and Japan

	1990	*2000*	*2013*	*2016*
GDP (% of US)	6.0	11.8	57.6	60.1
OFDI (% of US)	1.4	2.5	18.6	69.7
ODA (% of US)	n/a	12.8	34.8	n/a
CINC (% of US)	79.2	113.7	156.5	n/a
Vote shares in the WB (% of US)	21.6	17.0	36.0	27.9
Vote shares in the ADB (% of US)	49.1	42.8	42.9	42.7
GDP (% of JP)	11.5	24.8	186.3	227.7
OFDI (% of JP)	1.6	10.2	46.9	128.0
ODA (% of JP)	n/a	16.2	116.7	n/a
CINC (% of JP)	220.5	325.5	612.9	n/a
Vote shares in the WB (% of JP)	37.4	35.4	64.5	64.5
Vote shares in the ADB % (% of JP)	49.1	42.8	42.6	42.7

Source: GDP and OFDI data come from World Bank statistics; China's ODA data come from Dreher et al. (2017); US and Japanese ODA comes from OECD statistics; voting power data come from the World Bank's annual financial statements and the ADB's annual reports for those years.

Since the 2010s, China has been more ambitious in vying for influence in IFIs. When it was competing with Japan for leadership of the ADB, Beijing unusually failed to send its central bank head or finance minister to the annual IMF-World Bank meeting in October 2012 hosted by Japan, signaling its rejection of Japan's financial leadership in the region (Nakamichi, 2013). Beijing has also long criticized the way the West controls the IMF and the World Bank by means of voting powers and its occupation of the presidency, while emerging countries such as China have received scant attention (Vestergaard & Wade, 2013). Feeling this lack of respect, in 2012, China and its fellow BRICS (Brazil, Russia, India, China and South Africa) came up with the idea of a New Development Bank (NDB) (*The Financial Express*, 2012), which was established in 2014, just before the birth of the AIIB. Some Western diplomats were still unconvinced that China was ready for a leadership role in economic institutions (Davis, 2011). The IMF, the World Bank, and six other leading IFIs issued a joint statement hinting that the emerging AIIB and NDB might dilute the quality and sustainability of infrastructure investments fiscally, economically, socially and environmentally (The World Bank, 2014; Rowley, 2014).

Western sovereign rating agencies have been giving China's sovereign credit what Beijing considers to be biased ratings. While the US received a "Aaa" rating from Moody's even in the midst of the financial crisis of 2008, crisis-free China was only awarded an "A1." Deeming the rating unfair, China established the world's first non-Western credit rating agency, the Dagong Global Credit Rating, in 2010. In its first report, the China-led agency rated China and the emerging countries higher than the United States, France and other developed countries on account of their slow economic growth and heavy debt burden (*Xinhua*, 2010; K. Yao, 2013). Finally, during the early 2010s when Beijing was seeking to improve the renminbi's international status by having the currency included in the IMF's Special Drawing Right (SDR), Western countries, along with some emerging powers, were not supportive (Anderlini & Giles, 2011; Shah & Sikarwar, 2011). China's complaints and dissatisfaction with its under-recognized status can be shown by Xi Jinping's remark in March 2013 stating that the "global economic governance system must reflect the deep change of world economic structure and increase the representation and the say of emerging countries" (*People's Daily*, 2013). Western doubts about China's financial strength thus opened a gap between China's financial power and its status; this status deficit made China more prone to adopting power-seeking approaches.

The launch of the AIIB

As discussed, China was experiencing a status deficit in late 2013 when Xi Jinping first conceived the idea of the AIIB. While envisaging the trajectory of the new China-led IFI, a dissatisfied Beijing became more likely to accept power-maximizing logic for the creation of the bank and downplay the bank's cooperative potential. Such intention can be observed from the membership of the new bank, the degree of power wielded by China and the way in which the bank has been politicized in China's favor.

Regarding membership, the AIIB had options of either becoming an Asia-exclusive IFI or including other non-regional members. According to China's finance minister at the time, Lou Jiwei, the AIIB membership would be "regional first and non-regional later" (Zeng, 2015). On October 24, 2014, 21 countries – all members from the region – signed the Memorandum of Understanding on Establishing the AIIB (MOU). Later, in both the 1st and 2nd AIIB Chief Negotiators' Meetings, held in November of 2014 and January of 2015, there was no participation by non-regional members. At this stage, the AIIB looked like an exclusive club, as it remained unclear whether the bank would attract non-regional powers. Exclusive international organizations favor unequal power distribution and are easier for key members to control (Koremenos, Lipson, & Snidal, 2001). Arguably, China might have made efforts to lobby for the participation of Western countries in the beginning in order to seek status recognition from them. Should the European countries decide to follow Washington's rejection of the AIIB (Chen, 2018), it would further increase China's sense of status deficit. Thus, rather than becoming an IFI with worldwide membership, the AIIB was more likely to become an exclusive club that allowed China to have tighter control.

Regarding the concentration of power in China's hands, when the MOU was signed in 2014, China planned to contribute 50% of the bank's funds, which would allow it to dominate the AIIB (Sun, 2015). Admittedly, this might have been inevitable, as most Asian countries are developing economies that could only afford to subscribe to a minority of the AIIB's shares. Beijing might be the only country willing and financially capable of subscribing most of AIIB's authorized capital. Nonetheless, China had alternative ways to ease the financial burden of developing countries. It could lower the preliminary capital scale that allowed a higher percentage of shares to be purchased by prospective founding members that were financially limited. In fact, according to Lou Jiwei in early 2014, the preliminary capital scale of the bank was set at US$50 billion (*Xinhua*, 2014), only half of the final amount of US$100 billion. Alternatively, Beijing could have also persuaded financially rich developed countries, such as Brunei, Singapore or South Korea, to share more of the burden. Comparing the three countries' subscribed shares in the AIIB and ADB, in which the amounts of authorized capital are roughly the same at US$100 billion: the AIIB shares subscribed by Singapore and South Korea amount to only about half of the amount of their ADB subscriptions, while Brunei's AIIB share subscription is only about 10% of its ADB subscription. The distribution of shares did not appear to be proportional to the distribution of financial power of the prospective founding members. With regard to veto power, it is claimed that during the consultation stage, China planned to give itself veto powers in the bank's constitution (Pang, 2014). Veto powers are seen as a way in which risk-averse states protect themselves from unforeseen circumstances (Koremenos, Lipson, & Duncan, 2001, p. 792). In the early stages of the bank, when China was uncertain about the AIIB's positioning and future trajectory and unsure how other countries and IFIs would perceive and interact with it, it was quite rational for China to hold veto powers, thus guaranteeing that the bank would achieve Beijing's goals.

Finally, China originally sought to develop the AIIB as either an aid agency or a profit-seeking commercial bank (Sun, 2015). As an aid agency, the AIIB could be used by China to direct foreign aid in a way that served its own national interests. China could more easily make concessional loans to its strategic partners or allies, as well as putting money on the table in exchange for favors. The AIIB's proposals are often more attractive and competitive than those of the World Bank, which sometimes come with political or economic reform conditions attached. In this way, the AIIB had the potential to become China's multilateral policy bank. As a commercial entity, the bank would be more likely to finance commercial projects that serve China's own strategic interests than promote regional development. Thus, the bank would be less likely to prioritize economic and financial concerns in making investment decisions.

Before the AOA was finalized in June 2015, the AIIB might still have become a fairly exclusive multilateral policy bank dominated by Beijing. However, the bank soon received a positive reaction from the European powers. At the same time, the major IFIs started to think about raising China's status in the international financial system. China's voting shares in the IMF were increased and the renminbi was included in the IMF's SDR basket. The implications of being in the SDR are more political than economic, as inclusion signals that the IMF recognizes the currency's significance and its future (*Financial Times*, 2015). These moves might have reduced China's sense of status deficit. Under such circumstances, China became more satisfied with its international financial status and was thus more likely to play down power-competing implications in the final form of the AOA.

Although we saw the absence of non-regional countries in the first two Chief Negotiators' Meeting, three non-regional members (Luxembourg, Switzerland and the UK) participated in the 3rd meeting, and another 14 European countries, plus Brazil, Egypt and South Africa, joined the 4th and 5th meetings before the singing of the AOA (Lichtenstein, 2019, pp. 77–78). In fact, the scope of AIIB's membership has become more inclusive than its major competitor, the ADB. For regional members, the ADB excludes most Western Asian countries while the AIIB does not. Therefore, countries in the Middle East are eligible to apply for regional membership in the AIIB. For non-regional members, the ADB allows only developed countries while the AIIB has no such restriction.[1] Compared to the period of Asia-exclusive participation before 2015, the AIIB has, hence, become an inclusive IFI that permits worldwide membership applications.

Of the 57 founding members, 20 (35%) are from outside Asia. European countries, such as the UK, were heavily involved in drafting the AOA (O'Neill, 2015). Even experts from the U.S, which was suspicious and harshly critical of the AIIB, contributed to the process (Earl & Murray, 2015; Lichtenstein, 2019). Regarding the distribution of voting powers, the AIIB's initial authorized capital stock was set at US$100 billion, partly thanks to European participation. As China did not subscribe to 50% of the shares, it didn't increase its financial burden; instead, Beijing allowed European countries to share more financial burden. China also gave up its veto power over loan decisions (Wilson, 2017). However, Beijing still controls almost 30% of the shares, which gives it an initial voting power of 26.06%. Although China gave up its outright veto power over day-to-day operations (Magnier, 2015), it still holds veto powers for major issues that require a supermajority (75%) for passage.[2] So, the AIIB ended up as neither China's aid agency nor a commercial bank. Article 2 of the AOA stipulates that the function of the bank is to promote infrastructure development in particular; Article 31 states that the bank's loan decisions should be based on economic considerations and not influenced by political considerations. Although China still holds a certain degree of control in the AIIB, a China-dominant IFI free from constitutional constraints did not emerge.

Who joins the bank?

Undoubtedly, the AIIB attracted a great deal of attention from both regional and non-regional countries. It would be interesting to investigate what kinds of countries were more likely to have joined the AIIB as founding members and, of those that did, which had the greatest voting power. My quantitative findings are presented in the following section. The first dependent variable is a dummy variable: founding membership of the AIIB. The second dependent variable is the founding member's initial voting power based on that country's promised subscription of shares.

There are nine explanatory variables that might account for a country's wish to join the AIIB and to subscribe more shares. The first one is dissatisfaction with the current international financial governance system. I use voting power to GDP ratio in the World Bank as a proxy measure of each country's level of dissatisfaction with the international financial architecture (see Chapter 4 for more detail). The second and third factors are common interests and shared political characteristics. The literature suggests that states that are politically similar are less likely to be involved in conflicts; in other words, they are more likely to cooperate (Werner, 2000). Common interests are operationalized as the political affinity index, which measures dyadic voting pattern in the United Nations General Assembly (Voeten, Strezhnev, & Bailey, 2016). Political regime data comes from the widely used POLITY IV (Marshall, Gurr, & Jaggers, 2014). If the factor of political system similarity is significant, the results should show that authoritarian countries are more likely to join the bank and get a larger share of votes because China is currently an authoritarian political regime. The fourth factor is whether a certain country currently has a security alliance with China. I propose that if such an alliance exists, that country will have a more positive perception of a China-led AIIB, and will therefore be more likely to join and contribute more shares. A country is coded 1 if it has had a formal alliance with China since 1990 and 0 otherwise. Data comes from Gibler (2009).

The fifth and sixth factors imply that developing countries with urgent infrastructure needs are more likely to join the AIIB because they will be able to secure more funds through the bank for their infrastructure development. I use a dummy variable for this: a country is coded 1 if it is classified by the World Bank as a low-income economy, a lower-middle-income economy or an upper-middle-income economy; otherwise, the code is 0. In addition, I also use level of infrastructure as a proxy for the need for infrastructure development. This indicator comes from the World Bank's Logistics Performance Index.[3] The seventh and eighth factors reflect a country's economic dependence on China: if a country is highly dependent on Chinese manufactures and investments, it will be more likely to participate in China-led international financial projects. These factors are measured by volume of imports and inward foreign direct investment (FDI) from China.[4] Because a country with a larger economy would naturally be more dependent on China than a country with a smaller economy, the final factor is a country's economic weight, which is used to control for the size of a country's economy.

I use probit analysis in Models 1 and 2 to estimate the relationship between the probability of joining the AIIB and the explanatory variables. I use ordinary least square (OLS) regression analysis in Models 3 and 4 to account for the level of share subscription, which translates into each country's voting power in the AIIB. Results are reported in Table 3.2. Model 1 includes all countries for which data are available while Model 2 only includes Asian countries. The inclusion of a global analysis reflects a comment by Yan Xuetong, a prominent Chinese scholar, that the AIIB has unintentionally expanded from a regional to a global financial institution (*Nikkei*, 2015). The results show that from both a global and a regional perspective, countries are more likely to have joined the AIIB as founding members if they had a low power to GDP ratio in the World Bank, received more Chinese exports and FDI and had lower global economic weight. This coincides with the argument that the AIIB is an international organization whose members tend to be dissatisfied with the unequal distribution of voting power in the World Bank. Interestingly, those countries are not necessarily developing countries – there is no statistically significant association between being a developing country and joining the AIIB. Instead, they may be small but wealthy economies that have felt underrepresented in the World Bank. In terms of external economic relationships, those countries that import huge amounts of Chinese goods and receive a significant amount of Chinese FDI are more likely to accept a China-led AIIB. This, to some extent, demonstrates how China's economic offensive over the past few years has made the AIIB an attractive international organization that both developed and developing countries are keen to join (Lam, 2014; Wong & Lye, 2014; Zha, 2015, p. 134). Surprisingly, authoritarian countries or countries sharing similar global perspectives with China do not seem more likely to join the AIIB, albeit the effect of being an authoritarian regime approaches statistical significance at p-values 0.11 and 0.14 for models 1 and 2. Though less statistically significant, this factor seems plausible and is therefore deemed worthy of further research.

Models 3 and 4 focus on the countries that have higher initial voting power in the AIIB. Model 3 includes all AIIB members, while Model 4 comprises only the members from Asia. Interestingly, as shown in the first two models, whether a country joins the AIIB depends partly on whether it is dissatisfied with unequal voting powers in other major international financial organizations. But Models 3 and 4 show

Table 3.2 Who joins the AIIB and their relative voting power

	(1)	(2)	(3)	(4)
	AIIB Member	AIIB Member	Relative Power	Relative Power
Power/GDP (WB)	−0.194***	−0.561**	1.195***	1.162***
	(0.0699)	(0.224)	(0.217)	(0.245)
Affinity Score	1.929	0.856	−1.220	−1.021
	(1.924)	(2.331)	(2.169)	(2.444)
Polity IV	−0.0416	−0.0925	0.0317	0.0541
	(0.0265)	(0.0635)	(0.0463)	(0.0567)
Security Alliance	1.399***	−0.161	0.222	−0.129
	(0.529)	(0.790)	(0.773)	(0.918)
Developing country	0.0203	−2.052	−0.0732	0.0884
	(0.437)	(1.969)	(0.639)	(1.423)
Infrastructure	1.769***	0.297	−0.373	0.257
	(0.475)	(1.704)	(0.488)	(1.174)
China's exports (log)	1.137***	5.546***	1.101**	0.821
	(0.419)	(2.048)	(0.451)	(1.442)
China's outward FDI (log)	0.382***	1.382***	0.554**	0.659
	(0.145)	(0.498)	(0.255)	(0.806)
GDP (log)	−1.362***	−5.837***	−3.516***	−4.614***
	(0.524)	(2.000)	(0.746)	(1.387)
N	145	35	51	27
Adjusted R-Square	0.441	0.574	0.881	0.913

Note:

1 Numbers in parentheses are robust standard errors for models 1 and 2, and Huber-White standard errors for models 3 and 4.

2 $* p < 0.10, ** p < 0.05, *** p < 0.01$.

that, after controlling for many factors, the alleged voting power distribution problem still exists in the AIIB, from both a global and a regional perspective. Those countries that are overrepresented or underrepresented in the World Bank remain so in the AIIB. This suggests that, in terms of the distribution of voting power by economic weight, the AIIB is no different from the World Bank (refer to Chapter 4 for more details). However, countries with lower GDPs, no matter whether they are rich or poor, have a larger share of the votes in relation to their economic weight. But, this situation holds mainly for mini-states or the least developed countries, including Laos, Malta, Tajikistan, Kyrgyzstan and the Maldives. These countries simply have no decision-making power in any financial IOs. If we look only at the AIIB's top 30 members in terms of GDP, the effect of GDP vanishes.

Figure 3.1 displays the marginal effects of four variables in model 1. Holding other factors constant, countries that are properly represented in terms of their economic weight (power/GDP ratio=1) are about 13.8% more likely to join the AIIB than countries that are 400% overrepresented in the World Bank. The most underrepresented country in the World Bank, Vietnam (ratio=0.29), is about twice as likely to join the AIIB than a country with 560% overrepresentation, such as

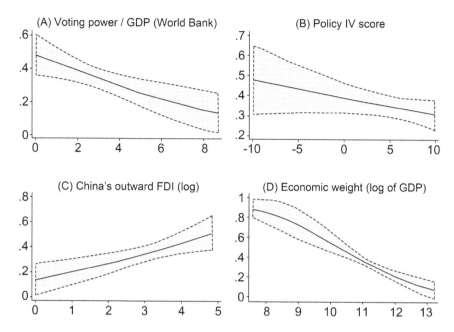

Figure 3.1 Predicted probability of joining the AIIB

the non-member Armenia (ratio=5.64).[5] Looking at the factor of regime type, the most authoritarian countries – e.g., Saudi Arabia or Uzbekistan – are 17.3% more likely to join the AIIB than the most democratic countries, such as Japan and the United States. In terms of FDI from China, countries receiving the most Chinese FDI are 3.82 times, or 38%, more likely to join the AIIB than those with no Chinese investment. Finally, countries with the lowest economic weight are 12 times, or 81.3%, more likely to join the AIIB than those with the largest economies.

The finding here leads to several interesting arguments. First, although countries may join the AIIB out of a sense of resentment at the governance systems of other IFIs, the same governance problems exist in the new bank too. There remains no improvement in the AIIB in terms of matching voting power to economic weight. This China-led financial vehicle has the same representation problems as other IFIs. Second, considering the effect of authoritarian regime, non-democratic countries may be more likely to join an organization like the AIIB which is led by China. Out of the 31 Asian members of the AIIB that account for 75% of the initial authorized capital, 21, or 68%, are non-democratic (polity score less than 6). They may be expected to cooperate with one another (Ambrosio, 2008; Peceny, Beer, & Sanchez-Terry, 2002) and form a strong financial alliance in the AIIB. However, one study shows that different kinds of authoritarian regimes may react differently to IMF financial programs (Fails & Woo, 2015). This finding implies that one should not take unity among the AIIB's non-democratic members for granted. In addition, lack of democracy is often associated with poor governance and corruption (Lederman, Loayza, & Soares, 2005), which conflicts with the financial best practice espoused by the AIIB's European members. According to Transparency International's Corruption Perceptions Index 2014, the top five emerging economies in the AIIB, which hold more than 3% of the voting power, experience serious corruption problems. Out of 175 countries, China ranked 100th on this list, while Russia was 136th, India 85th, Indonesia 107th and Brazil 69th (Transparency International, 2014). Together, these countries control more than 43% of the votes in the AIIB. In these circumstances, it will be a challenging task to establish best practice within the AIIB, including accountability and transparency (Biswas, 2015). Given their limited voting powers, it is doubtful whether the AIIB's European members will be able to get the AIIB to accept global standards. The above analysis indicates that the AIIB might not be as united as was imagined and may also be less likely to embrace global standards.

Third, the variable of political affinity, which measures the degree of agreement on global affairs between China and other countries, does not explain either a country's likelihood of joining the AIIB or its share of voting power. This factor reflects the degree to which AIIB members share China's views on various aspects of global affairs. If they do not, it would be problematic for China to mobilize enough support to challenge the current international financial system. The BRICS countries, which are probably the most important members of the AIIB, may differ in their views, just as they do in the New Development Bank (NDB) that they have created. Instead of differing with regard to the approach to economic development, these five countries have different international political agendas and divergent views concerning the NDB's financing role and the location of its headquarters (Wihtol, 2014, pp. 11–12). In addition to the problem of potential discord, studies found that IFIs that are subject to extensive competition, which results in more outside options, are more likely to experience institutional change to align with members' underlying interests (Lipscy, 2015a). More outside options tend to lead to members leaving the organization, which in turn, can force change. There is more extensive competition in the area of development aid – an area that the AIIB is involved in – than there is among institutions responsible for balance of payments lending, such as the IMF or the Chiang Mai Initiative; therefore, China may not always be able to dominate the AIIB. As the bank's funds increase, structural constraints may in fact weaken China's leadership. Satisfying as many members with divergent interests and global perspectives as possible is the key to the AIIB's survival.

Immediately after the bank was founded, it seemed as though the AIIB had the potential to become a political and strategic arm of the PRC, if that had been what Beijing intended. However, now that China's concerns about its status deficit have eased, will the AIIB seek to downplay speculation in the rest of the world concerning its revisionist ambitions? I will attempt to answer this question by examining the initial period of the bank's operations. Specifically, I will consider whether the AIIB has confirmed these initial suspicions by testing the validity of two arguments. The first argument, from a pessimistic perspective, is that China will engage in power competition through the AIIB for political and strategic purposes. To verify this, it is necessary to investigate whether most of the AIIB's loans have a political/strategic basis. The second argument relates to whether the AIIB has become a multilateral agency engaged in cooperation and reform.

Political and strategic loans?

Do China's political or strategic interests play an important role in deciding who gets an AIIB loan? If they do, we should be able to observe a concentration of AIIB loans going to countries that are diplomatically friendly, politically similar and strategically important to China. In addition, most loans should have political or strategic significance (Fallon, 2015; Rolland, 2017).

By the end of 2019, the AIIB had approved 56 country-level and 6 region-wide projects, with another 23 proposed projects under review. At least 8 of the proposed projects originally posted on the AIIB website had disappeared, which may indicate that they failed to get approval. The total value of the approved projects is estimated at US\$37.3 billion, and the AIIB is financing approximately US\$11.7 billion, or 31.3% of that total. The cost of most of the projects is shared among the AIIB, other IFIs and local governments or agencies.

Of the 62 approved projects, 20 are in the energy sector, 13 are in transportation, 8 are in water, 8 involve more than one sector, 7 are in the financial sector, 4 are in urban sector, 2 are in the telecommunication sector. Figure 3.2 shows how the loans are distributed across the sectors. The energy and transportation sectors together account for about 56% of total AIIB commitments so far. Both sectors are viewed as being politically and strategically sensitive. Energy projects help strengthen the creditor country's energy security while transportation projects help connect strategically important locations within its borders.

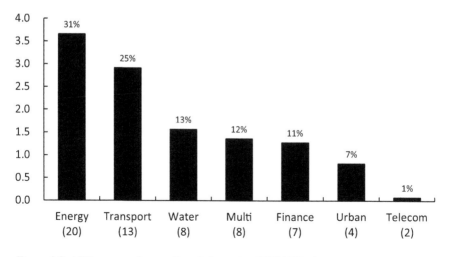

Figure 3.2 AIIB-approved commitments by sector (US\$ billion)

Table 3.3 shows the distribution of projects by country. By the end of 2019, 21 countries had secured project loans approved by the AIIB. India received the largest amount in loans. Although Azerbaijan's projects were worth more than India's in terms of total costs, the AIIB only bankrolled a relatively small portion. The Herfindahl-Hirschman Index (HHI) is adopted to measure the concentration of AIIB commitments by nation. The HHI equals 12%, which suggests that commitments have not been concentrated on any particular nation. However, the four largest loan recipients are AIIB members with relatively large voting powers. The question is, does the distribution of investment loans reflect China's political and strategic interests?

Next, I will test the political/strategic loans hypothesis by including four political/strategic variables, five economic variables and two variables regarding membership in quantitative models. There is extensive research showing that IFIs, such as the IMF and the World Bank, are politically maneuvered by Western countries

Table 3.3 AIIB projects by country, 2016–2019

Country	Number of projects	AIIB funds	Total costs	Vote share % (ranking)
India	13	2,954	7,578	7.6 (2)
Turkey	5	1,400	3,820	2.5 (10)
Regional	6	1,329	2,145	n/a
Indonesia	5	940	3,344	3.2 (8)
China	2	750	2,666	26.5 (1)
Egypt	3	649	1,599	0.8 (28)
Azerbaijan	1	600	8,600	0.4 (39)
Pakistan	4	512	1,700	1.1 (17)
Bangladesh	5	505	1,373	0.8 (27)
Russia	1	500	500	6.0 (3)
Oman	3	301	880	0.4 (38)
Sri Lanka	2	280	397	0.5 (36)
Philippines	1	208	500	1.1 (19)
Nepal	2	202	805	0.3 (46)
Georgia	1	114	315	0.3 (51)
Tajikistan	2	88	456	0.2 (57)
Uzbekistan	1	82	184	0.4 (42)
Cambodia	1	75	75	0.3 (50)
Hong Kong	1	75	75	0.8 (25)
Kazakhstan	1	47	136	0.9 (23)
Laos	1	40	128	0.3 (54)
Myanmar	1	20	20	0.4 (37)
Total	62	11,670	37,296	54.7%

Note:

1 The funds and costs are in million US$.

2 Projects included in this table were all approved before the end of 2019; the official vote-share data was released in December 2019.

3 The project "Egypt Round II Solar PV Feed-in Tariffs Program" included 11 similar sub-projects which were applied for and implemented at the same time. The AIIB originally counted them as 11 projects, but they later appeared on the website as one project. They are counted as one project here.

for projecting their interests. For an IFI to survive, it has to consider the economic situations of its investment targets for profitability and sustainability. Therefore, political and economic motivations are both likely to play a role in the success of development loan applications. The purpose of the quantitative analyses below is to investigate which factors might be more statistically significant.

The dependent variables in the model are the amounts of all proposed and approved loans, as well as only approved loans, received by the AIIB members. By the end of 2019, AIIB had already approved membership to 102 applicants, but only 75 members had ratified, accepted, or approved the AOA and subscribed to AIIB shares. Of those 102 members, the models exclude China and Hong Kong, as well as Cook Islands, Samoa, Tonga and Vanuatu due to the unavailability of data. As a result, there are 96 members included in the quantitative analyses.

The first political/strategic factor is the likelihood of the AIIB to offer loans to authoritarian regimes with poor human rights records, that is, countries in a similar human rights situation as China which have a hard time obtaining loans from other major IFIs (Rosenzweig, 2016). If it can be asserted that regimes with poor human rights records are more likely to receive loans from the AIIB, it could be assumed that the AIIB can act as a cash machine for authoritarian regimes. Not only do those regimes become more reliable to the China-led bank but might also project China's political influence in the recipient countries. I use the Freedom House aggregate score for civil liberties as a proxy for this variable. The second factor is the likelihood of the AIIB issuing loans to countries that have close diplomatic ties with China (Kaya & Woo, 2018). Existing literature found that the destinations of development loans issued by the international financial institutions are correlated with the donors' foreign policy interests. Countries whose foreign policy aligns closer to major powers of the international financial institutions tend to receive more loans (Fleck & Kilby, 2006; Kilby, 2006). Loans can be gifts from major powers in exchange for the support of foreign policy agendas. For this variable, I use the distance between the foreign policy ideal points of China and a given AIIB member represented by voting behavior in the UNGA (Bailey, Strezhnev, & Voeten, 2017). This index seeks to proxy bilateral foreign policy alignment.

The third factor is the likelihood of the AIIB financing infrastructure projects in important oil-exporting countries that would improve China's energy security (Swaine, 2015; S. Yao et al., 2017). Countries exporting a greater volume of crude petroleum to China should be seen by Beijing as strategically more important to China's energy security. As a consequence, the China-led bank may have greater incentive to support more loans to those countries in exchange for secured energy imports. For this, I use the log of exporting value (US$) of crude petroleum from the AIIB members to China as a proxy (Simoes & Hidalgo, 2011). The higher the value, the greater China's energy dependence on the AIIB members; therefore, those members might be able to receive more loans. The fourth factor is the AIIB's propensity to be more generous to members that feel they are underrepresented in other IFIs, such as the World Bank. As part of its effort to challenge the Bretton Woods system, China might want to use the AIIB to unite those countries that share China's dissatisfaction with other major IFIs. Therefore, issuing more loans to those countries could possibly make the AIIB more popular worldwide and gain greater momentum in the current international financial system. I use each member's voting power in 2015 to GDP percentage ratio in the World Bank as a proxy for their level of dissatisfaction with other IFIs (Chen, 2016). The lower the index, the greater the underrepresentation of that country in the World Bank. If the AIIB is being made use of in this way, it should be expected that there will be a higher rate of lending to members with a lower ratio. For the political/strategic hypothesis to be plausible, one or more of the aforementioned four variables should be significantly associated with the dependent variables.

For economic factors, the AIIB's loans may be more likely to go to countries that have a greater market potential as they generate greater trade and investment benefits, have higher infrastructure demands and have lower investment risks. A larger market indicates greater market potential and greater economic opportunities for China. I use a log of GDP in 2015 (current US$) to proxy economic scale. The data comes from the World Bank's World Development Indicators. Trade and investment potentials can be approximated by a gravity model of international trade, which predicts that bilateral trade flows are positively associated with economic scale (GDP) of and negatively associated with geographical distance between a dyad of countries. For both factors, I use a log of GDP and thousand kilometers of distance between the capitals of China and each of the AIIB members. The data of geographical distance comes from "the GeoDist database". In addition, I include each country's inward FDI stock from China as a measure of the factor of China's established investments, which may reflect China's economic interests in overseas investments. The data of FDI stocks comes from the *2015 Statistical Bulletin of China's Outward Foreign Direct Investment* published by the Ministry of Commerce of the People's Republic of China.

For the demands of infrastructure projects, I use each individual country's infrastructure level as a proxy. The AIIB project loans may be more lucrative to destinations with a lower level of infrastructure and have more urgent needs for outside funds. The data of infrastructure level comes from the World Bank's Logistics Performance Index 2016. Lastly, economic risk is an important consideration for any investment. The AIIB should favor a loan destination that has a lower economic risk. If a country is considered as high risk, the creditor may face sovereign default in the future. For operationalizing the economic risks, I use the BMI Economic Risk Index as a proxy. BMI Research is a part of the Fitch Group and produces a quarterly country-level economic risk index. This is an inverse risk index in which a higher score indicates a lower risk.

In addition to political/strategic and economic factors, I add another three control variables. The first is the dummy variable: whether the country is a regional member, as, in that case, it would be likely to receive more loans from the AIIB as the bank is mainly focused on enhancing connectivity in Asia. The second variable is the number of days the country had been a member of the AIIB as of December 31, 2019. Countries approved as prospective members do not have votes in the AIIB until they have completed domestic ratification and transferred their paid-in installment, so their days of membership is zero. It is intuitive to expect that those countries that have been members of the bank for longer would have more private information about business opportunities. The last control factor is a country's total amount of funds received from the World Bank since 2010. The rationale behind this last factor is that, as a newly-established IFI, the AIIB would be expected to choose projects that have already been screened and approved by other lenders, as that would allow them to build up an investment portfolio quickly. To test the effect of all variables, I use ordinary least square (OLS) analysis with robust standard errors for estimation.

Table 3.4 Political economy of AIIB commitments

	(1)	(2)
	All projects	*Approved projects*
Civil liberty	1.835	1.511
	(4.016)	(3.666)
Foreign policy difference	−123.7	−160.6
	(134.4)	(117.7)
Crude oil imports (log)	−3.895	−8.347*
	(4.935)	(4.300)
WB power-GDP ratio	18.30	6.672
	(13.50)	(11.17)
GDP (log)	146.6*	112.7*
	(76.74)	(66.13)
Geographical distance	−0.00753	−0.00942
	(0.0102)	(0.00867)
FDI stock (log)	−30.35*	−16.50
	(15.61)	(14.07)
Infrastructure level	44.51	−78.90
	(93.90)	(82.85)
Economic risk	−1.889	2.031
	(3.538)	(3.369)
Regional member	143.5	92.29
	(99.64)	(78.62)
Days of membership	0.0763	0.0361
	(0.0689)	(0.0581)
World Bank commitment (log)	14.31**	6.701*
	(5.467)	(3.858)
N	96	96
Adjusted R-square	0.269	0.216

Note:

1 Numbers in parentheses are robust standard errors.
2 * $p < 0.10$, ** $p < 0.05$, *** $p < 0.01$.

Table 3.4 presents the results. Model 1 uses each member's total number of proposed and approved AIIB-funded projects as the dependent variable while Model 2 includes only approved projects. For the political/strategic factors, the results appear to be mixed and statistically insignificant. Controlling for all other factors, political regime and foreign policy alignment have opposite effects in Models 1 and 2, while all four political/strategic variables fail to pass significance tests. The results suggest that political/strategic factors did not play an important role in the first wave of loans decisions of the AIIB. For the economic factor, the quantitative results appear to be more consistent and significant. The scale of market potentials for trade and investments has a positive and statistically significant association with loan destinations. Such association also finds some statistical support in the factor of FDI stock. The rest of the economic factors are statistically insignificant and consistent. In regard to the control variables, there is a strong association between the amount of commitments countries received from the World Bank and the investments received from the AIIB. To sum up, the quantitative results suggest that, after the AIIB started to operate, neither political nor economic factors appear to be consistent and significant in the AIIB's loan decisions. No strong evidence supports claims that the AIIB has been maneuvered in projecting China's political and strategic ambitions.

Toward a multilateral institution

Engaging in international collaboration is another way in which the AIIB could help China improve its reputation. The AIIB has indeed attracted plenty of members from outside the region – 20 out of the 57 initial signatories, or 35.1%. Of the 45 additional membership applications approved by the end of 2019, 30 (66.7%) were from outside the region; non-regional countries will soon account for 49% of AIIB membership. This makes the AIIB a truly international IFI (Li, 2016).

The AIIB has also shown itself willing to cooperate with other IFIs. As of the end of 2019, 30 out of the 62 AIIB-approved projects were co-financed with other IFIs, and only 3 of the 30 clearly designated the AIIB as the lead source of finance. The other 27 had another institution or unspecified agency as the lead. The ADB presides over 4 projects, the European Bank for Reconstruction and Development (EBRD) 2, the European Investment Bank 1, and the World Bank and its sister institutions 18. According to official documentation, most of the non-AIIB lead financiers administer the loans on the AIIB's behalf, which may include procurement, disbursements, environmental and social compliance, and project monitoring and reporting. In other words, most AIIB projects are influenced by the rules and standards adopted by other IFIs. The AIIB has committed a total of US$4.9 billion to the 30 projects involving other institutions, which is about 19.8 billion less than its co-investors. Judging from the distribution of funding sources, the AIIB has not emerged as a formidable rival of the other IFIs.

The AIIB appears to be actively collaborating with other IFIs. By the end of 2019, as Table 3.5 shows, the bank had established formal collaborations with

Table 3.5 The AIIB's international collaboration

Date	Partners	Form
May 2, 2016	Asian Development Bank	MOU
May 11, 2016	EBRD	MOU
May 12, 2016	European Investment Bank	MOU
Feb. 9, 2017	International Financial Corporation	ISDA Master Agreement
April 1, 2017	New Development Bank	MOU
April 23, 2017	World Bank	MOU
May 16, 2017	Inter-American Development Bank	MOU
April 18, 2018	African Development Bank	MOU
June 25, 2018	Islamic Development Bank Group	MOU
Oct. 31, 2018	Eurasian Development Bank	MOU

at least ten other IFIs, covering co-financing, high-level consultations, exchange of information, the enhancement of investment capacity in emerging markets, managing interest rate and currency risks, enhancing mutual coordination and promoting implementation of the Sustainable Development Goals and the COP21 climate agreement, etc. Aside from cooperating with major IFIs, the AIIB has demonstrated its intention to fight corruption by voluntarily adopting the list of sanctioned firms and individuals under the Agreement for Mutual Enforcement of Debarment Decisions, which means that the bank will follow five leading multilateral development banks in debarring listed parties from participating in AIIB projects (Asian Infrastructure Investment Bank, 2017a). It also joined other international organizations in celebrating the United Nations' International Anti-Corruption Day and signaled its commitment to ensuring a clean AIIB (Asian Infrastructure Investment Bank, 2017b).

It is clear that the AIIB has not appeared to disregard other similar institutions. Instead, currently it intends to follow the lead of the other major IFIs, such as the ADB and the World Bank, in many investment projects. It is also recognized by its renowned counterparts as an important partner. These efforts further elevate the international status of the AIIB.

The AIIB and the Belt and Road Initiative

Although the preceding discussion shows that, in many aspects, the AIIB has appeared to be more cooperative to the established international rules than once imagined, many have still worried that it may emerge as a financing arm of China's BRI.[6] Therefore, I compare the funds distribution below to show whether the bank has evolved as such.

First, energy is one of the most sensitive and exploitative sectors for IFIs to consider for investment. While the BRI concentrates about 40% of funds in the energy sector, the AIIB spends 31% of its total funds in the sector. Of those energy project investments, the AIIB has yet to approve any energy projects related to

Table 3.6 Top countries and sectors receiving the most funds (US$ billion)

AIIB				BRI			
Country	*Fund*	*Sector*	*Fund*	*Country*	*Fund*	*Sector*	*Fund*
India	7.6	Energy	3.7	Pakistan	39.5	Energy	172.9
Turkey	3.8	Transport	2.9	Malaysia	31.0	Transport	100.1
Indonesia	3.3	Water	1.6	Singapore	28.1	Real estate	44.3
China	2.7	Multi	1.4	Indonesia	25.0	Metals	15.0
Egypt	1.6	Finance	1.3	Russia	24.3	Logistics	12.2
Azerbaijan	8.6	Urban	0.8	Bangladesh	21.1	Utilities	10.7
Pakistan	1.7	Telecom	0.1	UAE	17.8	Agriculture	10.0
Bangladesh	1.4			Laos	17.8	Chemicals	8.4
Russia	0.5			Egypt	17.2	Tourism	8.0
Oman	0.9			Iran	13.0	Technology	7.9
Total	11.7	Total	11.7	Total	421.0	Total	421.0

Note: BRI data is from "China Global Investment Tracker", which is compiled by the American Enterprise Institute and the Heritage Foundation. Retrieved from www.aei.org/china-global-investment-tracker/

coal, while 25% of the BRI's energy projects involved coal. The AIIB's selection of energy projects suggests that the bank, at least so far, seeks to contrast itself to the BRI and has shied away from environmentally-unfriendly energy projects. Second, the BRI was criticized as serving China's grand political and strategic ambition. It has bankrolled a great deal of transportation infrastructure in many strategically sensitive locations regardless of the financial strength of the borrowing countries, which in the end, must submit to China's debt-for-equity swap. The proportion of investment in the transportation sector in the AIIB is about 25%, similar to the BRI's 24%. However, the AIIB's approved transportation projects are either co-financed with major IFIs, like the World Bank, confined within a national scale, or are quality improvements, which are less strategically sensitive, such as the BRI projects.

Third, while India sat out the BRI due to fears of China's geopolitical ambitions, it has participated in the AIIB and has secured about 31% of all AIIB funds so far. New Delhi distinguishes the AIIB from the BRI. For the Indian government, the former appears to be a multilateral institution with a board, membership and voting rights and which allowed India to participate in the beginning, while the BRI speaks solely to China's strategic interests. (Stacey, Mundy, & Feng, 2018). As China's geopolitical foe, India should be more vigilant than others in regard to the AIIB. India's participation suggests that at least so far, the bank has not acted as a financial arm to the BRI (please refer to Chapter 5 for a detailed case study on India). Fourth, while India has received the most funds from the AIIB, Pakistan, which is considered an important political and strategic partner to China, is the largest recipient of the BRI funds. These analyses suggest that the distributions of funds from the AIIB and the BRI are quite different. Unlike the AIIB's distancing from China's political/strategic implications, the projects and countries funded by the BRI more closely reflect China's own interests.

Conclusion

The evidence presented suggests that, when the idea of creating the AIIB emerged, China was dissatisfied with its status deficit situation and was likely to opt for a power competing IFI. As the AIIB continued to evolve, China's status deficit improved with its status improvement in the international financial system as well as the willingness of developed countries to join the AIIB. Constitutionally, the AIIB became a cooperative and reform-minded multilateral agency. After it started to operate in 2016, pessimistic perspectives of the AIIB were not supported by the evidence presented here. No strong evidence supports the claims that the AIIB has been maneuvered to project China's political and strategic ambitions. In seeking outside collaboration, the AIIB follows the lead of other major IFIs and is recognized as an important partner. Compared with the BRI, the AIIB appears to be less geopolitically sensitive.

Observing the AIIB in practice for its first four years, one may wonder whether the AIIB is destined to become a multilateral bank on which China can no longer project its preference and influence. Although the AIIB's current development leads many to have positive expectations, China still holds substantial power in deciding the AIIB's future trajectory. As a result, while envisaging the AIIB's future, it may be more realistic and pertinent to recognize the importance of China that is always faced with both power competition and collaboration options. As this chapter finds, a more satisfied China with lower status deficit will be more likely to shape the bank as a complementary IFI that follows established international norms and regulations. Conversely, should China become unsatisfied, the AIIB will be more likely to become an IFI that answers more to China's national interests and challenges current international financial system. Rather than judging the AIIB dichotomously as either satisfying China's own self-interests or regional benefits, one should keep in mind that the future of the bank may be dynamic. The AIIB will evolve according to how China perceives its current status in the international financial system.

Notes

1 Please refer to the both Article 3 of ADB's and AIIB's AOA.
2 Please refer to the Articles 4, 5, 25, 29, 38, 41, 43 and 53 of the AIIB's AOA.
3 Developing country is coded according to the World Bank's classification. The information is available at http://data.worldbank.org/about/country-and-lending-groups. A higher Logistics Performance Index represents a higher level of infrastructure. The data can be accessed at http://lpi.worldbank.org/international/global?sort=asc&order=Infrastructure.
4 Data are available at http://data.worldbank.org/.
5 Later, Armenia applied for AIIB membership and was approved by the bank on March 23, 2017.
6 I thank the external reviewer for bringing up the necessity of discussing such a possibility.

4   AIIB in comparative perspectives

The previous chapter investigates the evolving trajectory of the AIIB, with a focus on comparing the before and after of its creation. This chapter investigates possible motivations behind the establishment of the AIIB and the bank's actual behaviors by comparing the AIIB with the ADB and the World Bank. After China announced the AIIB plan, some considered the bank to be a byproduct of, and financing agency for the Belt and Road Initiative (BRI), which seeks economic cooperation with countries along the Silk Road economic belt through Central Asia and the "maritime Silk Road." At the same time, the bank would promote political trust, economic harmonization and cultural tolerance. At the time of the bank's founding, Perspectives in China focused on the positive influence that the AIIB was likely to have as a financial instrument for accelerating regional communications, connections and infrastructure building. This allows China to export its surplus factors of production, ease domestic pressure for macroeconomic control and solve its unemployment problem. In addition, the AIIB contributes to the internationalization of the renminbi by lending in that currency (Huang, Tan, & Lei, 2013).

Views from outsiders, however, are more divergent. On the one hand, many consider that the creation of the AIIB demonstrates China's dissatisfaction with the US-led system of global financial governance, which does not offer equal representation for all countries. The AIIB thus becomes an instrument through which China can address this inequality. Since 2007, China has been a donor to the International Development Association and is ready to take greater responsibility in the World Bank. There has been little progress on this front, however, mainly due to objections from the US Congress. The refusal of the United States and Japan to join the AIIB reflects concerns that China would like to see the new bank replace other major IFIs. On the other hand, optimists see the establishment of the bank as a sign that China intends to become a responsible stakeholder and is willing to conform to global best practice regarding the financing of development projects. China can raise its global reputation by improving its often-criticized low standards of financial diplomacy by means of the AIIB (Xu & Carey, 2015).

This chapter seeks to join this debate and investigate whether the AIIB is following a pessimistic or optimistic trajectory by comparing the bank with the ADB and the World Bank in four aspects, which includes their power structures, institutional design regarding power potential, observance to the best practices in environmental and social safeguards and competition in financial commitments. By comparison, one can understand the AIIB in a more appropriate context. Although there is nothing wrong with focusing the debate on whether a China-led AIIB is doing things rightly or wrongly, it may be more pertinent to evaluate that, if the AIIB is bad, is it worse than its main competitors in the region? If so, how much worse is that? Studying in a comparative perspective can lead us to a more impartial assessment. The next section consists of a brief review of the debates surrounding the AIIB based on Chapter 2. The following four sections will provide empirical evidence regarding the aforementioned four comparative dimensions. The last section concludes and provides tentative observations.

Debates surrounding the AIIB

Although most of the AIIB's founding members signed its Articles of Agreement on June 29, 2015, in Beijing, there is an intensive debate concerning China's underlying intentions and the bank's future. In addition to the question of who will benefit economically from the bank, two contrasting views can be identified. The first line of argument is a relatively pessimistic one that sees the AIIB as a tool in China's bid to challenge the existing international financial system. It attributes the establishment of the AIIB to dissatisfaction among emerging countries with the existing US-dominated Bretton Woods system. There is plenty of evidence that the lending decisions of the IMF and the World Bank are associated with the interests of the United States. Non-permanent members of the UN Security Council have been known to trade their votes for better lending deals (Dreher, Sturm, & Vreeland, 2009, 2015); countries more closely aligned with the United States have received more loans or loans with fewer conditions (Andersen, Hansen, & Markussen, 2006; Thacker, 1999); and countries with more top economic policy-makers trained in the United States or Europe have received more generous and less onerous lending deals (Nelson, 2014). The United States and its allies apparently use the direct and indirect power they possess in IFIs to exert a powerful influence on financial allocations. Emerging countries that have accumulated huge amounts of wealth but have only limited decision-making power in the major IFIs have found this situation troubling.

At the beginning of the 2008 global financial crisis, emerging economies, including China, expressed their intention to contribute more to the IMF and the World Bank in order to increase their financing capability. It was thought that this would inevitably result in a redistribution of the shares of authorized capital and a subsequent adjustment of voting powers that would give the emerging economies more power in the major IFIs. However, this adjustment did not happen and the current voting structure still does not properly reflect the economic weights of member-countries. For example, China only secured 4.85% of the votes in the World Bank in 2015 despite accounting for 13.51% of global GDP in 2014. Although the G20 leaders agreed to shift at least 5% of the voting power in the IMF and 3% in the World Bank from the developed to the developing countries, the US Congress has repeatedly rejected the White House's reform proposal, which has in turn impeded the progress of reform in the two international organizations (Vestergaard & Wade, 2015). Faced with this stalemate, China and other emerging powers put forward a number of new proposals, such as the BRICS countries' New Development Bank (NDB) and the China-led AIIB and Silk Road Fund, in order to bypass the US-dominated global financial system and get more support from others in the region (Cook, 2015). Thus it is believed that the AIIB can address the problem of vote distribution and court discontented members of other financial institutions with more attractive and easy-going lending terms that some fear could lead to a "race to the bottom" in financial standards (Wolf Jr., 2015). The contrast between Europe's enthusiasm for the AIIB and the lukewarm reception it received from the United States has also invoked fears that it might erode transatlantic harmony (Renard, 2015a). If this were to happen, the AIIB would have the effect of reshaping the current system to serve China's geopolitical and geoeconomic interests. According to this argument, the AIIB could become the institution that allows the creation of a China-led alliance to challenge the current system.

The second line of argument adopts a more favorable view of the AIIB and treats it as supplementary to the major IFIs. According to this way of thinking, the AIIB will not only act as a responsible stakeholder providing international public goods for investment in infrastructure but is likely also to encourage China to abide by current financial governance standards. The ADB has estimated that Asia will require about US$8 trillion-worth of investment in overall national infrastructure in the years 2010–2020 (Asian Development Bank Institute, 2009). There is evidence that improved infrastructure will benefit national economic development (Calderón & Servén, 2004), but currently available funds are far from sufficient. While Asia might need US$800 billion annually, the major regional source of finance, the ADB, could only contribute US$21 billion in 2013. As a responsible stakeholder, China's AIIB could narrow the infrastructure investment gap in Asia and contribute to economic growth in the region (Dai & Li, 2015). Regional economic development led by the AIIB will, in turn, help China secure the friends that it desperately needs as an emerging regional power (Heydarian, 2015). In addition to regional economic concerns, the growing number of complex global issues calls for more specialized IFIs. Whereas the ADB's mission is one of poverty reduction, the AIIB is designed to focus on the financing of infrastructure (Wihtol, 2014, pp. 6–13). If this is the case, rather than being a threat, the AIIB could be a valuable regional asset that will cooperate with other regional financial institutions (Lam, 2014, p. 135). The AIIB will not crowd out the influence of the ADB and the World Bank. Instead, it will only bring additional benefits for the region.

In addition to the material benefits it may bring, many observers see the establishment of the AIIB as a chance to further lock China into the Bretton Woods financial governance system that operates in line with global best practice (Desai & Vreeland, 2015). China recently adopted the IMF's Special Data Dissemination Standard, which signals Beijing's willingness to abide by best practice in terms of transparency, encouraging the optimistic view that China is ready to accept international financial standards. As a consequence of this, the AIIB is unlikely to challenge or move away too much from best practice (Xu & Carey, 2015). China may be encouraged to accept international standards by the fact that the area of development aid has become extremely competitive. If shareholders find that the AIIB is tilting toward China's interests at the expense of others, they will withdraw their funds and transfer them to other agencies. This kind of competition can check any Chinese tendency toward domination (Lipscy, 2015a, 2015b). The initial success of the AIIB itself reflects shareholders' dissatisfaction with the World Bank and the ADB.

These contrasting arguments yield two predictions. China will either become a challenger state that, having secured a dominant position in the AIIB, will try to outperform the Bretton Woods system, or it will become a responsible stakeholder that will put development ahead of politics and embrace global standards (Liao, 2015). The first possibility explains the reluctance of the United States and Japan to endorse the AIIB. The economies of both of these countries remain sluggish and they may not be willing to take on an extra burden. Strategically, if the United States and Japan were to join the AIIB, this might weaken the influence of the World Bank and the ADB, institutions which they dominate. Geopolitically, their participation might signal their acceptance of Beijing's dominance in the region and raise China's global reputation. If the AIIB succeeds, it will fuel China's determination to be a challenger. From this point of view, it is in the interests of the United States and Japan to do whatever they can to sabotage the AIIB. Other observers argue that these concerns are exaggerated. The AIIB is still too weak to challenge the current system, they claim, and Tokyo and Washington should join the bank and help China take its place within the established financial governance structure. China can then become a reliable provider of global financial goods and cooperate with Japan and the United States in regional development.

While it seems too early to judge which of the two scenarios is correct, comparing the AIIB with the World Bank and the ADB should provide some clues as to how the AIIB is likely to develop. If the AIIB has been created as a reformist institution designed to fix the problems that beset the current system, there are some characteristics we should be able to observe. First, its voting power structure should be fairer than that of the other IFIs. Second, its institutional design should be such as to check China's power and allow other emerging countries and funding recipients to have stronger voices. Third, the bank should embrace established financial best practice. Fourth, we should be able to find evidence of complementarity rather than competition among the three IFIs. If the AIIB does not display these characteristics, it is more likely to become a Trojan horse with a hidden agenda. These arguments are tested with comparative empirical analyses in the following four sections.

Power structures comparison

In this section, I compare the distribution of votes, the concentration of voting power and veto power in the World Bank, the ADB and the AIIB. This comparison can help readers understand the implications of the power distribution in the AIIB, China's probable intentions and potential influence and the likely future of the AIIB.

Voting power distribution in 2015

One of the main reasons why China established the AIIB was in response to complaints by developing countries about underrepresentation in the major IFIs, a situation that made these agencies unaccountable (Woods, 2000). In 2009, G20 leaders from emerging countries put forward a proposal for reform of the voting systems of the IMF and the World Bank (International Monetary Fund, 2010). According to this proposal, at least 5% of the votes allocated to developed countries in the IMF and 3% of those in the World Bank would be transferred to developing countries. Although this reform program was approved by many members of the World Bank, the US Congress has been unable to agree to any reform that would see a reduction in the United States' current 16.21% of the votes, which gives it de facto veto power on major constitutional issues. European countries share similar worries about votes being allocated according to states' economic weight or GDP instead of their standard of financial governance, including transparency (Vestergaard & Wade, 2015, pp. 2–3). It seems that most countries have recognized the need to reform the governance structure of the World Bank, but there is still a huge gap between the developed and developing countries when it comes to how this reform should be carried out. The associated discontent among the emerging countries is considered to have been an important factor in China's decision to establish the AIIB.

The developing countries' concerns appear plausible, but if one compares the voting shares of the major developed and developing countries, the situation does not appear as inequitable as is claimed. Table 4.1 shows the voting shares of the BRICS countries in the World Bank and their shares of global GDP in 2015, right before the AIIB came on the scene. The ratio of these two indexes will show the level of these countries' representation in that institution relative to their global economic weight. A ratio exceeding "1" implies power overrepresentation in the institution while below "1" implies underrepresentation. Interestingly, judging from their economic weight, only two of the BRICS – China and Brazil – were underrepresented in the World Bank. China's voting power was only 36% of its global economic weight in 2015 and Brazil's was 63%. Russia, India and South Africa have, respectively, 1.17, 1.13 and 1.74 times more voting power than they should have according to their economic weight. As a group, the five BRICS countries were about 39% underrepresented back then; but if China is excluded, the four other BRICS countries were quite fairly represented in the World Bank. Therefore, of the major emerging countries, only China and Brazil suffer from the underrepresentation problem that developing countries complain about and only China was seriously underrepresented.

In view of China's underrepresentation, another question we can ask is, were the developed countries overrepresented in the World Bank? Of the top ten

Table 4.1 BRICS countries' voting power in the World Bank, 2015

	Vote power%	Global GDP share%	Ratio
Brazil	1.91	3.06	0.62
Russia	2.82	2.43	1.16
India	3.04	2.70	1.13
China	4.82	13.51	0.36
South Africa	0.80	0.46	1.74
Total	13.39	22.16	0.60
Total (excluding China)	8.57	8.65	0.99

Source:

1 Voting power data are from World Bank, "International Bank for Reconstruction and Development Subscriptions and Voting Power of Member Countries," available at http://siteresources.worldbank.org/BODINT/Resources/278027-1215524804501/IBRDCountryVotingTable.pdf
2 GDP data comes from the World Bank, available at http://data.worldbank.org/indicator/NY.GDP.MKTP.CD

Table 4.2 Top ten non-BRICS countries' voting power in the World Bank, 2015

	Vote power %	Global GDP share %	Ratio
United States	16.21	22.72	0.71
Japan	7.51	6.00	1.25
Germany	4.40	5.03	0.88
France	3.95	3.69	1.07
United Kingdom	3.95	3.84	1.03
Saudi Arabia	3.04	0.97	3.12
Canada	2.67	2.33	1.15
Italy	2.48	2.80	0.89
Spain	1.94	1.83	1.06
Netherlands	1.92	1.13	1.69
Total	48.07	50.34	0.95
Total (excluding Saudi)	45.03	49.37	0.91

Source: Please refer to Table 4.1

non-BRICS countries in terms of voting power, eight were from North America or Europe and the other two were Washington's staunch allies in East Asia (Japan) and the Middle East (Saudi Arabia) (see Table 4.2). Together, this US-centered bloc of three countries held 48.07% of the voting power and was responsible for 50.31% of global GDP; in terms of the ratio of voting power to global GDP, they were in fact 5% underrepresented in the World Bank. Germany and Italy were more fairly represented than the United States. Among the seven overrepresented countries, Saudi Arabia, another major emerging country, had 3.12 times the voting power it should have, although its share was not decisive. Other US allies had 1.03 to 1.69 times more votes than they should have according to their share of global GDP, making them only slightly overrepresented; this was to some extent balanced by the United States' underrepresentation. If one excludes Saudi Arabia as a non-Western emerging power, Japan and eight Western, developed economies were slightly underrepresented in the World Bank. Despite this underrepresentation, there is no denying that the United States still dominates the organization.

A comparison of the data in Tables 4.1 and 4.2 reveals that, of the major developed and developing countries in the World Bank, only China and the United States were underrepresented in terms of voting power. This problem did not seem to greatly affect other prominent members. At face value, a more legitimate argument is that, among the major economies, China had been the most underrepresented in the World Bank, but the United States had been in a similar situation. If votes were to be allocated according to economic weight, China would indeed secure a substantial increase in its share, but the United States should also be given more votes, which would strengthen its current power base still further. Vestergaard and Wade (2015) demonstrated that, even if the bank were to implement its current version of reform, the improvement would still be very limited.

The Asian Development Bank (ADB) is another international financial institution criticized for its unequal distribution of voting power and political domination by major donors (Kilby, 2006). Japan's voting power in the ADB has continuously been greater than it should have been as measured against its GDP share, while the United States' power was weaker. As an Asian regional financial institution, major shareholders and lenders from outside the region – mainly the United States and EU countries – control only one-third of the votes; this situation has not changed much since 2000. Asian regional members together control about two-thirds of the voting power. But criticism of Japan's dominant position is legitimate. Since 2000, Japan's GDP share has declined, but its voting power has not decreased proportionately, meaning that its ratio of power to GDP has increased from 1.23 to 1.74. Additionally, the president of the ADB has always been a Japanese national (Howes, Davies, & Betteridge, 2013). In contrast to Japan's overrepresentation, China had been severely underrepresented in the ADB as it had been in the World Bank. In 2000, in proportion to its economic weight, China was 52% underrepresented, and that representation gap had subsequently increased to 67%.

To summarize, criticism of the ADB's power structure is justified where its two most powerful members are concerned. The main target of criticism, the United States, was in fact underrepresented in the World Bank, although China's complaints concerning Japan are justified. Therefore, the power distribution problem in the ADB seems mainly to involve Tokyo and Beijing.

Having investigated the situation in the World Bank and the ADB, we can see that concerns about power distribution in Asia's international finance system were legitimate and serious from China's perspective. As illustrated in Table 4.4, the situation has not changed much since the birth of the AIIB. China is even more underrepresented. This has less to do with the slight decline in China's voting power than with the growth in its GDP share. Since the World Bank and ADB have not undergone any satisfactory restructuring, it is plausible that the AIIB was designed by China to deal with this unfairness. If this is the case, it would be interesting to find out whether the power distribution in the AIIB provides any solutions.

Table 4.3 Voting power of top regional and non-regional members of the ADB

Country	2015			2000		
	Power%	*GDP%*	*Ratio*	*Power%*	*GDP%*	*Ratio*
Japan	12.84	7.38	1.74	13.05	10.60	1.23
China	5.48	16.62	0.33	5.59	11.65	0.48
India	5.39	3.32	1.62	5.50	3.29	1.67
Australia	4.95	2.33	2.12	5.05	2.20	2.30
Other regional (44)	36.47	9.50	3.84	36.32	8.42	4.31
Total	**65.12**	**39.15**	**1.66**	**65.51**	**36.15**	**1.81**
United States	12.75	27.95	0.46	13.05	28.85	0.45
Canada	4.50	2.87	1.57	4.60	3.11	1.48
Germany	3.78	6.18	0.61	3.86	6.58	0.59
France	2.17	4.54	0.48	2.24	5.10	0.44
Other non-regional (15)	11.69	19.31	0.61	10.73	20.20	0.53
Total	**34.89**	**60.85**	**0.57**	**34.48**	**63.85**	**0.54**

Source: Voting power data from the ADB's annual reports in 2000 and 2015, available at www.adb.org/documents/series/adb-annual-reports; GDP data from the World Bank.

Table 4.4 Comparison of power/GDP ratio of the great powers in the World Bank and ADB

	World Bank power/GDP ratio		*ADB power/GDP ratio*	
	2015	*2019*	*2015*	*2018*
China	0.36	0.34	0.33	0.28
Japan	1.25	1.53	1.74	1.81
US	0.71	0.73	0.46	0.44

Source: Please refer to Table 4.1 and Table 4.3.

Next, I will investigate the initial power distribution among the AIIB's founding members as recorded in the Articles of Agreement first released in mid-2015. The member-countries with the highest voting power to total GDP ratio were all minor regional countries, such as the Maldives, Kyrgyzstan, Tajikistan and Laos (plus one non-regional member, Malta), which together have less than 10% of the voting power. The other 33 regional members in Table 4.5 have 63% greater representation than they should have according to their economic weight, as they account for only 17.5% of the total GDP of all the AIIB founding members. A comparison of the voting power of the AIIB's regional and non-regional members produces a very similar result to the findings for the ADB (see Table 4.3). Asian countries had a greater share of votes than they should have had if votes were distributed according to GDP share, while non-regional members were severely underrepresented. Another similarity is that the lead country in the ADB (Japan) and the leader of the AIIB (China) were both overrepresented as measured by their economic weight. While Japan's level of overrepresentation (power/GDP ratio = 1.74) in the ADB was greater than that of China in the AIIB (power/GDP

Table 4.5 Voting power of the top regional and non-regional members of the AIIB

Country	2015 (56 members)		2019 (75 members)	
	Power%	*Power/GDP*	*Power%*	*Power/GDP*
China	26.06	1.12	26.51	0.98
India	7.51	1.62	7.60	1.41
Russia	5.93	1.42	5.98	1.82
South Korea	3.50	1.11	3.51	1.09
Other regional	28.60	1.63	30.29	1.66
Total	**71.60**	**1.36**	**73.90**	**1.29**
Germany	4.15	0.48	4.17	0.53
France	3.19	0.50	3.19	0.58
Brazil	3.02	0.57	n/a	n/a
United Kingdom	2.91	0.44	2.91	0.51
Other non-regional	15.14	0.74	15.82	0.66
Total	**28.41**	**0.60**	**26.10**	**0.61**

Source: AIIB data is based on author's collection; GDP data comes from the World Bank.

ratio = 1.12), the latter controlled more than a quarter of the votes. The situation had not changed to any significant extent when the AIIB had been running for four years. China's representation declined slightly in 2019, and China became underrepresented given its economic scale. This was due to the addition of more members that diluted the founding members' vote shares, as well as China's growing share of global economic weight. Finally, if one measures the average power/GDP ratios of all the countries accounting for more than 1% of the GDP membership of all three bank members' total GDP, the World Bank scores 0.95, the ADB 1.09 and the AIIB 1.03. In other words, all three have quite similar and equal voting power structures.

To summarize, the AIIB has not fixed any of the power distribution problems that afflict IFIs, apart from the problem of China's underrepresentation in the World Bank and the ADB. Neither has the emergence of the AIIB triggered effective global pressure for reforming the power representation issue in the World Bank and ADB. This leads one to suspect that the AIIB may develop into a policy instrument of one major power, no different from the other institutions that have been so harshly criticized by China.

Concentration of voting powers

Another common accusation directed at the ADB and the World Bank is that power has been overly concentrated. Here the often-used Herfindahl-Hirschman Index (HHI) is borrowed to measure the level of competition within these institutions. The HHI is the sum of squares of the share percentage in a specific market. A high HHI indicates a highly monopolized market structure, which in this case would mean that voting power is highly concentrated among a few members. Typically, an HHI of below 1% suggests a high level of competition; 1% to 15%

suggests no concentration; 15% to 25% suggests moderate concentration; 25% or more suggests a highly concentrated structure.

The arrangement of data in Table 4.6 reflects the fact that the United States and its security allies often stick together in major IFIs and thus exert a great deal of control (Wade, 2002). The results in row 2 (Voting power HHI A) of Table 4.6 show that, treating each country independently, there does not seem to be a voting power concentration problem in any of the three organizations, albeit the AIIB's power structure is slightly more concentrated than the others as a result of China's dominant share of more than 26%. The second largest initial share – a mere 7.51% – is that of India. The results in row 3 of Table 4.6 demonstrate that, in the AIIB, voting power was more concentrated among the top ten members than in the World Bank or the ADB in 2015. However, if we add in the United States and its allies as a single player, as shown in row 4, voting power is highly concentrated in the ADB and the World Bank while only moderately concentrated in the AIIB. This shows that, even though many European countries have been enthusiastic about becoming founding members of the AIIB, they do not constitute a strong force within the organization, which allows Beijing to keep a tighter hold on power and shield the AIIB from Western influence.

Another interesting finding is that, as the level of power concentration in both the World Bank and ADB has declined with the increase in their membership, the AIIB's level of concentration has grown slightly as more countries have joined. This raises the question of whether the power structure of the bank will become less concentrated as more non-regional members are admitted. To summarize, China might be partly correct about the unfair concentration of power in the existing major IFIs, but the AIIB does not perform any better on that count. The only real change is the lower concentration of power in the hands of Western countries.

Judging from the power structure of the World Bank and the ADB, it appears that only China might have had plausible incentive to change the status quo by establishing a new institution, which not only allows it to exert greater control but is also shielded from Western influence. But do other dissatisfied non-Western countries have more voting power in the AIIB? Table 4.7 displays the power/GDP ratio of members of the World Bank and the ADB as compared to the AIIB. Of the

Table 4.6 Herfindahl-Hirschman Indices of the World Bank, ADB and AIIB

	World Bank			ADB			AIIB	
	1947	*2015*	*2019*	*1966*	*2015*	*2018*	*2015*	*2019*
Number of members	45	188	188	32	67	67	57	75
Voting power HHI A (%)	15.3	4.7	4.4	8.3	5.3	5.3	9.0	9.1
Voting power HHI B (%)	23.8	15.5	15.4	16.1	13.2	13.2	21.5	22.0
Voting power HHI C (%)	54.2	40.4	39.8	43.1	30.6	30.0	15.7	17.1

Notes: Voting power HHI A (%): all members; Voting power HHI B (%): top ten members; Voting power HHI C (%): combined voting power of US, EU, Japan, Australia, New Zealand and Israel (US-centered bloc) as percentage share of the top sixty members.

Table 4.7 Number of countries with greater voting power/GDP ratio in the AIIB

	World Bank	%	ADB	%
Increase	34	59.6%	8	19.0%
Decrease	23	40.4%	34	81.0%
Total number of members	57	100.0%	42	100.0%

57 founding members of the AIIB, 34 enjoyed more voting power in comparison to their global economic weight than they do in the World Bank system. The top ten in terms of improvement in voting power are the Maldives, Kyrgyzstan, Laos, Mongolia, Tajikistan, Cambodia, Malta, Nepal, Georgia and Iceland, which are all insignificant members of either the World Bank or the AIIB. The positions of major emerging economies, such as Iran, South Africa or Brazil, are no better in the AIIB.

The situation seems even worse if we compare the AIIB with the ADB. The second column in Table 4.7 indicates that among the 42 founding members of the AIIB that are also ADB members, only eight countries have a better power/ GDP ratio in the AIIB. Those eight countries in order of degree of improvement are Turkey, China, Spain, Vietnam, the United Kingdom, France, Italy and Sweden. More than half are European allies of the United States. As many as 81% percent of AIIB members do not have greater power/GDP ratios than they do in the ADB. Comparing these indicators leads to a conclusion that, although they have consistently criticized the existing global financial governance structure and tried to make a case for the AIIB, the major emerging economies do not enjoy any greater power within the AIIB. In reality, it is China, some small developing countries and several European countries that do better in the AIIB.

Institutional design

In this section, I compare the institutional design of the AIIB with that of the ADB and the World Bank. I focus on how the AIIB performs in areas in which other IFIs are recognized as needing reform. Beginning with a comparison of the configuration of the three IFIs, it is common to see that, when a new international organization is in the process of establishment, powerful countries will seek to consolidate their power by assigning their nationals to leadership positions and locating the headquarters in their capital. From this point of view, the US and China have been more successful in taking charge of the World Bank and the AIIB than Japan has with the ADB. Japan managed to keep Japanese nationals at the helm of the ADB but failed to keep its headquarters in Tokyo. Although there is no mention of the nationality of the IFI's president in the charters of any of the three institutions, both the AIIB and the ADB stipulate that the president shall be a national of a regional member-country. In reality, previous presidents of the

Table 4.8 Configuration of AIIB, ADB and the World Bank

	AIIB	ADB	World Bank
Headquarters	Beijing, China	Manila, Philippines	Washington, DC, US
Nationality of the president	Chinese	Japanese	United States
Membership	Toward global	Regional	Global
Minimum percentage of regional shareholding	75%	60%	n/a

World Bank have all been US nationals and the ADB has been continuously led by the Japanese. The first AIIB president is a Chinese national, Jin Liqun. This is understandable since China's share subscription is the largest, thus giving Beijing enough power to decide who should be the bank's president.

Membership of the World Bank includes all countries regardless of region. On the other hand, the ADB, although it is open to both regional and non-regional countries, has set the minimum shareholding for regional countries at 60%, while the shareholding of the non-regional membership as a whole shall not exceed 40%. The ADB charter differs from that of the AIIB on two points. First, the definition of regional membership of the ADB includes members of the UN Economic and Social Commission for Asia and the Pacific, which was succeeded by the Economic and Social Commission for Asia and the Pacific. Second, only "developed" non-regional countries are welcome in the ADB, and there is no mention of "developing" countries outside the region. The bank is limited to financing projects within its own region. Non-regional members are, therefore, wealthy countries able to commit financial resources rather than wanting to borrow money. The scope of the membership of the AIIB appears to be larger than that of the ADB. In general, regional membership of the AIIB is open to countries classified by the United Nations as being in Asia or Oceania. In addition, there is no mention, either implied or explicit, of conditions for or discrimination against prospective non-regional members. Although the AIIB seems to be more inclusive than the ADB, the minimum shareholding for regional countries is 75%, which is more effective in limiting non-regional influence than the ADB's configuration. However, the AIIB permits changes to the regional shareholding percentage, although such a change requires 75% agreement.

Altogether, while the World Bank is a global financial institution controlled by the US, the ADB remains a regional institution focusing on regional financing. However, it is not as shielded from non-regional influences as the AIIB, which makes the ADB look like a regional bank controlled by non-regional donors. The AIIB's conditions for both regional and non-regional membership are not so strict as those of the ADB, but they do ensure that the former group retains sufficient power. The non-regional membership of the AIIB includes not only wealthy donors but also developing countries that are seeking external financial assistance. This design makes the AIIB look more like a regional vehicle for lifting the developing South out of economic disadvantage. It remains to be seen how far the AIIB can move forward.

In the following section, I will explore the AIIB's performance in areas in which other IFIs are recognized as needing reform and whether the AIIB has performed better in those areas. There are at least five identifiable problems afflicting the World Bank: (1) unbalanced distribution of voting powers; (2) inefficient management and redundant procedure; (3) Western monopolization of the presidency; (4) loan conditionality; and (5) a lack of experts from a variety of disciplines (Chin, 2016; Chow, 2016; Evans & Finnemore, 2001; Malkin & Momani, 2016; Ong, 2017; Zedillo, 2009).

Veto power

First, the AIIB does not seem to have addressed the unbalanced voting-power distribution problem. When the AIIB's Articles of Agreement were signed in mid-2015 by the 57 founding members in Beijing, China held a 26.06% share of the votes (assuming that all parties completed the required procedure for effective membership). In 2016, China's voting power increased to 29.88% because 11 signatories failed to achieve domestic ratification of their membership or make payment of the first installment of their subscription. They are Brazil, Egypt, Iran, Italy, Kuwait, Malaysia, the Philippines, Portugal, South Africa, Spain and Uzbekistan. In 2017, nine more states fulfilled the membership requirements, diluting China's voting power by a marginal amount. By the end of 2019, China's voting power was as high as 26.51%.

During the period 2016–2019, the AIIB approved 45 new applications for membership, increasing its membership to 102. Since the bank has not increased its number of shares, these new members will have to make do with the unallocated 8% of shares. According to author's calculation based on the AIIB's rules, Beijing will continue to hold more than 25% of voting shares, even if the membership increases to 200. Unless China gives up some of its shares or the AIIB increases the number of shares for subscription, this situation will not change. But with more than 25% of the votes, China alone can veto any proposal to increase the authorized capital stock, which requires a supermajority vote of 75%. Although China has repeatedly promised not to abuse its veto power, it remains to be seen whether it will keep that promise (He, 2016, pp. 268–269). No one country holds more than 13% of the votes in the ADB or more than 17% in the World Bank.

This indicates that the AIIB is not the answer to the problem of developing countries being underrepresented in the World Bank (Chen, 2016). However, Article 28 of the AIIB AOA states that each member's basic votes shall be the number of votes that results from the equal distribution among all the members of 12% of the aggregate sum of the basic votes, share votes and founding member votes of all the members. This formula increases the total number of votes allocated to smaller countries. In comparison, the percentage of basic votes in the World Bank decreased from 11% at the time of its inception to 2.86% in 2009 (Ong, 2017, p. 552). The AIIB is also the first IFI designed to have a predominantly Asian membership.

Table 4.9 Veto power in the World Bank, ADB and AIIB

Bank	Lowest veto threshold	Veto power(s)
World Bank	15%	US controls 16.21% voting share
ADB	25%	US and Japan control 25.59% voting share
AIIB	25%	China controls 26.06% voting share

Instead of looking at the absolute level of power by counting the votes, it is also important to look at the banks' charters and compare the voting shares with the voting threshold required for the approval of critical agenda items, as this is what really matters. For example, the highest vote threshold in the AIIB is a supermajority of three-fourths of the total voting power. However, the admission of new members only requires a simple majority, more than half. Table 4.9 lists the highest voting thresholds and the lowest veto thresholds in the AIIB, ADB and World Bank. Some suggest that the problem of veto power enjoyed by the United States in the World Bank and Japan in the ADB was China's justification for establishing the AIIB. According to Article VIII of the World Bank AOA, modifications of the agreement must be accepted by three-fifths of the members having 85% of the total voting power. Therefore, without the approval of the United States, the World Bank cannot implement its ambitious reform plan that will involve the revision of the bank's charter. According to the Agreement Establishing the Asian Development Bank, major issues, such as the admission of new members (Article 3), increasing authorized capital (Article 4), special funding programs (Article 19), deciding a country's level of development (Article 28), suspension of membership (Article 42), termination of operations (Article 45), asset distribution (Article 47) and amendment (Article 59), cannot be approved if they are opposed by the United States and Japan acting in concert.

The veto-power problem does not appear to have been rectified in the AIIB either. According to the AIIB AOA, major issues require a supermajority of 75% in order to be passed, just as they do in the ADB. But, unlike the ADB, which requires close alignment of the United States and Japan for a veto, in the AIIB, China, which holds more than 25% of the voting power, can unilaterally veto any important matter, such as an increase in authorized capital (Article 4), subscription of shares (Article 5), composition of the board of directors (Article 25), election of the AIIB's president (Article 29), suspension of membership (Article 38), termination of operations (Article 41), distribution of assets (Article 43) and amendment (Article 53). According to the comparisons drawn by Lichtenstein (2019, pp. 157–160), the AIIB stipulates a high total voting power for more items than the ADB or the World Bank. A change in the percentage of the regional shareholding, assistance to non-members, an increase in limitations on operations and allocating net income to other purposes all require a supermajority in the AIIB, whereas these items have no such requirement in the other two IFIs. An increase in a member's subscription and the election of the president require a supermajority in the AIIB but only a simple majority in the ADB. The World Bank has the fewest items requiring a high voting threshold.

These comparisons suggest that the AIIB's institutional design and the fact that China holds over 25% of the votes give Beijing more opportunities to veto decisions than any one state has in the other two IFIs, regardless of whether it actually wants to use its veto power. An examination of the voting power of AIIB members suggests that, by the end of 2019, the next possible veto bloc may consist of 25 non-regional members from Africa, Europe and North America. Another possible veto bloc would be the six regional members with the largest voting power after China (India, Russia, South Korea, Australia, Indonesia and Turkey). Both of these groups appear to be too internally divergent to unite in opposition to China. As a result, although the governance structures of the ADB and the AIIB are not significantly different in terms of the distribution of power among members, China enjoys autonomous veto power in the AIIB, while the ADB requires Japan and the US to cooperate.

Comparing the institutional design regarding power structure of the World Bank and the ADB with that of the AIIB, it is clear that China has not resolved the problems of the US-led global financial system that it used to complain about. The main difference China strived to make is that in the AIIB, China, as the most important provider of funds, can exercise the greatest influence. As a consequence, it is not plausible to argue that China set up the AIIB because it was dissatisfied with global power politics in existing IFIs and was seeking a revolution. What really troubles China is who leads the current system. Beijing seems more interested in replacing the current leader while keeping the existing rules of the game of power politics. Its goal in establishing the AIIB may be to join in the competition and weaken the US-dominated international financial system, rather than to actively attempt to replace the whole system with a new one that addresses alleged problems. The slogan "reforming governance structure" might be merely a convenient ploy aimed at garnering support.

Inefficient management

Now, we will investigate whether the AIIB's governance structure addresses the problem of inefficiency that besets other IFIs. The 25-member Board of Directors of the World Bank is criticized for being too unwieldy, and it has been suggested that more non-European chairs from developing and transition countries should be appointed (Zedillo, 2009). Besides, the design of the resident board of directors acts as a strong check on the World Bank's management team and sometimes delays the review process and operations (Callaghan & Hubbard, 2016; Chin, 2016). The board members may also try to influence loan decisions in a way that favors their own countries (Malan, 2018). The AIIB addresses this issue by limiting its Board of Directors to 12 members, which is the same as that of the ADB. In addition, the AIIB's board is non-resident and the directors receive no remuneration from the bank, while the boards of the ADB and the World Bank perform their duties full-time with remuneration. Instead of holding regular meetings, the AIIB Board of Directors may hold "virtual" meetings as required (Ong, 2017, p. 553). These procedures are cheaper and more efficient than having a resident board. Also, according to Article 26 (ii) of the AIIB AOA, the AIIB board is only involved in deciding major operational and financial policies; decisions on loans to the bank's management team are delegated. In contrast, according to Article 31(ii) of the Agreement Establishing the Asian Development Bank, the ADB board has to make decisions concerning loans, guarantees, investments in equity capital, ADB borrowing, the furnishing of technical assistance and other operations of the bank. The AIIB appears to be bolder than the ADB and the World Bank in addressing the problem of inefficiency.

Monopolization of the presidency

The issue of Japanese, American and European monopolization of the presidency is one that has attracted criticism for the ADB, IMF and the World Bank. According to Article 29 of the AOA, the AIIB president is elected by a supermajority of its Board of Governors (75%). The president must be a national of a regional member and he or she may be re-elected once. In contrast, the president of the ADB may be elected by a simple majority (50%) of its Board of Governors. In other words, China can veto any AIIB presidential candidate, whereas the US plus Japan cannot veto candidates for the presidency of the ADB. While the AIIB president can only serve two terms, there is no term limit for the ADB president, albeit no president has ever served more than eight years. As mentioned above, the current president of the AIIB is a Chinese national, Jin Liqun, who started his five-year term in 2016. He has five vice presidents recommended by the president and selected by the Board of Directors. Currently two of the five vice presidents are Europeans, coming from the UK and Germany, while the other two come from regional member countries, India, Indonesia and Russia. Whether a non-Chinese will ever be elected president remains to be seen, but China can veto any candidate it does not approve of.

Up to the end of 2019, the AIIB Board of Directors had met 29 times. According to the minutes of these meetings, the board has, in general, supported the president's recommendations and policies. Of the 62 investments put forward for consideration, 61 were approved as recommended by Jin Liqun. The only project that was not approved was a proposed preference-shares investment in Bayfront Infrastructure Management of Singapore for a Project Infrastructure Private Capital Mobilization Platform. This was deferred at the request of one director in July 2019. On other items, such as the annual plan and budget, the establishment of policies, decisions concerning operations, the supervision of the management and the establishment of an oversight mechanism, the president's recommendations were, in general, supported. All of this suggests that the president of the AIIB has a lot of power to direct the bank's policies and trajectories. The board, rather than being a supervisor, acts more as a supportive partner.

Loan conditionality

The World Bank has been criticized for placing policy conditions, such as the implementation of privatization or deregulation, on its loans, some of which are inimical to developing countries (Stiglitz, 2002). Researchers have also found that the World Bank makes loans for political and strategic purposes (Dreher et al., 2015; Malan, 2018). In this regard, both the AIIB and the ADB stipulate that loan decisions should be made on economic grounds alone. However, Kilby (2006) finds that the ADB's loan decisions tend to reflect the interests of the major donors (Japan and the US), which would make the ADB a "political" IFI. The ADB also has its own guidelines for policy-based lending which are tied to a neoliberal reform agenda (Raman, 2009). From its inception, the AIIB has claimed that, compared to the World Bank, it will issue loans with fewer strings attached and will not ask borrowers to adopt free-market economic policies, such as privatization or deregulation (Koh, 2015). So far, there has been no sign of any neoliberal policy conditions being applied to AIIB loans. In addition, the findings reported in Chapter 3 do not offer strong support for the contention that the AIIB's financial commitments are based on political/strategic considerations.

Variety of disciplines

Finally, is the AIIB hiring experts from disciplines other than economics? The IMF and the World Bank have been criticized for tending to recruit relatively inexperienced economists, freshly graduated from esteemed universities in the US or the UK which are strongholds of neoliberalism. As such, they lack the knowledge and experience necessary to address local or regional differences and deal with practical issues. More social scientists or practitioners from different regions with backgrounds in disciplines other than economics are required (Malkin & Momani, 2016). The AIIB has a Young Professionals Program (YPP) with a maximum age limit of 32, which is designed to cultivate future leaders of IFIs. Applicants are required to have two years of professional experience. The ADB and the World Bank have similar programs with the same upper age limit. The length of professional experience required by applicants is three years for the World Bank and two for the ADB. Unlike the AIIB and the World Bank, the ADB does not require applicants to have a master's degree. The ADB and the World Bank welcome applicants with a social science background, while the AIIB does not include social scientists but does admit those with qualifications in the public policy field. The AIIB is not interested in anthropologists, political scientists or sociologists, despite the fact that they could make a significant contribution to social and environmental assessments (Li, 2011; Malkin & Momani, 2016). From this evidence, the AIIB does not appear to be encouraging greater intellectual diversification than the other two IFIs. So far, the bank has focused more on traditional recruiting methods and has not come up with any innovative human resources initiatives.

The preceding analysis suggests that the area in which the AIIB has made the most significant progress is that of institutional design which has allowed it to address the inefficiency problems that have beset other IFIs. The AIIB is leaner than its counterparts. Although the AIIB has slightly different standards from the other IFIs where monopolization of the presidency and policy conditionality are concerned, it remains to be seen whether these concerns can be addressed in practice. Regarding unbalanced representation and lack of disciplinary diversity, the AIIB does not appear to be any better than either the ADB or the World Bank. The AIIB's achievements so far have received recognition from outside agencies. Moody's, Fitch and S&P have all assigned the AIIB a triple-A long-term issuer default rating in recognition of the strength of its governance framework and the adequacy of its capital (*Asia Times*, 2017). The Basel Committee on Banking Supervision also assigned eligible AIIB liabilities a 0% risk weighting and a high-quality liquid assets Level One designation (Asian Infrastructure Investment Bank, 2017c). Recognitions from outside agencies will elevate China's status and reduce its sense of status deficit. If this trajectory is maintained, we may observe a more reform-minded AIIB that can exert greater influence on the international financial system.

A race to the bottom?

This section examines whether the AIIB may encourage a race to the bottom in the international financial system. Many are worried that the AIIB will compete with other IFIs by lowering prevailing international standards and supporting more environmentally and socially unfriendly projects rejected by other IFIs (Wihtol, 2015). For this to happen, the AIIB's policies would have to deviate observably from IFI best practice and AIIB projects would have to cause a negative impact on the environment and society. Now, I will focus on environmental and social standards and compare the AIIB with other IFIs.

In his first speech as AIIB president in January 2016, Jin Liqun committed the bank to the "highest possible standards" (Zheng, 2016). Testing this commitment requires a comparison between the AIIB's Environmental and Social Framework and those of other IFIs. In certain areas, the AIIB appears to have higher standards. For example, it goes further than the World Bank in refusing to finance commercial logging operations in tropical or old-growth forests (Larsen & Gilbert, 2016). The AIIB also conforms to other established standards. For instance, it has adopted the World Bank's Environmental, Health and Safety Guidelines. Myanmar's proposal for the Myingyan 225 MW combined cycle gas turbine (CCGT) power plant project was an early test of the AIIB's adherence to best practice as it was considered to be a politically and strategically sensitive project. In its evaluation of the project's environmental and social impact, the AIIB finally decided to follow the International Finance Corporation's (IFC) Performance Standard on Environmental and Social Sustainability. The IFC is a member of the World Bank Group.

However, in other areas, the AIIB's standards are ambiguous. For example, in explaining how to mitigate adverse effects on the environment, the IFC uses concepts such as "no net loss of biodiversity" and "set-asides" while the AIIB simply requires as "measures acceptable to the Bank" (Kim, 2016). According to its Environmental and Social Framework, the AIIB stipulates that it will not "will not knowingly finance projects involving" activities or items specified in its Environmental and Social Exclusion List (ESEL). The use of the word "knowingly" makes the AIIB's ESEL weaker than those of other multilateral banks (see Table 4.10). In addition, when the AIIB issued the first draft of its ESEL in 2015, it was criticized for failing to include bans on projects that involved (1) radioactive materials, (2) nuclear reactors, (3) forced labor, (4) child labor, (5) the production or trade in wood or other forestry products other than those from sustainably managed forests, (6) involuntary resettlement, (7) the conversion or degradation of critical natural habitats or (8) the conversion or degradation of critical forest area (Fried, 2015). The latest version of the ESEL, which was approved in February 2016 and amended in February 2019, addresses points (3), (4) and (5) but does nothing about the others.

The following part will now compare the environmental and social impacts of AIIB projects with those of other IFIs. The ADB, for example, adopts four categories to assess the impact of its projects on three different dimensions: the environment, involuntary resettlement and the impact on indigenous peoples. The four categories are A, B, C and FI. Category A projects are considered to have

Table 4.10 Environmental and social exclusion lists of the AIIB and other IFIs

Environmental & Social Exclusions	AIIB	ADB	World Bank
Wording	*will not "knowingly" finance . . .*	*. . . do not qualify for ADB financing*	*Does not lend directly for investment in . . .; prohibit . . .*
(1) radioactive materials		√	√
(2) nuclear reactors		√	√
(3) exploiting forced labor	√	√	√
(4) child labor	√	√	√
(5) production or trade in wood or other forestry products other than from sustainably managed forests	√		√
(6) involuntary resettlement			√
(7) conversion or degradation of critical natural habitats			√
(8) conversion or degradation of forest area		√	√

a significant adverse environmental impact; Category B projects are those considered to have limited number of potentially adverse environmental and social impacts; Category C projects are those judged to have minimal or no adverse impact. Category FI projects involve investment through a financial intermediary, which is delegated by the bank. In this book, I only include the first three categories. The AIIB's grading system is similar, although its evaluation standards and process are different. The AIIB combines the impacts on involuntary resettlement and indigenous peoples with environmental impact rather than treating them as separate items. This makes it more difficult to see the environmental and social impacts of AIIB projects independently.

Table 4.11 shows the annual change in the impact level of AIIB projects. Compared to its first year, the AIIB has approved a smaller proportion of projects with a significant adverse impact since 2017. Since then, the distribution of impact categories has not changed much, with about 36% of projects having significant adverse impact and 64% having potentially adverse impacts. So far, there is only one AIIB project in category C (not much impact). This relatively harmless project is the Sultanate of Oman Railway System Preparation Project which, according to the official project summary, "is a preparatory phase that supports studies, institutional development and capacity building, and no physical works are to be carried out during these studies." In other words, adverse impacts are likely to follow once physical construction gets underway. Next, let us compare the performance of the AIIB with other IFIs.

To improve the relevance of the comparison between ADB and AIIB grading, I have only included ADB projects approved in 2016, 2017 and 2018 as well as projects involving loans in four sectors (agriculture, natural resources and rural development; energy; transport; water and other urban infrastructure and services) (see Table 4.12). The percentages of 148 ADB projects judged to have a significant adverse impact on the environment, indigenous peoples and involuntary resettlement are 15%, 1% and 30%, respectively. By the end of 2019, of the 62 approved AIIB projects, 38% are assessed as causing significant adverse environmental and social impact, a higher percentage than the ADB. It is interesting to note that of the 30 projects under review, 60% have been assessed as resulting in significant adverse environmental impact while none are considered to have minimal or no adverse impact. Should these projects be approved, the AIIB's percentage of category A projects would rise to 46%.

Table 4.11 Environmental and social impacts of AIIB projects by year

Category	2016	2017	2018	2019	Total
A	4(44%)	4(33%)	3(38%)	7(37%)	18(38%)
B	4(44%)	8(67%)	5(63%)	12(63%)	29(60%)
C	1(11%)	0(0%)	0(0%)	0(0%)	1(2%)
Total	9(100%)	12(100%)	8(100%)	19(100%)	48(100%)

Note: I exclude the category of financial intermediary (FI) due to the nature of its lower sensitivity to the impacts.

Table 4.12 Environmental and social impacts of ADB and AIIB projects

Category	ADB			AIIB	
	Environment	Indigenous Peoples	Involuntary Resettlement	Environment (approved)	Environment (proposed)
A	22(15%)	2(1%)	37(30%)	18(38%)	18(60%)
B	112(76%)	27(18%)	49(39%)	29(60%)	12(40%)
C	14(9%)	119(80%)	39(31%)	1(2%)	0(0%)
Total	148(100%)	148(100%)	148(100%)	48(100%)	30(100%)

Note: I exclude the category of financial intermediary (FI) due to the nature of its lower sensitivity to the impacts.

Table 4.13 ADB, IFC, WB, and AIIB energy-related projects: degrees of alignment with the Paris Agreement

Categories	ADB	IFC	WB	AIIB
Aligned	26(29%)	32(50%)	28(25%)	5(26%)
Conditional	46(51%)	12(19%)	69(61%)	12(63%)
Misaligned	3(3%)	7(11%)	3(3%)	0(0%)
Controversial	15(17%)	13(20%)	12(11%)	2(11%)
Total	90(100%)	64(100%)	112(100%)	19(100%)

Source: ADB, IFC and WB data taken from the World Resources Institute (Christianson et al., 2017).

Another issue of widespread concern regarding the AIIB's environmental credentials is whether the bank would be more likely than other IFIs to finance coal-fired power plants in the region. The World Resources Institute assessed energy-related projects financed by the major IFIs, dividing them into four categories according to their degree of alignment with the Paris Agreement on Climate Change (see Table 4.13). The four categories are: (1) aligned (renewable energy projects); (2) conditional (natural gas-fired power or electricity transmission and distribution infrastructure); (3) misaligned (new coal-fired power plants); (4) controversial (sometimes involve significant environmental and social risks). The results show that by the end of 2019, 26% of the AIIB's energy projects were aligned with the Paris Agreement, which is roughly the same as the ADB and the World Bank. It is interesting to note that before the end of 2018, the AIIB had only approved one renewable energy project aligned with the Paris Agreement (8% of the total). However, four new renewable energy projects were approved in 2019 alone.

Several regional members of the AIIB, including India and Indonesia, have been seeking outside funding for relatively cheap coal-fired plants and have been rejected by other IFIs. For example, the ADB shows little interest in investing in coal-fired plants (Chin, 2016; Otto, 2015). Although the AIIB says that it aims to be "clean, lean and green," the bank has yet to place restrictions on financing coal-fired plants (Kynge, 2017). By 2019, however, the AIIB has yet to approve any "misaligned" projects related to coal, but China itself was involved in 240 non-AIIB coal-fired projects between 2001 and 2016 via, for example, the Export-Import Bank of China and China Construction Bank (Rolland, 2017). India, Indonesia, Mongolia, Vietnam and Turkey are the top five recipients of non-AIIB Chinese funds for such projects (Feng, 2017). Should the AIIB give the green light to any coal-fired power projects in the future, it may well lead to a "race to the bottom" in Asia's infrastructure investment market and hinder the enforcement of best practice in the region. It appears, therefore, that the AIIB intends to follow the other IFIs in minimizing environmental impact.

Regarding the minimization of social impacts, the AIIB's performance is similar to that of the IFC, which conforms to the Core Labor Standards on child labor, forced labor, freedom of association and collective bargaining as well as discrimination in employment and occupation. Kim (2016) points out three differences, however: (1) although the AIIB conforms to the International Labour Organization's Minimum Age Convention for child labor, it does not conform to the Worst Forms of Child Labour Convention that specifically proscribes hazardous working environments for child labor; (2) rather than protecting general freedom of association, the AIIB merely urges its private sector clients to comply with national laws on labor organizations and collective bargaining; and (3) according to the AIIB's Environmental and Social Framework, the bank only offers limited protection against discrimination for women and migrant workers.

Regarding transparency policies, the AIIB was expected to upgrade its Draft Policy on Public Information issued in January 2016 (Rosenzweig, 2016), but this has yet to be done. Problems with the policy identified by outside agencies include the scope of proactive publication, an overly broad regime of exceptions, a lack of procedural rules governing the Draft Policy, no provision for appeal to an independent oversight body and failure to process requests for information (Mendel & Summers, 2016).

Legally speaking, the AIIB does not appear to comply fully with best practice. But as a rookie bank that has been running for only four years, there is no clear evidence that it is encouraging the international financial system into a "race to the bottom" and trying to crowd out other IFIs by adopting lower standards. Many observers recognize that the AIIB is at least signaling that it has a strong commitment to high global standards in the financing of infrastructure and positive results are expected (Kim, 2016; LaForgia, 2017; Schiefelbein, 2016). However, it is still uncertain whether the AIIB will live up to its promises (Callaghan & Hubbard, 2016).

To summarize, although the AIIB appears to deviate to some extent from international standards both legally and in practice, which may risk a race to the bottom in Asia, currently the bank itself does not appear to be a norm challenger. In fact, most of the AIIB's internal policies follow those of its more experienced Western-dominated counterparts. There is little sign that the AIIB is being manipulated by China to undercut the other major IFIs. At least for now, the bank is acting like a compliant partner of other parties involved.

Competition for loans

In this section I dissect the heated debate over whether the emergence of the AIIB will influence the loans and grants issued by other IFIs, especially the ADB, the EBRD and the World Bank, whose areas of operation largely overlap with that of the AIIB. If the answer is yes, what does this influence look like? In addition, will countries change the structure of their external financial assistance after they join the AIIB? If the AIIB emerges as a challenger, these changes should be reflected in the other IFIs' loan structures. However, if the AIIB behaves in a complementary fashion, the other IFIs should behave as before.

According to officially released data on those three IFIs displayed in Table 4.14, total regional infrastructure loans amounted to US$45.8 billion even before the AIIB was established in 2015. Although the ADB's total commitments in 2016 dropped by 17.9%, the bank saw massive growth in the following two years. In 2018, the ADB's total financial assistance had caught up with the World Bank's financial commitments in the Asia-Pacific region. The ADB's increase may have been part of a Japan-initiated policy to counter the potential rise of the AIIB, a theory which is discussed in Chapter 7. While the ADB has seen a considerable increase, the World Bank has not. Its commitments registered a negative growth rate for two consecutive years after 2015. Although the World Bank increased its total financial commitments in 2017 and 2018, the scale of the increase was insignificant, and it still did not reach the amount for 2014. Although total commitments from the EBRD declined by 10.9% in 2016, there does not appear to be a significant downward trend for that bank. The average annual growth rate in commitments since 2015 for the AIIB was 37.3%; whereas, for the ADB it was 12.0%, -4.0% for the World Bank and -1.6% for the EBRD. Although the AIIB has

Table 4.14 Approved funds from AIIB, ADB and the World Bank (US$ billion)

Year	AIIB		ADB		World Bank		EBRD		Total		HHI (%)	Inverse HHI
	$bil	Δ%	$bil	Δ%	$bil	Δ%	$bil	Δ%	$bil	Δ%		
2011	n/a	n/a	12.9	n/a	20.6	n/a	8.5	n/a	42.0	n/a	37.6	2.7
2012	n/a	n/a	12.5	−3.1	16.4	−20.4	8.0	−6.5	36.9	−12.1	35.9	2.8
2013	n/a	n/a	14.1	12.8	17.3	5.5	7.0	−12.6	38.4	4.1	37.1	2.7
2014	n/a	n/a	13.5	−4.3	23.3	34.7	7.3	4.9	44.1	14.8	40.0	2.5
2015	n/a	n/a	16.2	20.0	22.3	−4.3	7.3	−0.8	45.8	3.9	38.8	2.6
2016	1.7	n/a	13.3	−17.9	20.1	−9.9	6.5	−10.9	41.6	−9.2	36.2	2.8
2017	2.3	35.3	19.7	48.1	20.7	3.0	7.3	13.1	50.0	20.2	35.0	2.9
2018	3.2	39.1	21.6	9.6	21.8	5.3	6.6	−9.4	53.2	6.4	35.2	2.8
2019	4.4	37.5	21.6	0.3	18.7	−14.2	7.0	6.6	51.8	−2.6	33.1	3.0

Note:

1 World Bank data only include projects for the Asia-Pacific region.
2 EBRD data only include investment projects in Eastern Europe and the Caucasus, Central Asia, southern and eastern Mediterranean, Turkey and Russia.
3 ADB and World Bank data include both loans and grants.

performed significantly better than the others, the scale of its commitments cannot match those of the other three IFIs, which fund far more projects than the AIIB annually. As a result, the change of total funds approved and shown in Table 4.14 is more a reflection of the observable growth in the ADB and moderate decline in the EBRD and World Bank. The HHI suggests that the level of concentration has not changed much either. The multiplicative inverse of the HHI here suggests that the effective number of IFIs in the Asia-Pacific region has slightly increased since the AIIB came on the scene, albeit the effect has not yet been substantial.

Table 4.15 presents a breakdown of types of funding into loans and grants for the ADB and the World Bank, as well as how this funding is distributed across the three sectors that currently account for the largest proportion of loans approved by the AIIB – energy, transportation and water (see Figure 3.2 in Chapter 3). As shown in the previous section, the ADB has accelerated its financing while the World Bank has slowed somewhat. Variation in the scale of grants has also changed quite substantially in the ADB since the arrival of the AIIB in 2015. By any of the three methods used in Table 4.15 to compare the change in grants from both institutions before and after 2016 (see the note to Table 4.15), considerable growth in the ADB and massive decline in the World Bank can be observed over a longer period. The structural change in financial assistance in terms of non-repayable grants has been more substantial than it has been with loans. Grant decisions are typically based on major donors' attitudes and perceptions and given to countries in desperate financial and social distress. The observable change may reflect the fact that the ADB's major donors, especially Japan, refocused their concern on those countries. In 2017, the ADB's president, Takehiko Nakao, pushed

Table 4.15 ADB and World Bank loans and grants (US$ billion)

Year	Loans+Grants		Grants		Energy		Transportation		Water	
	WB	ADB	WB	ADB	WB	ADB	WB	ADB	WB	ADB
2011	20.6	12.9	0.6	0.0	1.0	4.5	3.6	6.2	3.6	2.5
2012	16.4	12.5	0.7	0.0	2.0	3.0	3.0	5.3	1.8	1.1
2013	17.3	14.1	0.9	0.0	1.7	3.3	3.4	4.6	2.1	1.5
2014	23.3	13.5	1.2	0.3	3.9	2.6	1.9	5.1	3.9	1.0
2015	22.3	16.2	0.9	0.6	2.1	5.8	2.5	3.0	4.1	1.2
2016	20.1	13.3	0.6	0.5	2.0	5.6	3.7	5.2	1.8	1.2
2017	20.7	19.7	0.8	0.2	2.7	3.6	1.8	9.4	2.0	1.0
2018	21.8	21.6	0.5	1.4	1.8	3.0	2.2	2.5	2.1	1.5
2019	18.7	21.6	0.2	0.8	0.9	2.3	1.3	9.1	1.4	0.5
Δ1%	−9.6	−17.9	−32.1	−16.7	−1.5	−2.7	46.9	72.2	−55.9	3.7
Δ2%	1.8	37.6	−39.8	302.8	−13.3	−4.8	−22.1	35.0	−37.7	−27.2
Δ3%	−8.7	17.6	−43.9	20.8	−10.6	−36.9	−11.3	118.3	−54.5	−7.8

Note: "Δ1%" is the growth rate for 2016 compared to 2015 after the AIIB was established; "Δ2%" is the growth rate in the average amount from 2016 to 2019 relative to the average amount from 2011 to 2015; "Δ3%" measures the growth rate in the average amount from 2016 to 2019 relative to the amount in 2015.

for the merger of the Asian Development Fund (ADF) and the Ordinary Capital Resources as a way of competing with the rising AIIB. The new grant-only ADF envisaged itself increasing the ADB's commitments geared toward infrastructure in 18 lower-income, developing member-countries in the region (Cheng, 2017).

Energy, transportation and water sectors received the largest amount of funds from the AIIB. The former two are considered more politically and strategically sensitive as well as potentially socially and environmentally harmful. The energy and transportation sectors also received the greatest portion of funds from the ADB throughout the 2010s – a combined total of 55.7% in 2015. The increase in funding for these two sectors should be seen as a reflection of the total increase in ADB commitments rather than a change in the distribution across sectors. The lending structure of the World Bank is slightly different from that of the AIIB and ADB. Water, sanitation and flood protection received the largest portion of funds both globally and in the Asia-Pacific region. Compared to total commitments in 2015, the World Bank's lending and grants have dropped substantially. Although energy and transportation remain important sectors for the World Bank, the level of commitments is not as high as it is in the ADB. Both sectors have encountered a moderate decline in funds received from the World Bank. According to the author's calculations based on official data, the percentage of total commitments devoted to those three sectors combined in the Asia-Pacific region decreased from 39% in 2015 to 19.5% in 2019. The percentage devoted to the information and communications technology (ICT) sector has surged, however. These figures may suggest that the AIIB plays a complementary role in those three sectors. The AIIB's input combined with the increase in the ADB's funding means that the World Bank can shift focus to other sectors. From the evidence, therefore, it would be premature to suggest that the ADB and the World Bank are currently competing with the AIIB in lending to sensitive sectors in the region.

Another interesting question is whether a country's decision to join the AIIB affects the amount of funds it receives from other IFIs. Although the data presented in Table 3.3 in Chapter 3 suggests that politics has not played a visible role in determining AIIB lending so far, this may not be the case with other IFIs when they are considering funding applications from AIIB members. Will other IFIs "punish" AIIB members by limiting funding for them? Or will they funnel more funds to them to counteract the AIIB's growing influence? Table 4.16 lists all AIIB members in order of the financial commitment they had received by the end of 2019. So far, 21 members have secured AIIB loans. Evidently, almost all of these countries have faced a substantial decline in the grants offered by the World Bank, although the change in ADB grants is less clear. It is apparent that after the AIIB started lending to its members, most of them (13 out of 16) have also received increasing amounts of funds from the ADB in terms of both loans and grants. This corresponds to the previous finding that the ADB has accelerated its lending since the AIIB was created. The situation with the World Bank is a little different: 10 out of 21 the AIIB loan recipient countries have received greater financial commitments from the World Bank, but the other 9, or 42.9%, have seen a decline in World Bank assistance. The proposition that the emergence of the

Table 4.16 Changes in ADB- and WB-approved funding for AIIB members

Country	AIIB Commitment	Δ Loans+Grants %		Δ Grants %	
		WB	ADB	WB	ADB
India	2,954	−22.4	−3.6	−63.8	219.4
Turkey	1,400	−17.6	n/a	641.2	n/a
Indonesia	940	−9.9	88.7	−66.9	−100.0
China	750	10.1	23.8	34.7	−100.0
Egypt	649	55.6	n/a	−98.1	n/a
Azerbaijan	600	−68.6	119.4	−93.1	0.0
Pakistan	512	20.9	46.7	−31.5	374.7
Bangladesh	505	3.4	77.0	−97.7	7.0
Russia	500	−100.0	n/a	−100.0	n/a
Oman	301	n/a	n/a	n/a	n/a
Sri Lanka	280	37.9	25.0	−93.0	228.5
Philippines	208	−33.7	170.9	−49.6	−26.0
Nepal	202	37.7	48.4	36.7	−77.3
Georgia	114	−48.7	27.1	−93.9	n/a
Tajikistan	88	116.8	−4.9	−41.3	−5.1
Uzbekistan	82	110.4	6.3	−96.9	0.0
Cambodia	75	724.4	65.9	−89.5	81.7
Hong Kong	75	n/a	n/a	n/a	n/a
Kazakhstan	47	−46.5	−39.8	−85.8	0.0
Laos	40	41.2	20.0	−69.9	50.3
Myanmar	20	−48.5	32.3	14,586.4	653.5

Source: Official projects data statistics from the ADB and the World Bank

Note: Δ is the rate change of average funding approved (both banks compare the 2011–2015 average with 2016–2019).

AIIB has politically and strategically crowded out the regional visibility of other institutions and influenced the distribution of lending across countries appears to be more valid for the World Bank but less likely to be the case for the ADB.

The situation with the World Bank can be shown more clearly by using the difference-in-differences (DiD) design presented in Figure 4.1. This helps to estimate the causal effect of AIIB membership and the lending opportunities from the World Bank. The design first identifies the 140 World Bank members that have received at least one financial commitment since 2012. Those countries are then divided into the treatment group (AIIB members) and the control group (non-AIIB members). The pre-treatment period is 2012–2015, before the AIIB came into being, and the post-treatment period covers 2016–2019. Then each country's total World Bank-committed funding in both periods is divided by that country's population, which controls for the effect of the size of the country. For both groups, the means of the total amount of World Bank funds per capita for both the control and treatment groups in the pre- and post-treatment periods are measured. Finally, DiD compares World Bank funds received by both the control and treatment groups in the two periods, which are four years before and four years after the AIIB started to operate.

For example, plot A in Figure 4.1 shows that from 2012 to 2015, the average amount of World Bank-committed funds to sixty approved AIIB members (treatment group) was about US$100 per capita. From 2016 to 2019, the average amount committed increased slightly to US$117 (solid black line). However, for the other eighty non-AIIB members, the average amount improved significantly from US$101 to US$253 per capita, a significant 2.5-fold increase (dashed black line). A counterfactual estimate (dotted grey line) suggests that the DiD estimate is −135, which means that, statistically speaking, after these countries became members of the AIIB, they received, on average, US$135 per capita less from the World Bank than non-AIIB members. In other words, the average World Bank commitment to those sixty AIIB members would, like non-members, have been raised to US$252 per capita, a 2.5-fold increase, if they had not become AIIB members. Plots B to D suggest the same pattern. Regardless of how the AIIB membership is treated in this DiD estimate (see the note to figure 4.1), it appears that the growth of World Bank financial assistance per capita to AIIB members lags far behind that to non-AIIB members. This DiD estimation suggests that the effect of AIIB membership on the amount of World Bank commitments is negative.

To summarize, the findings suggest that the amount and structure of financial commitments from the ADB and the World Bank have changed since the birth

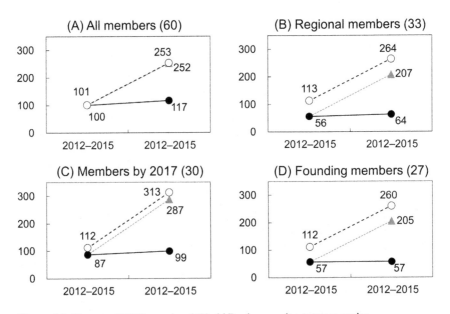

Figure 4.1 Change of AIIB members' World Bank commitments per capita

Note: For the treatment group, plot A includes all approved members by 2019; plot B includes all approved regional members by 2019; plot C include countries with AIIB membership and voting power after completing all official admission requirements by 2017; plot D includes 27 AIIB founding members that have received World Bank funds since 2012.

of the AIIB. While the total amount of commitments to regional infrastructure projects from the three institutions has risen, support from the ADB appears to be stronger than that from the World Bank, which, in effect, slowed down its lending in the region. In addition, the scale of the variation is larger in grants than it is in loans from both the ADB and the World Bank. Looking at individual sectors, there is no clear evidence that the three institutions are competing to bankroll sensitive sectors in exchange for political benefits. At a national level, however, some variation can be observed. While most AIIB members have received more commitments from the ADB, some of them have secured less from the World Bank. In addition, most AIIB members are receiving less in grants from both institutions. Finally, although the World Bank has, on average, committed more to both members and non-members of the AIIB, the growth rate for the former lags way behind that for the latter group of countries. The gap appears to be significant. It requires further detailed study to investigate whether this phenomenon is a result of the World Bank "punishing" countries for joining the AIIB, or simply a desire to divert more financial resources to countries not covered by the AIIB.

Conclusion

In this chapter, through comparing the AIIB with the ADB and the World Bank, I show that criticism of the current international financial governance structure coming from emerging countries might not be as legitimate as it seems. The problem of representation is salient only with China and the United States in the World Bank and China and Japan in the ADB. Other than that, there is not much difference in the voting structure of the three banks. The AIIB is just another development financing vehicle with the same power structure problem. The only difference is that it is structured to ensure that China is in the lead. Furthermore, compared to the ADB and the World Bank, the AIIB has the highest power concentration among its top ten members. Veto power is also a problem in the AIIB. Not only does China have stronger veto power in the AIIB, there are also more occasions when it can use its veto. Even if Japan and the United States were to take up the unallocated shares as a regional member and a non-regional member, respectively, they would each only get a 1.58% and a 0.40% share of the votes, while China's voting power cannot fall below 25%. The fact that it requires a supermajority to increase the level of authorized capital stock required to vote would make it unlikely that Washington or Tokyo could easily increase their voting power. Consequently, even if the European members of the AIIB were to align with the United States, China would retain its veto power.

Aside from veto power, the power of the president of the AIIB is greater than that of the presidents of other IFIs without a resident board. The president of the AIIB can recommend vice presidential candidates for approval by the board of directors, which allows the formation of a senior management team subject to manipulation by the president. In addition, China retains a de facto veto power on major issues that require a supermajority (75%) in order to be passed. As a result, as long as the president of the AIIB continues to be a Chinese national with the power to form a compliant senior management team and China has de facto veto power, Beijing will be able to control the trajectory of the AIIB should it wish to do so.

From an institutional perspective, the AIIB does not appear to be a norm challenger as some have suggested. But, although the AIIB's institutional design does not appear to address the problems of monopolization of the presidency, unbalanced representation and lack of disciplinary diversity that have been identified in other IFIs, it does address certain inefficiency problems. Also, compared with the other two Bretton Woods IFIs, it has deviated slightly from established standards both legally and in practice. There is, however, no evidence to suggest that a serious race to the bottom problem will emerge anytime soon. As for the issue of loan competition, the evidence suggests that the ADB has reacted by boosting its financial capacity in several respects, while the World Bank's reaction is less clear. Although the World Bank's financial commitments to most AIIB members increased, the growth in these commitments has been significantly lower than it has been for non-AIIB members. This is an interesting development requiring further research. All of this seems to suggest that the AIIB is behaving more like a new development agency controlled by a new dominant global power. In its present incarnation, this China-led bank has the potential to challenge the status quo.

However, China's ambitions in this respect may yet be thwarted. The AIIB is not providing solutions to the problems that countries are having with the World Bank. The problem of equality of representation remains. If the AIIB does not correct this problem, underrepresented countries may threaten to walk away. Furthermore, even if China intends for the AIIB to adopt global best practice in order to retain its competitiveness, it is doubtful whether other authoritarian regimes would cooperate with China in such reform. After all, some countries may be joining the AIIB in the expectation of easy access to funds with less stringent conditions; they may have no interest in adopting global best practice. All of this suggests that it will be hard for China to initiate the kind of collective agenda it wants. Finally, Washington and Tokyo are probably starting to curb the bank's influence by not only refusing to join but also by engaging in intense loan competition in the development finance market. To summarize, the AIIB may demonstrate China's intention to challenge or reform, but its weak potential for alliance formation and an increasingly competitive environment will further complicate the situation.

Part II
Global responses to the AIIB

5 Asia-Pacific participation in the AIIB

This chapter examines how Asian countries are responding to the creation of the AIIB. According to the bank's Articles of Agreement, "the purpose of the bank shall be to improve infrastructure connectivity in Asia [and] . . . promote regional cooperation and partnership in addressing development challenges." The total subscription of shares held by the regional members of the AIIB cannot fall below 75%. This threshold guarantees that Asian countries will remain firmly in control; although by the end of 2019, regional countries only accounted 50% (fifty out of one hundred) of the membership. Although the shareholding of regional members is more than the threshold, their voting power is slightly below 75%. With China in the driving seat, the bank remains firmly in regional control. Most regional countries have expressed a high degree of interest in further cooperation with the bank. In this chapter, I will first investigate the general trend in regional participation and discuss the similarities and differences in regional members' approaches to the bank. Most countries in the Asia-Pacific region are developing economies desperate for AIIB loans, although they differ in terms of national capability, national wealth, type of political regime and the nature of their bilateral relationship with China. The following in-depth case studies of India, Kazakhstan, Indonesia and the Pacific Island countries will demonstrate the different circumstances faced by each and how these differences influence their participation in Asia's regional development initiative.

How Asia and Oceania view the AIIB

While the AIIB was China's idea, the bank was expected to become a regional institution that would concentrate on improving regional infrastructure. In defining what it means by "regional members," the AIIB has adopted the United Nations (UN) definition of geographic regions. So, its regional membership consists of countries in Asia or Oceania, or as otherwise decided by the bank's Board of Governors. According to that definition, the total number of qualified countries amounts to 52 in Asia and 15 in Oceania.[1] When the first "Memorandum of Understanding on Establishing the Asian Infrastructure Investment Bank" was signed on October 24, 2014, all of the 21 signatories were Asian countries. With the exception of three wealthy oil-producing countries (Brunei, Kuwait and

Oman), they were all developing economies in desperate need of the upgraded infrastructure necessary to promote economic growth. Even though Beijing managed to persuade some European countries to join as non-regional members, 37 out of the 57 founding members (65%) came from the region, either from Asia or Oceania. As it has evolved, the bank's scope has extended to other parts of the world, reducing the percentage of regional members to 50% (50 out of 100) by the end of 2019. Apart from the 57 founding members, the bank has approved 13 regional and 30 non-regional memberships, and in September 2017, the AIIB started to approve loans to non-regional members. Egypt, the first non-regional beneficiary, received loans for two projects.[2] By the end of 2019, 59 of the bank's 62 approved project loans went to countries in the region. In general, the membership distribution of the AIIB makes it look like a global, rather than a regional, financial institution, despite the fact that most of its operations still take place within the region.

Of the 67 countries in the Asia and Oceania region, as defined by the AIIB, 50 (75%) have become regional or prospective regional members. The remaining 17 regional countries without AIIB membership include Taiwan and the six Pacific states that still recognized the Republic of China (Taiwan) as of mid-2019. The remaining ten non-AIIB members in the region are Bhutan, Iraq, Japan, Macau, Micronesia, North Korea, Palestine, Syria, Turkmenistan and Yemen. Although the AIIB has attracted a high percentage of regional participation, these members are quite diverse in terms of their populations, levels of development, levels of infrastructure, types of political regime, bilateral relations with China, governance, etc. Their level of participation and the actual benefits they may receive will differ according to their different strategic and developmental considerations.

Table 5.2 demonstrates the differences between individual countries in Asia and Oceania. The region has the world's biggest countries in terms of population or

Table 5.1 AIIB's regional and non-regional memberships (by December 31, 2019)

Founding members	Regional	Non-regional	Total
	37	20	57
2015	12	6	18
2016	22	10	32
2017	6	5	11
2018	4	4	8
2019	0	6	6
Prospective members	6	19	25
Total	50	50	100

Note:

1 The total number in the last row sum the number of membership from 2015 to 2019 and the number of prospective members.

2 Prospective members are those whose membership application has been approved by the AIIB Board of Governors, but who have yet to finish domestic processes and to deposit their first capital installments with the bank.

Table 5.2 Varieties of Asian countries

	Max	Min	Mean	Median	Std. dev.
Population (million)	1,379	0.009	69	8	232
GDP (million US$)	9,490,586	39	460,278	40,000	1,398,511
GDP/capita (US$)	64,303	571	12,859	4,303	16,233
Infrastructure (1~5)	4.1	1.6	2.8	2.8	0.6
Political regime (-10~10)	10.0	−10.0	1.0	3.0	7.2
Foreign policy difference	3.1	0	0.7	0.4	0.7

Note:

1 The data for population, GDP and GDP/capita comes from the World Bank and is in 2016; infrastructure data comes from 2016 "Logistic Performance Index" of the World Bank; political regime data comes from the polity score of POLITY IV in 2016; foreign policy is the difference of ideal foreign policy point between China and its counterpart (Bailey, Strezhnev, & Voeten, 2017).

economic scale, such as China, India, Indonesia and Russia. It also includes some of the world's smallest countries, like the Oceanic states of Tuvalu, Nauru and Palau. The emerging countries are seeking greater power in the region. However, most of them are not the richest or the most developed ones. Therefore, like most developing countries, they are actively seeking global investment and advanced technology to develop their domestic infrastructure and economies. They are keen to participate in international organizations and want to play a part in writing the rules of global governance. These emerging regional members have more to gain from the AIIB. Strategically, they are more alert than other countries to changes in regional power distribution as the China-led AIIB evolves. On the other hand, the mini-states of Oceania may be too financially vulnerable to participate in the AIIB to any substantial extent. What they are looking for is simply financial support for projects concerned with the fight against the effects of global warming or the upgrading of roads or ports to improve the livelihoods of their populations. Although their ambitions are limited, some of them are in important strategic locations, a situation which puts them in a better bargaining position when it comes to striking financial deals with the great powers in the region.

The region also has some of the world's richest countries, already blessed with advanced infrastructure, such as Qatar, Singapore and New Zealand. It also has some of the most unstable, underdeveloped and poorest states, like Afghanistan, Nepal and Yemen. The rich countries do not need project loans from the AIIB. Instead, they subscribe a larger proportion of the shares. Together with China and the European countries, they constitute another major regional financier. Their financial and technological contribution to the region can improve the level of regional infrastructure, which in turn will benefit their own regional economic engagement. In addition, their engagement with the bank could bring them new business opportunities in the form of participation in AIIB projects. Their reasons for joining the bank are similar to those of the European countries, although they differ from Europe in that their strategic concerns are influenced by their proximity to China. While more AIIB infrastructure projects are welcome in general, these countries may be wary if China cultivates them at the expense of their own interests or concerns. As a result, they may be wondering how they can tactfully contain China's power and ambitions in the AIIB. For the poor and underdeveloped countries, the AIIB serves as an alternative source of funding to the other major IFIs, such as the World Bank or the ADB. Seeing the AIIB as complementary rather than in competition with the other IFI, even Washington's regional allies are enthusiastically backing it and not worrying about political pressure from their US patron (Kim, 2020). Besides, diversifying the sources of development loans may increase these countries' bargaining power when they apply for loans from traditional lenders. Their priority is to accelerate economic growth by speeding up infrastructure projects that will connect them more closely with the region. Since they are too weak to contain China in the AIIB, some of them are choosing to jump on the bandwagon with China. Political alignment with China may yield more preferential deals from the China-led bank, which would not be possible in other IFIs.

From a political point of view, the region has a lot of democracies whose foreign policy positions are different from China's, such as Australia, Israel and New Zealand, as well as some authoritarian regimes whose foreign policies are more aligned with Beijing's. The contribution of the more developed democracies to regional development includes not only capital, business acumen or technology but also expertise in how to govern international financial institutions. They hope that their participation in the AIIB will encourage the bank to adhere to global best practice. They want the AIIB to become an open and transparent financial agency abiding by existing rules. Therefore, they are likely to intensify their cooperation with their European fellow-members and bid for senior management positions. Since they are also actively engaged with the World Bank and the ADB, their membership can help prevent fierce competition breaking out between the three institutions. The authoritarian regimes in the region, in contrast, appear to be more willing to align with China in return for Beijing's political support, especially the poorer autocracies. However, some of these countries are oil-producing states in Central Asia or the Middle East. Their natural resources are not only a source of national wealth but also give them greater bargaining power when negotiating with the AIIB. What they care about most may not be the bank's governance standards but whether they can obtain the loans they want with no strings attached. They are not obedient followers of Western standards. In order to facilitate wealth creation and consolidation of political power, authoritarian regimes tend to be more tolerant of risky infrastructure projects detrimental to the environment and society. Their behavior in the AIIB may conflict with that of the developed democracies.

The AIIB prescribes that regional countries shall hold more than 75% of shares. When the bank was founded in mid-2015, regional founding members were allocated 733,850 subscribed shares, which accounted for 74.8%, a little below the threshold. When the bank started to operate in 2016, the regional portion soon increased to 81.4%. As more non-regional members joined, the regional share declined, reaching 76.4% in 2019. The same pattern is also apparent in regional voting power, which consists of share votes as well as basic votes and founding member votes. The total regional vote power amounted to 73.3% in 2015, subsequently climbed to 79.7% and then declined to 74% in 2019. Judging from the structure of votes, regional members remain powerful in terms of the governing structure, even though the AIIB has in effect become a global financial institution. However, for critical motions that require a supermajority of 75%, the board of governors requires cooperation from at least one non-regional member in control of more than 1% of the vote power. At the end of 2019, the top ten AIIB regional members were China, India, Russia, South Korea, Australia, Indonesia, Turkey, Saudi Arabia, Iran and Thailand. In the senior management team, Jin Liqun, who is a Chinese national, has served as the president of the bank since 2016. Two out of the five vice presidents come from within the region. They are D. J. Pandian from India (vice president and chief investment officer) and Luky Eko Wuryanto from Indonesia (vice president and chief administration officer). In 2019, three out of the five vice presidents came from the region. In addition to Wuryanto and Pandian, the third regional vice president is Konstantin Limitovskiy from Russia who is in charge of investment operations. Judging from the management structure, it is clear that the AIIB is controlled by regional members.

By the end of 2019, as shown in Table 5.3, the AIIB had approved 59 projects in Asia or Oceania, either in a single member-country or for cross-border regional development as a whole. These projects account for 94% of the total loans from

Table 5.3 AIIB project loans by regional members (US$ million)

Country	Item	Total	2019	2018	2017	2016
India	13	2,954	885	995	1074	-
Turkey	5	1,400	600	800	-	-
Regional	6	1,329	679	500	150	-
Indonesia	5	940	-	498	225	217
China	2	750	500	-	250	-
Azerbaijan	1	600	-	-	0	600
Pakistan	4	512	112	-	0	400
Bangladesh	5	505	220	60	60	165
Russia	1	500	500	-	-	-
Oman	3	301	-	-	-	301
Sri Lanka	2	280	280	-	-	-
Philippines	1	208	-	-	208	-
Nepal	2	202	202	-	-	-
Georgia	1	114	-	-	114	-
Tajikistan	2	88	-	-	60	28
Uzbekistan	1	82	82	-	-	-
Cambodia	1	75	75	-	-	-
Hong Kong	1	75	75	-	-	-
Kazakhstan	1	47	47	-	-	-
Laos	1	40	40	-	-	-
Myanmar	1	20	-	-	-	20
Total	59	11,021	4,297	2,853	2,141	1,730

the AIIB. The annual growth rate of loans issued has increased year on year: by 24% in 2017, 33% in 2018 and 51% in 2019. Among the regional beneficiaries, India secured the largest number of loans either in terms of the number of items or loans. It is followed by another two major regional players, Turkey and Indonesia. More than half of the funding recipients are emerging countries hungry for infrastructure investment. As well as their greater voting power that may give them institutional advantages when applying for loans, they also have enhanced bureaucratic capacity that facilitates their loan application process. Most of these approved loans, as mentioned in a previous chapter, went to the energy and transportation sectors.

In general, although the regional members of the AIIB account for only 50% of the membership, the bank's main focus so far has been on infrastructure projects within the region. New non-regional members that are also eager for infrastructure projects have not yet consumed many of the bank's resources. Regardless of this regional focus, divergence among regional members means that they have different views of the AIIB and different levels of participation. In the following sections, four case studies are presented, those of India, Kazakhstan, Indonesia and Oceania. Each case has its distinct perspectives and degree of participation in the bank. Oceania is treated as a single case here since most countries in that region share similar traits and perspectives.

India: participation and restraint

India is an emerging global power hungry for inward investment in its infrastructure. Although the level of India's physical and social infrastructure tops that of other South Asian developing countries, it still lags behind its fellow BRICS (Brazil, Russia, India, China, South Africa). Where it is most lacking is in access to electric power, internet access, level of air travel and quality of seaports. The elimination of poverty and access to health care, education and vocational training are also pressing items on the national agenda (Agrawal, 2015). According to the Global Competitiveness Report, India's overall infrastructure performance ranked 68th out the 138 countries or economies surveyed (Schwab, 2016). Although its transportation facilities, especially rail, outperform many developing economies, it only ranks 88th in terms of electric power supply, putting it in the 36th percentile. The situation is even worse in rural areas. Instead of the construction or upgrading of basic transportation networks, efficient, reliable and affordable electricity supplies are critical to the country's economic growth (Allcott, Collard-Wexler, & O'Connell, 2016). To sustain economic momentum, India is seeking to build closer connections with both the East and the West. Improving air, land and sea connectivity to the East is expected to generate trade and investment opportunities. Integration with countries to the west will open up more business opportunities and ensure a supply of oil from the Middle East across the Arabian Sea for this energy-hungry country. In 2018, India's top four oil suppliers were in the Middle East (Abdi, 2018). The structure of India's external trade relations demonstrates the importance of improving regional connectivity. According to official data, most of India's top trading partners are in East Asia or the Middle East.[3] Improving linkages with these regional countries is India's main challenge.

This major regional and global power had the world's second largest population (1.31 billion) and was its seventh largest economy in 2018.[4] Since 1990, China and India have been considered to be the two most promising emerging powers in Asia. They were numbered among the BRICS by Goldman Sachs for their outstanding economic growth (O'Neill, 2011). At the beginning of the 1990s, India's GDP rivaled China's GDP, both of which were around US$350 billion (in current US$). Due to its smaller population, India had a higher GDP per capita in the early 1990s. Since the mid-1990s, however, China's GDP has rapidly surpassed that of India, making it the world's second largest economy, producing five times more than India both in total and per capita. In terms of military spending, India spent a little more than China, although both countries spent about US$10 billion. Since then, the gap has widened rapidly. In 2018, China spent US$250 billion on its military, 3.76 times more than India.[5] If one accepts that a state's national power includes both economic scale and military power, the power gap between China and India has widened between the 1990s and the 2010s. Faced with China's ever-increasing dominance in the region and Beijing's geopolitical and geo-economic expansion, some Indian scholars took the attitude that "if you can't beat them, join them." They considered that while India must be alert to any threat that China poses to its national security, New Delhi should cooperate with Beijing's economic development planning in the region (Garlick, 2017). With China both raising strategic concerns and offering economic opportunities, India has a tough choice to make (Das, 2017). In such a situation, India is hesitant about either jumping on China's bandwagon or turning down China's invitation (Sachdeva, 2018; Jacob, 2017; Nanwani, 2019).

Regardless of its policy of looking East or linking with the West, India's regional strategy will overlap with China's Belt and Road Initiative (BRI). The country cannot turn a blind eye to China's engagement in South Asia. Although national security concerns are slowing down India's engagement in China's regional integration plan, New Delhi cannot afford to reject the economic bonanza offered by China, as it has the potential to help it sustain its domestic economic growth. So India, while aware of the potential security costs, is showing interest in the opportunities provided by China's engagement in its neighborhood (Sachdeva, 2018). As China is putting enormous efforts into improving regional connectivity, India has been seeking acceptable ways of introducing Chinese loans and investments to improve its domestic infrastructure.

When the US and Japan rejected the BRI and refused to apply for AIIB membership, the other two pillars of Washington's Indo-Pacific strategy, India and Australia, behaved more pragmatically. Responding to the BRI, the Indian Ministry of External Affairs stated that, although it recognized the potential benefits of the BRI in improving regional connectivity, India would not be joining. This was because the BRI's flagship project, the China-Pakistan Economic Corridor, is a collaboration between its two main regional rivals. Rather than having a geo-economic purpose, this corridor project is seen by many as a geopolitical instrument that will enable China to hedge against India. It could encroach on India's sovereignty and territorial integrity and may threaten India's interests in the Indian Ocean region (Garlick, 2018). Despite its rejection of the BRI, India, together with Australia, became a founding member of the AIIB. It was one of the 21 Asian countries that signed the "Memorandum of Understanding on Establishing the Asian Infrastructure Investment Bank" on October 24, 2014. It sent representatives to all five chief negotiators' meetings before the bank came into being in June 2015 and hosted the second such meeting in Mumbai.

India became the second most powerful member of the bank and its share subscription (83,673) was second only to that of China. When Usha Titus, the joint secretary of the Economic Affairs Division of the Ministry of Finance, signed the MOU on behalf of India, she said that "India's view is that the new bank provides rich resource capital base for infrastructure financing . . . playing a complementary role along with other financial institutions . . . and work[ing] for good governance." When asked what her views were about the as yet undecided governing structure of the bank, she expressed confidence that those issues "would be decided . . . in consultations with other members" (*The Economic Times*, 2014). When he participated in the AIIB's opening ceremony in January 2016, Prime Minister Narendra Modi said that he thought the AIIB would play a big role in India's upcoming infrastructure programs and that he was confident that it would become a partner in the Indian economy and be an invaluable instrument of regional prosperity (Asian Infrastructure Investment Bank, 2016). Later, Prime Minister Modi asked senior officials to approach the AIIB for loans to finance projects in agriculture, rural housing and railways (Chaudhury, 2016).

India's refusal to join the BRI while embracing the AIIB is a typical case through which we can understand regional powers' responses to China's grand strategy in the region. India saw the BRI as a unilateral Chinese geopolitical initiative which ruled out multilateral involvement. India was willing, however, to join a multilateral institution which would abide by international norms and good governance (Panda, 2018). The BRI has no effective multilateral consultative platform. Other participants are too weak to influence China's behavior, and each BRI cooperation scheme is bilateral in nature and favors China's interests. Furthermore, the negative political and economic consequences of the BRI suffered by other participants, such as debt traps or environmental and social impacts, acted as a wake-up call for other states that might contemplate joining (Belt & Road News, 2019). Regional powers like India do not entirely reject contributions from other states to the expansion of regional infrastructure programs; their concern is that China's grand plan should not be carried out at the expense of their own national interests. The BRI could be harmful unless it abides by international best practice and adopts transparent consultative processes. Unlike the BRI, the AIIB is seen as a China-led international organization that facilitates regional infrastructure financing through constructive cooperation among emerging economies (Aneja, 2015). It also follows international norms universally recognized by other IFIs. India's involvement in the bank's creation has reassured the Indian government of the AIIB's multilateralism and addressed any suspicions of the unilateralism that it saw in the BRI (Jaishankar, 2015). Despite the ongoing geopolitical rivalry between India and China, India's active engagement in the AIIB demonstrates its intention to intensify its economic engagement with China (Iwanek, 2019).

By the end of 2019, India was the biggest beneficiary among AIIB members. It has the second largest share subscription and voting power. India's share of global GDP was consistent with its voting power in the World Bank, though its voting power in the ADB lagged behind its share of Asian GDP. New Delhi appears to have made up for this by its increased power in the AIIB (see Table 5.4). This may help ease emerging countries' complaints regarding the West's rejection of their demands for greater influence in international organizations (Sehrawat, 2019). In addition to voting power, India has also benefitted by receiving the largest number of approved loans. Of the AIIB's twenty loan recipients, India has had a total of US$2.954 billion in loans approved (26.8% of the total). This percentage far exceeds what would be commensurate with India's subscribed shares. One interesting question is whether AIIB loans have had a negative effect on India's loan opportunities from other IFIs. Table 5.5 shows India's total annual loans approved by three institutions since 2014. Although the increase in the total amount received

Table 5.4 India's power in three international financial institutions

	World Bank	*ADB*	*AIIB*
Subscribed capital	3.11%	6.33%	8.69%
Voting power	2.96%	5.35%	7.62%

Note:

1 In 2018, India's GDP share is about 3.16% worldwide and 7.77% in Asia and Oceania.
2 The World Bank and AIIB data is in 2019; the ADB is in 2018.

Table 5.5 India's loans from international financial institutions (US$ billion)

Institutions	*Unit*	*2013*	*2014*	*2015*	*2016*	*2017*	*2018*
A. World Bank	($bil.)	2.84	3.53	5.30	2.36	2.89	3.47
	(%)	8.4	7.1	11.2	6.2	6.3	7.5
B. ADB	($bil.)	3.50	3.78	1.52	3.09	3.15	2.58
	(%)	24.0	26.9	9.7	16.7	14.9	16.0
C. AIIB	($bil.)	-	-	-	0.00	1.07	1.00
	(%)	-	-	-	0.0	45.9	31.6
D. FDI from China	($bil.)	2.70	0.84	1.97	0.91	2.80	3.84
	(%)	1.9	0.5	1.0	0.3	1.0	1.9
A+B+C	($bil.)	6.34	7.31	6.82	5.45	7.11	7.05
	(%)	13.1	11.4	10.9	9.3	10.3	10.7
A+B+C+D	($bil.)	9.04	8.15	8.79	6.36	9.91	10.89
	(%)	18.7	12.7	14.0	10.9	14.4	16.6

Note: The data was compiled by the author using official open data from the World Bank and the ADB. For China's investment data, please refer to endnote 6.

from all three has been quite stable at about 10% per year, moderate changes have occurred in different institutions. The amount India secured from the World Bank increased, but loans from the ADB dropped significantly in 2015 when the AIIB was established. Compared to World Bank and ADB loans received in 2013 and 2014, the amount from both institutions saw a moderate decline in 2015 and 2016. The AIIB approved most of its loans to India in 2017 and 2018, and in those years, both the World Bank and the ADB also increased their loans fractionally. While India has refused to join the BRI, Chinese multilateral corporations have, in effect, invested in many infrastructure projects in India even though they are not designated BRI projects. With significant input from the AIIB and Chinese investors, India's total funds received returned to, or even exceeded if one adds in other Chinese investments, their pre-2015 scale. It remains to be seen whether these changes were the result of India's active engagement in the AIIB putting New Delhi at a disadvantage with the other IFIs.

By the end of 2019, India's 13 AIIB-approved loan projects included five in transportation, four in energy, two in financial intermediary and two in water, while one was a multi-sector project. Transportation and energy accounted for the majority in terms of the number of items and amount. Those two areas are also considered to be potentially the most detrimental to the environment and society in terms of pollution and forced migration of populations without appropriate compensation. Environmentalists worry that the AIIB might be a channel for funding dirty projects that the Western-dominated IFI's might reject, but which emerging countries seeking relatively inexpensive quick fixes might find attractive. If the AIIB were to give the green light to harmful projects, such as coal-fired power plants, India might increase its participation in the AIIB at the expense of the interests of its own population (Kumar & Munroe, 2014). Since 2015, when it was created, the AIIB has not approved any coal-fired power projects in India or any other member-country, and the same can be said of China's multinational energy corporations, although they did frequently undertake such investments before then.[6] In the light of China's ambitious funding of coal-fired projects in South Asia (Watts, 2019), as well as India's high demand for low-cost energy, it is notable that New Delhi and the AIIB have resisted the temptation to embrace highly polluting energy investments. Such resistance may be the result of New Delhi's policy barring foreign participation in coal-fired projects, as well as the fact that it signed the Paris Agreement in 2016 (Feng, 2017). All energy-related AIIB investments in India relate to improvements to the power distribution system, renewable energy and green funds.

Nevertheless, 30% of India's AIIB projects, excluding projects for financial intermediary, are Category A projects which are likely to have significant adverse environmental and social impacts; the remaining 70% are in Category B, in that they may potentially lead to adverse impacts. Two Category A projects are in the transportation sector – the Bangalore Metro Rail Project and the Mumbai Urban Transport Project. The other Category A project is the Andhra Pradesh Urban Water Supply and Septage Management Improvement Project, which aims to provide a safely piped supply of drinking water to 3.3 million people in Andhra

Pradesh. A lot of AIIB projects are collaborations with other IFIs that abide by best practice, such as the World Bank and the ADB, but two of the three Category A projects are solely funded by the AIIB and India's local governments. It appears that the AIIB may become a source of finance for India when its most harmful projects are rejected by other agencies. This leads us to wonder whether the advent of the AIIB might result in an aggravation of environmental and social degradation among the loan recipients, which may result in a subsequent increase in the financing of harmful projects by the AIIB's competitors. In other words, will there be a race to the bottom in terms of environmental and social impacts? Table 5.6 shows the distribution of safeguard categories among India's ADB projects since 2015. For Category A projects that are likely to have a significant adverse impact in three areas, no apparent increase can be observed. The same applies to Category B (moderate impact). Indeed, projects in Category C (minimal or no adverse impact) have slightly increased since 2015. So it appears that the ADB has not lowered its environmental and social standards in an effort to compete with the AIIB.

To summarize, unlike China's other great power competitors in the region, such as Japan and the US, both of which have sufficient funds and knowledge to support their national economies, India, as a developing giant, has been hungry for outside resources. It has certainly welcomed China's economic engagement and the way the Chinese have contributed to regional integration. A higher level of regional integration made possible by either the BRI or the AIIB will benefit India. However, in India's eyes, engagement should be multilateral, consultative, open, transparent and in line with recognized international norms. India had to make sure that the AIIB came up to those standards before it decided to participate actively. If these standards are applied, membership of the AIIB will not conflict with India's democratic governance, and New Delhi will be reassured that China's behavior in the AIIB can be constrained. This analysis of India's early engagement indicates that the AIIB appears to be behaving as India had expected, and the Indian government seems to be satisfied with its role and status in the bank. India's strong opposition to the BRI has not been reflected in its attitude to the

Table 5.6 The safeguard categories of India's ADB loans

Safeguard	Category	2015	2016	2017	2018
Environment (ADB)	A	0.0%	11.1%	0.0%	0.0%
	B	100.0%	77.8%	8.3%	7.7%
	C	0.0%	11.1%	91.7%	92.3%
Indigenous People (ADB)	A	0.0%	0.0%	0.0%	0.0%
	B	28.6%	0.0%	25.0%	38.5%
	C	71.4%	100.0%	83.3%	61.5%
Resettlement (ADB)	A	28.6%	44.4%	25.0%	23.1%
	B	42.9%	33.3%	33.3%	46.2%
	C	28.6%	22.2%	41.7%	30.8%

Note: I exclude the category of financial intermediary (FI) due to the nature of its lower sensitivity to the impacts.

AIIB. If the AIIB continues to evolve in the expected way, India will likely remain a powerful and cooperative member that will continue to deepen its involvement. But, if China tries to use its dominant position to take the AIIB on an unexpected course, India will not remain tame and silent.

Kazakhstan: joining for an admission ticket

Kazakhstan is a major power in Central Asia and an important oil producer globally. Although it is not the most populous country in Central Asia, its GDP, at US$180 billion in 2018, tops those of its regional neighbors. The most populous and second largest economy in the region, Uzbekistan, generated only about one-fourth of Kazakhstan's GDP. Although in terms of macroeconomic scale Kazakhstan cannot compete with either China or India, it is one of the richest countries in the region. The Kazakh people's gross national income (GNI) per capita reached US$8,070 in 2018. Average earnings for Kazakhs in 2014, before the oil price crashed in the middle of the year, were US$12,090. It is clear that the economic performance of Kazakhstan is extremely sensitive to changes in the price of oil. In the early 2000s, thanks to rising oil prices, Kazakhstan saw a consistent annual economic growth rate of about 10%, although growth has slowed down since then. Its current growth still eclipses that of other countries in the region. According to the Global Competitiveness Report, Kazakhstan ranked 63rd out of 138 countries in terms of infrastructure performance, which makes it similar to India (Schwab, 2016). Most of its Soviet era infrastructure is now in need of upgrading or replacement. Fixing infrastructure problems is critical to speeding up national economic development. Sectors in most urgent need of upgrading are the district heating systems, electric power supply, solid waste management, water supply and sanitation and urban public transport. In particular, roads, ports and airports require attention in order to deal with growing traffic demand and air pollution control (OECD, 2017, pp. 102–107).

Modernizing Kazakhstan's national transport infrastructure network will help integrate both the domestic and the regional market (Molokovitch, 2019). Geopolitically, Kazakhstan is in an ideal strategic location to connect with the fast-growing regions of East and South Asia, with the Commonwealth of Independent States (CIS) countries and the developed economies of Europe. China particularly values Kazakh participation in BRI projects that will offer accelerated rail transportation routes to Europe. The Khorgos Free Economic Zone along the China-Kazakhstan border was a flagship BRI project, involving the creation of the biggest dry port for exporting Chinese goods to the Middle East, Europe and Africa (Dave & Kobayashi, 2018). In fact, it was in Kazakhstan that Xi Jinping first unveiled his "Silk Road Economic Belt initiative," which later morphed into the "One Belt One Road" and then the current BRI. This demonstrated Beijing's warm relationship with Astana and showed that the Chinese consider Kazakhstan to have the potential to develop into the most important Asia-Europe transit hub in Central Asia. China's ambitious engagement in Kazakhstan has motivated other great powers, such as Russia and the US, to renew their interest in the region, which may allow Astana to regain its regional status (Standish, 2019a). Such a position would help the Kazakhs diversify their domestic economy to reduce their reliance on oil wealth, an unreliable situation given the volatility of global oil prices.

Being an oil producer, Kazakhstan is a major energy supplier. According to the US Energy Information Administration, Kazakhstan produced about 2% of total petroleum and other liquids worldwide in 2018. Its oil reserves, the second largest among the CIS countries, have attracted China's national oil companies. Since 1997, the China National Petroleum Corporation (CNPC) has been a major player in exploring for oil reserves and has engaged actively in the oil business. China has also been keen to build a Kazakh-China oil pipeline to facilitate oil imports from Central Asia. As China's own energy production cannot meet surging domestic demand, close cooperation with its oil-rich neighbor is important if it is to sustain its economic growth. For Kazakhstan, a deepening collaboration with China can help break Russia's monopsony over its oil business (Liao, 2019). In the power sector, Kazakhstan enjoys a surplus. As part of the integrated Central Asia Power System, Kazakhstan actively seeks to increase its electricity exports to neighbors that are experiencing power shortages and to large consumers such as China, Russia and Pakistan. To achieve this end, it is necessary for Astana to reform its power sector, improve energy intensity and attract inward investment to upgrade its domestic power network (Aldayarov, Dobozi, & Nikolakakis, 2017). China's planned regional integration of transportation and energy serves Astana's interests appropriately.

In terms of diplomatic relations, China and Kazakhstan are economically, geopolitically and politically complementary. They share similar views on global political affairs and both give priority to consolidating their authoritarian regimes. They strive to avoid actions that might threaten each other's security. The creation of a strategic partnership between Beijing and Astana, which was proposed by Hu Jintao in 2015, has created further opportunities for mutual economic benefit and cooperation in energy security. The two sides have forged an understanding regarding recognition of the legitimacy of their authoritarian regimes, pledging not to intervene in each other's domestic affairs and to fight extremism, separatism and terrorism at home. China's developmental model of rapid economic growth combined with tight social and political control was of particular interest to President Nursultan Nazarbayev, who exercised authoritarian rule in Kazakhstan from 1989 to March 2019 (Kembayev, 2018). The two sides do have a few issues, including Russian intervention and public worries about the poor quality and problematic processes of Chinese BRI investments. In addition, the mistreatment of Chinese Muslims in Xinjiang provoked public fear in Khorgos, which straddles the border, when China's internment camps encroached on the city (Standish, 2019b). Nonetheless, at the state-to-state level, agreement and complementarity between China and Kazakhstan so far appear to outweigh any potential discord.

As China's close strategic partner, Kazakhstan expressed a high degree of interest in the AIIB. In May 2014, the Kazakh minister of economy and budget planning, Erbolat Dossaev, met with China's finance minister, Lou Jiwei, the main official spokesman for the AIIB plan, in Astana. Hoping to be able to export the country's surplus electricity to neighboring countries, Dossaev stated that "the initiative such as the creation of an 'Asian Infrastructure Investment Bank' will allow [us] to deeper implement such projects" (Mukhtarov, 2014). Following India and 19 other Asian countries, the Kazakh government sent Dossaev as its representative to sign the MOU on October 24, 2014. Kazakhstan hosted the 3rd chief negotiators' meeting in Almaty and did not miss any of these meetings, which were held before the AIIB was created. When Xi Jinping visited Kazakhstan in May 2015, before the finalization of the AIIB Articles of Agreement, Nazarbayev expressed devoted friendship with China and committed Kazakhstan to aligning with China's regional developmental initiatives. Nazarbayev said "Kazakhstan backs China's initiative and stands ready to be an important partner of China to build the Silk Road Economic Belt . . . [it] is ready to work more closely with China under the framework of AIIB" (Witte, 2015).

On August 8, 2015, the Kazakh National Budget Commission approved the funds necessary for its annual AIIB membership fee. In January 2016, President Nazarbayev signed into law the AIIB ratification agreement, in which Kazakhstan's initial subscribed capital amounted to US$729.3 million (Zhumabayeva, 2016). Nazarbayev appointed the minister of national economy, Kuandyk Bishimbayev, as an AIIB governor. While participating in the first annual meeting of the board of the governors in June 2016, Bishimbayev said that "Kazakhstan attaches great importance to the modern infrastructure development in Asia to strengthen inter-regional trade and economic cooperation" (*Interfax*, 2016). In October 2017, Nazarbayev amended a law so that Kazakh laws and regulations regarding borrowing and depositing funds would align with AIIB regulations (*Kazinform*, 2017). This gesture signified the importance of the AIIB to the Kazakh government. Unlike India, whose perception of the BRI differed from its attitude toward the AIIB, Kazakhstan has not appeared to discriminate against the BRI. It has not shared India's suspicions regarding the strategic threat posed by that initiative. Astana embraces both the BRI and the AIIB.

Although Kazakhstan is very enthusiastic about the AIIB, it does not have significant power in the bank. It ranks only 23rd in terms of its shareholding (0.75% of capital shares), which gave it a 0.85% voting power in 2019. This makes it commensurate with Switzerland and Israel. Although not a major shareholder, Kazakhstan's power in the AIIB exceeds its share of Asian GDP. Interestingly, Kazakhstan's AIIB vote share has declined compared to its share in the ADB (Table 5.7). Judging from Astana's attitude to the AIIB, it does not seem to be troubled about its trivial power. Unlike India, which is seeking a bigger role to ensure that the AIIB behaves itself, Kazakhstan does not show any such concerns. What it cares about most is jumping on the AIIB bandwagon and making sure it benefits from China's regional initiatives. The two countries' convergence of economic and political interests has made Astana indifferent to Beijing's domination of the AIIB.

Has participation in the AIIB given Kazakhstan more access to global financial resources? An interesting pattern is apparent from Table 5.8. In 2015 when the

Table 5.7 Kazakhstan's power in three international financial institutions

	World Bank	*ADB*	*AIIB*
Subscribed capital	0.19%	0.81%	0.75%
Voting power	0.21%	0.94%	0.85%

Note:

1 In 2018, Kazakhstan's global GDP share is about 0.21% and 0.46% in Asia and Oceania.
2 The World Bank and AIIB data is in 2019; the ADB is in 2018.

Table 5.8 Kazakhstan's loans from international financial institutions (US$ billion)

Institutions	Unit	2013	2014	2015	2016	2017	2018
A. World Bank	($bil.)	0.12	0.15	1.14	1.06	0.07	0.00
	(%)	0.4	0.3	2.4	2.8	0.1	0.0
B. ADB	($bil.)	0.12	0.23	1.00	0.44	0.01	0.00
	(%)	0.8	1.6	6.4	2.4	0.0	0.0
C. AIIB	($bil.)	-	-	-	0.00	0.00	0.00
	(%)	-	-	-	0.0	0.0	0.0
D. BRI	($bil.)	-	3.22	2.49	0.52	3.81	1.90
	(%)	-	2.7	1.9	0.4	3.2	1.5
A+B+C	($bil.)	0.25	0.37	2.14	1.51	0.07	0.00
	(%)	0.5	0.6	3.4	2.6	0.1	0.0
A+B+C+D	($bil.)	0.25	3.59	4.63	2.03	3.88	1.90
	(%)	0.3	2.0	2.4	1.1	2.1	1.0

Note: The data was compiled by the author using official open data from the World Bank and the ADB. For China's investment data, please refer to endnote 6.

AIIB was created, there was a significant increase in loans to Kazakhstan from both the World Bank (7.6 times the 2014 level) and the ADB (4.3 times that of 2014). This increase was repeated in 2016. However, since 2017, Kazakhstan has received almost nothing from either of these IFIs. From 2016 to 2018, Astana received no loans from the AIIB either. By the end of 2019, its only approved AIIB project was the Zhanatas 100 MW Wind Power Plant which was financed to the tune of US$46.7 million. Although Astana has not actively pursued financial assistance from IFIs, it has secured a lot more investments from China's BRI. In 2014, when the BRI started, Beijing supplied Kazakhstan with 8.7 times more funds than the World Bank and the ADB together. Since then, the BRI has become the single most important source of funds for Kazakhstan.

Most of the BRI funds went to the sectors of energy (32%), transportation (28%), chemicals (19%) and metals (15%). Some of these projects provoked public concern about debt traps, land grabbing, displacement, human rights abuses, adverse environmental impact and public health and labor rights violations. In 2016, when the Nazarbayev administration announced its intention to revise the land law to extend the length of time farmland can be leased to foreign nationals from 10 years to 25 years in order to accommodate China's BRI investments, a strong grassroots protest erupted (*GRAIN*, 2019). In September 2019, when the new president, Kassym-Jomart Tokayev, paid a friendly visit to Beijing, anti-China protests erupted in reaction to the trip and China's exploitative investments (Lin, 2019). The changing structure of financial resources from abroad suggests that Astana considers the BRI to be the most critical source of external funding, since BRI projects are not required to abide by universally recognized best practice.

Compared to the BRI, the ADB has approved five projects for Kazakhstan from 2013 to the present. Three of them concern creating funding opportunities for developing small and medium enterprises, one is about public sector management for countercyclical support and the fifth is for modernizing the transport system: none is classed as having a significant adverse environmental or social impact. The environmentally friendly wind power plant is the only project Kazakhstan has had approved by the AIIB since joining the bank in 2015. It did apply for another renewable energy scheme, the 40 MW Gulshat PV Solar Power Plant Project (AIIB project number 000017), early on, but that was not approved and has now disappeared from the records. Despite the AIIB being another resource supported by a strategic partner, the evidence suggests that the BRI is far more useful to Kazakhstan than the AIIB is. Although the AIIB is much more compliant with global best practice and tries to minimize the adverse impacts of its projects, the process of applying for loans from the AIIB and other IFIs can sometimes be costly and cumbersome.

In conclusion, Kazakhstan, like India, has been seeking external funds and resources to sustain its economic development. However, its national economy depends more on exploitative sectors which tend not to be welcomed by either the established institutions or the AIIB. As a close strategic partner, Kazakhstan supports both of China's grand plans – the AIIB and the BRI – as it appreciates the opportunities they provide. However, what actual benefits Astana can obtain from participation in the AIIB appear to be uncertain. The BRI should bring more, and less troublesome, opportunities for the authoritarian Kazakh regime. The evidence suggests that, although the Kazakh government cheered the birth of the AIIB, the bank may only play a minor role in China's engagement with Kazakhstan. In contrast to the situation with New Delhi, the current shape of the AIIB has failed to persuade Astana to become more involved. Only if the AIIB moves away from the other IFIs to be more like the BRI will Kazakhstan see the bank as a window of opportunity.

Indonesia: obsession with infrastructure funding

Indonesia is an emerging country with the largest population and economy in Southeast Asia. In a fast-growing region, Indonesia's average economic growth of 5.5% from 2010 to 2017 is above that for ASEAN (Association of Southeast Asian Nations) as a whole. However, the country's US$3,894 GDP per capita leaves it ample room for further growth. As the world largest archipelagic country, consisting of more than seventeen thousand islands, Indonesia is geographically fragmented. Poor transportation infrastructure connecting the different regions has slowed down growth of the national economy. There is evidence that growth of the non-tradable sector is the current engine of the economy, as lack of infrastructure and high logistics costs have prevented growth in the tradable sectors (Horridge et al., 2016). Logistics costs are estimated to account for 24% of its GDP (Muna, 2018). According to the Global Competitiveness Report 2016–2017, Indonesia ranked 60th out of 138 countries in infrastructure performance, with its lowest score being for the quality of the overall infrastructure, quality of port infrastructure and the quality of electricity supply (Schwab, 2016). Its performance as regards infrastructure remains poor compared to other countries in Southeast Asia. Improving the quality of roads, constructing a railway network, facilitating inter-island shipping and extending and upgrading the power network are the keys to economic growth and poverty reduction. Under the presidency of Susilo Bambang Yudhoyono, the level of infrastructure spending was considered insufficient, something the current president, Joko Widodo (Jokowi), promised during his election campaign to remedy by building ports and other key facilities (Mietzner, 2015). Despite emerging political risks, Jokowi has secured parliamentary support for prioritizing and accelerating infrastructure construction (Lane, 2015).

China is Indonesia's largest trading partner in terms of both exports and imports. China is also the country's second- or sometimes third-largest foreign investor. This close economic relationship allows Beijing to sell its regional initiative to Jakarta. Japan is another important economic partner and the biggest investor in Indonesia. From a political point of view, Jakarta was the first place in Southeast Asia that Xi Jinping visited after becoming president. During the trip, the two countries announced that they would upgrade their bilateral relationship into a "comprehensive strategic partnership" for intensifying strategic cooperation. In addition, it was in Jakarta that Xi proposed his "Vision and Action on Jointly Building a Silk Road Economic Belt for the 21st Century Maritime Silk Road" which subsequently became part of the "One Belt One Road" and the AIIB. Aside from improving trade, investment and foreign relations with Indonesia, China has also replaced Japan as the country's largest source of infrastructure financing (Weatherbee, 2017). Although Indonesia is not entirely uninvolved in sovereignty disputes with China in the South China Sea, both Jakarta and Beijing have avoided further escalation. The two governments have quarreled over fishing rights in the exclusive economic zone of the Natuna Islands, but when clashes have occurred, they have resolved the issues between themselves and have denied that there is any territorial dispute between them. Unlike some of the South China Sea claimants who seek the support of other parties in the dispute and other regional powers in their bargaining with China, Jakarta does not want outsiders to be involved in the Natuna dispute. The spokesperson of the Chinese Foreign Ministry, Hua Chunying, has even stated that "the sovereignty of the Natuna Islands belongs to Indonesia." Geopolitical interests do not seem to be impeding the overall improvement in bilateral relations at all levels (Suryadinata, 2016).

Like India and Kazakhstan, Indonesia was actively involved in the creation of the AIIB. It was not among the first 21 Asian countries to sign the MOU in October 2014 due to the transition of presidential power. After Jokowi assumed the presidency on October 20 that year, Indonesia's finance minister, Bambang Brodjonegoro, officially signed the agreement to join the AIIB. He said that "Indonesia attaches great importance to the establishment of the bank and could not sign earlier because of the country's change in government" (Feng, 2014). Although absent from the signing, Indonesia participated in all five chief negotiators' meetings before the bank was formally established in June 2015. In addition, Jakarta hosted the 8th chief negotiators' meeting on November 3, 2015. During the meeting, President Jokowi met with the then president-designate of the AIIB, Jin Liqun, and stated, "Indonesia attaches great importance to this new bank . . . helping to meet the infrastructure financing needs of the entire Asian region" (Asian Infrastructure Investment Bank, 2015). One of Jokowi's national development goals is to attract investment in Indonesia's infrastructure to improve connectivity throughout the archipelago. He had high hopes that the AIIB would help him reach his economic growth target (Brummitt & Amin, 2016). The AIIB became an important complementary funding agency pursued by Jakarta. Recognizing the inadequacy of development funds from the ADB and the World Bank, Finance Minister Brodjonegoro said that "the AIIB will target 'big-scale infrastructure projects' only . . . [and] complement existing multilateral lenders such as the ADB and the World Bank." In addition to financing big projects, Brodjonegoro also expected the AIIB to approve controversial projects refused by the traditional IFIs. He said "the ADB will not be interested in a big power plant . . . but the AIIB would fund a 2,000-megawatt coal-fired power plant" (Otto, 2015).

As an emerging country, Indonesia has sought a greater role in the AIIB. Jakarta subscribed 33,607 capital shares, which amounted to US$3 billion. As a result, Indonesia holds a 3.17% share of voting power in the AIIB. Commenting on the possible inequitable power problem before the AIIB was created, Brodjonegoro said that the AIIB's "voting rights will likely be determined by gross domestic product, so China will have the highest share of votes, but that's not strange . . . in the World Bank, who can be the president other than a US citizen, right? Same with ADB: who can be president other than a Japanese citizen? IMF, European." Despite his optimism, Brodjonegoro was suspicious of the participation of non-Asian countries, saying, "We don't want to repeat what happened in ADB . . . where somehow the power of the US and Europe is too strong." He ascribed China's eagerness to create its own bank to its failure to be given a greater role in the ADB, which was controlled by Western countries (Otto, 2015). Compared to its 3.2% share of the GDP of the Asia and Oceania regions, Indonesia's representation appears to be balanced and satisfactory. It is the eighth most powerful member of the AIIB. With a global GDP share of about 1.2%, Jakarta's voting power in the World Bank seems appropriate, too, and Indonesia enjoys greater power in the ADB. When we look at its voting power in the three IFIs (see Table 5.9), it is apparent that Indonesia's participation in the AIIB was not motivated by discontent regarding the unequal power distribution in the traditional IFIs.

Jakarta does not care too much about the bank's internal politics. What it concentrates on is maximizing its benefits through active participation. Jakarta's offer to host the AIIB was rejected by Beijing; despite this, Brodjonegoro's

Table 5.9 Indonesia's power in three international financial institutions

	World Bank	ADB	AIIB
Subscribed capital	0.98%	5.43%	3.47%
Voting power	0.95%	4.65%	3.17%

Note:

1 In 2018, Indonesia's global GDP share is about 1.2% and 3.21% in Asia and Oceania.
2 The World Bank and AIIB data is in 2019; the ADB is in 2018.

strategy for optimizing the AIIB's support for Indonesia's infrastructure projects is to place Indonesian nationals in senior management positions (Diela, 2016). One of these, Luky Eko Wuryanto, has been a successful vice president and chief administration officer since the beginning of operations in 2016. Following India and Turkey, Indonesia was the third largest recipient of AIIB funds by the end of 2019, with total loans worth US$939.9 million. Among the five approved projects, two are in urban development, two in irrigation and water management and one concerns the creation of a fund for regional infrastructure development. The National Slum Upgrading Project was one of the first four projects approved by the AIIB on June 24, 2016. Although the total amount in loans Indonesia has received from the AIIB still falls short of the amount it can obtain from the ADB and the World Bank, Jakarta remains optimistic that this figure will increase in the future (Dwinanda, 2018).

Has Indonesia's involvement in the AIIB influenced the support it has received from other IFIs? According to Table 5.10, there has been a significant increase in Indonesia's approved loans from both the ADB and the World Bank since 2016 when the AIIB opened for business. Total loans from the three institutions increased from US$1.98 billion in 2013 to US$3.9 billion in 2018, which is about a two-fold increase. Among these projects, the AIIB's Mandalika Urban and Tourism Infrastructure Project was the only Category A project that may result in significant adverse environmental and social impacts. The AIIB has not yet given the green light to Indonesia's coal-fired power plant project. Indonesia is one of the most important active regional countries that is asking the IFIs to bankroll its coal projects. It should have stronger bargaining power to pit the ADB against the AIIB and persuade the former to invest in dirty projects. However, as Table 5.11 shows, none of the 15 ADB commitments from 2015 to 2018 is classified as having an adverse environmental impact, although one project addressing the problem of deforestation will have an adverse impact on indigenous people and one flood management project will have an adverse impact regarding resettlement. As expected, no dirty energy projects have been approved by the AIIB or the World Bank, either. This shows that Indonesia's active engagement in the AIIB has not affected its cooperation with traditional institutions. The AIIB, together with others, has helped Indonesia maximize the external financial resources it can obtain for infrastructure development without too detrimental an impact on the country's environment and society.

Table 5.10 Indonesia's loans from international financial institutions (US$ billion)

Institutions	Unit	2013	2014	2015	2016	2017	2018
A. World Bank	($bil.)	1.26	1.23	0.50	1.85	1.44	1.70
	(%)	3.7	2.5	1.1	4.8	3.2	3.7
B. ADB	($bil.)	0.72	0.16	1.38	0.76	1.90	1.70
	(%)	5.0	1.1	8.8	4.1	9.0	10.6
C. AIIB	($bil.)	-	-	-	0.22	0.23	0.50
	(%)	-	-	-	12.5	9.6	15.8
D. BRI	($bil.)	1.08	4.97	8.55	3.77	7.38	3.30
	(%)	3.9	4.1	6.5	2.9	6.3	2.6
A+B+C	($bil.)	1.98	1.39	1.88	2.83	3.57	3.90
	(%)	4.1	2.2	3.0	4.8	5.2	5.9
A+B+C+D	($bil.)	3.06	6.36	10.43	6.60	10.95	7.20
	(%)	4.0	3.5	5.4	3.5	5.9	3.8

Note: The data was compiled by the author using official open data from the World Bank and the ADB. For China's investment data, please refer to footnote 6.

Table 5.11 The safeguard categories of Indonesia's ADB loans

Safeguard	Category	2015	2016	2017	2018
Environment (ADB)	A	0%	0%	0%	0%
	B	67%	50%	75%	25%
	C	33%	50%	25%	75%
Indigenous People (ADB)	A	0%	25%	0%	0%
	B	0%	0%	50%	0%
	C	100%	75%	50%	100%
Resettlement (ADB)	A	0%	25%	0%	0%
	B	33%	25%	50%	0%
	C	67%	50%	50%	100%

Note: I exclude the category of financial intermediary (FI) due to the nature of its lower sensitivity to the impacts.

However, the Indonesian government sometimes prefers to go to the AIIB because of its efficiency, flexibility and compatibility. When the ADB and AIIB both expressed a high degree of interest in financing a US$31 billion project to relocate Indonesia's capital from Jakarta to East Kalimantan in Borneo, the deputy minister for infrastructure affairs, Kennedy Simanjuntak, said, "If I need it, I will go first to the AIIB . . . . If we utilize old-style multilaterals, we cannot achieve our target . . . it [the AIIB] is more flexible . . . with old-style banks, I'm worried . . . they're very slow" (Palma, 2019). This relocation project is expected to be complete by 2024. The Indonesian government can only contribute 19% of the total cost, with the rest coming from external sources (Lyons, 2019). Environmentalists are concerned that the relocation will have a serious environmental impact on the rainforest habitat of Borneo where deforestation is already a serious problem (Cassidy & Hamzah, 2019; Bendix, 2019). For the Jokowi administration, the

AIIB can offer a better solution for projects with tight budgets and time pressures as well as potential environmental ramifications.

Indonesia is also looking for external funding opportunities for projects that are not acceptable to traditional institutions like the ADB or the World Bank. China's BRI has emerged as Indonesia's largest external financier since 2014. As shown in Table 5.10, the BRI's contribution to Indonesia exceeded that of the World Bank, ADB and AIIB combined from 2014 to 2017. In 2017 alone, the amount of funds Jakarta obtained from the BRI was at least two times that obtained from the three IFIs. Unlike India, Indonesia has embraced the initiative and secured BRI investments for environmentally and socially controversial projects. According to the American Enterprise Institute (AEI) data, the BRI has financed 27 energy projects in Indonesia since 2013, 16 of which are coal-fired projects and 5 of which are hydro projects.[7] The energy sector has absorbed 57.6% of the BRI, of which 52.6% ends up in coal-fired projects. As the Jokowi administration strives for domestic infrastructure development often involving negative externalities, BRI projects, which are financed through China's policy banks, can allow Indonesia to circumvent the environmental safeguards imposed by the IFIs. In addition to dirty energy projects, the mega BRI transportation project connecting Jakarta to Bandung has come up against land ownership issues while another BRI hydropower plant built in the heart of the Batang Toru rainforest on the island of Sumatra may endanger the Tapanuli orangutans. Complying with development finance best practice by giving displaced populations their rightful compensation and minimizing environmental impacts can be costly and time-consuming. Although the BRI may be problematic for Jakarta in terms of procedures and financial planning (Earl, 2019), the initiative offers a faster way of obtaining development finance. Although BRI projects in neighboring countries have been political and economic disasters, Indonesia has continued to ask for funding from China's BRI (Parameswaran, 2019).

Despite the government's active pursuit of economic engagement with China, Indonesian society has been alarmed by the opaque nature of this engagement. In October 2015 when Jakarta decided to give the contract for the Jakarta-Bandung High Speed Railway project to China, public concern about the likely negative externalities, such as a flood of Chinese laborers to Indonesia, helped fuel anti-China sentiment (Herlijanto, 2017). In addition, a Southeast Asian regional survey report prepared by the Singapore-based ISEAS-Yusof Ishak Institute shows that the Indonesian public has a more negative perception of the BRI than the average among ASEAN countries. When asked about their views of BRI proposals in Indonesia in light of problematic projects in Sri Lanka (Hambantota Port) and Malaysia (East Coast Rail Link), 72.6% of Indonesian respondents said "my government should be cautious in negotiating BRI projects to avoid getting into unsustainable financial debts with China" (Tang et al., 2019). The widening gap in perception of the BRI between government and society might hamper China's engagement in Indonesia.

To summarize, Indonesia is currently eager to pursue increased Chinese economic engagement without worrying too much about the strategic disadvantages.

There is evidence that Jakarta's active engagement in the AIIB has not damaged its relationship with other traditional development financiers. It has not been discriminated against by any other IFIs. In fact, problems of social inequality and poverty in Indonesia's rural areas give the government no choice but to maximize its external financial resources. Unlike India with its strong strategic concerns or Kazakhstan with its lucrative natural resources that allow it to ignore the ADB and the World Bank, Indonesia cannot afford to lose any important source of financial support.

Oceania: too weak to refuse

The AIIB covers Oceania as well as Asia. This section will discuss the 12 Pacific Island countries of Oceania: the Cook Islands, Fiji, Kiribati, the Marshall Islands, Micronesia, Nauru, Palau, Samoa, the Solomon Islands, Tonga, Tuvalu and Vanuatu. This is a general analysis illustrated by relevant country-based examples. This region is geographically remote with a small population, which greatly limits the scale of these countries' domestic economies. In addition, these island nations are vulnerable to natural disasters and climate change. Poor infrastructure remains a problem both within and across countries. Developing sustainable and resilient infrastructure on the islands would improve their capacity to deal with the challenges they face. Since the Pacific Islands exist in such challenging circumstances, the ADB recommends that the following areas should be prioritized: access to electric power, maritime transportation, better quality and safer air transportation, innovative ways to reduce the cost of building roads, access to potable water, enhanced rural sanitation and efforts to address climate change (Rajasingham, 2017). Due to limited economic scale and the high costs involved in almost any kind of economic activity, the Pacific Island countries require outside financial assistance.

The geographical remoteness of these countries distances them from the major political battlegrounds. In addition, even if they were to form a single political entity, it would be too small and weak to compete with its regional counterparts. However, some are in valuable strategic locations, which enables them to capitalize on competition between the great powers. The great powers sometimes have to offer political or economic favors in order to win the support of these small countries. Currently, they have been left in something of a political vacuum by traditional donors. Major regional powers like Australia and New Zealand are not interested in further Pacific engagement, which leaves a gap which China can fill. Australia, however, has accused the Chinese of funding white elephant projects that are not only useless but have also created a potential debt crisis. Responding to China's ambitious activities, Australia once again focused its attention on financing infrastructure development in the region. Canberra intends to provide new concessional loans and launch an Australian Infrastructure Financing Facility for the Pacific (AIFFP) worth A$2 billion (Hornby & Smyth, 2018; Rajah, Dayant, & Pryke, 2019). The US is worried that China's footprint in the Pacific region presents a strategic military risk to itself (Rust, 2019). The region has also been a diplomatic battlefield for China and Taiwan. As of 2018, there were six Pacific Island countries that recognized the Republic of China (Taiwan) rather than the People's Republic of China (China). In September 2019, China used financial incentives to persuade the Solomon Islands and Kiribati to cut diplomatic relations with Taiwan (Teng, 2019). Since then, Taiwan has only had four diplomatic allies in the region: the Marshall Islands, Nauru, Palau and Tuvalu, and there has been no let-up in China's financial offensive.

None of the 12 countries of Oceania was a founding member of the AIIB. Fiji was the first Pacific Island country to join the bank after completing its domestic ratification process and depositing the first installment of its subscribed capital. It was followed by Samoa and Vanuatu in 2018. The Cook Islands and Tonga have applied to join and their applications have been approved by the AIIB. They are now waiting to complete domestic ratification. The remaining seven countries had not submitted membership applications as of the end of 2019. With the exception of Micronesia, these were all Taiwan's diplomatic allies when the AIIB was created in 2015. It has been found that diplomatic allies of Taiwan may receive less funding from China for aid projects (Dreher et al., 2015). As a result, Taiwan may be a critical factor in determining the Pacific Island countries' access to the AIIB. Although more than half of the Pacific Island countries are not AIIB members, all of them, together with Taiwan, are members of the ADB. Due to the size of their economies, they do not have the resources to subscribe more capital shares in the ADB. All of them have less than 0.5% voting power. Fiji holds the greatest voting power and received the most loans among the Pacific Island countries in the ADB and is the most powerful among the four AIIB members in the region. Since 2000, most development financing from the ADB and other traditional donors, like Australia, has taken the form of grants rather than loans (Rajah, Dayant, & Jonathan,

Table 5.12 Pacific Island countries in the ADB and AIIB

	ADB funds	ADB power	Taiwan	AIIB	AIIB power
Cook Is.	99.4	0.30%	-	Yes	0.1468%
Fiji	746.6	0.35%	-	Yes	0.1574%
Kiribati	75.7	0.30%	-	-	-
Marshall Is.	52.3	0.30%	Yes	-	-
Micronesia	72.4	0.30%	-	-	-
Nauru	63.7	0.30%	Yes	-	-
Palau	105.8	0.30%	Yes	-	-
Samoa	292.0	0.30%	-	Yes	0.1482%
Solomon Is.	220.0	0.30%	-	-	-
Tonga	126.4	0.30%	-	Yes	-
Tuvalu	73.2	0.30%	Yes	-	-
Vanuatu	112.5	0.30%	-	Yes	0.1468%

Note: Each dimension refers, respectively, to total ADB funds received from 2005 to 2019 (US$ million), voting power in the ADB, diplomatic relationship with Taiwan, AIIB membership and voting power in the AIIB (as of October 2020).

2019). Transportation, water-related infrastructure, public sector management and energy account for more than 80% of ADB funds. These infrastructure projects feature adaptation and resilience to climate change and natural disasters. In addition, a large portion of them are environmentally friendly and socially beneficial Category C projects.

Although no Pacific Island countries have had any loan projects approved by the AIIB, their views of the bank are generally positive. Fiji sent a delegation led by its permanent secretary for finance, Makereta Konrote, to participate in the first AIIB annual meeting in mid-2016. The Fijian delegation expressed interest in acquiring innovative and competitive financial options provided by the AIIB (*Fiji Sun*, 2016). In addition to the AIIB, non-AIIB funding, such as that provided by the BRI or other kinds of Chinese investment, was also welcome in the region. Right after severing diplomatic relations with Taiwan in June 2019, Manasseh Sogavare, the prime minister of the Solomon Islands, received generous financial "gifts" from Beijing, including BRI funding for building infrastructure, roads, bridges and power plants (Cavanough, 2019). It is alleged that a Chinese company was proposing a strategic cooperation agreement with the Solomon Islands to lease the entire island of Tulagi (Cave, 2019). A similar scenario unfolded on January 6, 2020, when Kiribati, which had switched diplomatic recognition from Taiwan to China, signed an MOU with the Chinese agreeing to more Chinese investment and tourism in Kiribati under the BRI (Lyons, 2020).

In the case of Vanuatu, Prime Minister Charlot Salwai Tabimasmas expressed an urgent need for his country to make use of the BRI for infrastructure development during his first official visit to Beijing in May 2019. He said that "whether through grants or through loans we have to have money to build our infrastructure, we want to invest this money into economic sectors" (Greenfield, 2019). Although Micronesia is not an AIIB member, President David Panuelo pledged to expand bilateral cooperation in infrastructure construction under the BRI infrastructure-building initiative when he met with Xi Jinping in December 2019 in Beijing. Micronesia is close to the US naval base on Guam, so China's plans are setting off alarm bells in Washington. In addition to strategic concerns, China's active engagement also creates uneasiness among those aware of problematic BRI projects elsewhere. Micronesia is already troubled by indebtedness, and that could get worse if Chinese checks are no better than those of traditional donors and institutions (Engel, 2018). According to one study, Tonga, Samoa and Vanuatu are the Pacific countries most heavily indebted to China, and all of them are, or are soon to be, AIIB members. It is clear that the Pacific Island nations are the most vulnerable to China's debt diplomacy (Rajah, Dayant, & Pryke, 2019).

To conclude, China's regional initiative through the AIIB and the BRI is proving to be attractive to the Pacific Island countries, especially those without diplomatic relations with Taiwan. China is providing a timely plug in the financial gap left by traditional players. The Pacific countries cannot afford to subscribe more capital to increase their power in the AIIB. In fact, they are not interested in the AIIB power game at all. What they seek are generous loans or investments that can boost infrastructure development without landing them in debt traps. Regional powers such as Australia and the US are increasing their affordable financial assistance to these states in an effort to defend against China's strategic encroachment in the region. As more resources and choices emerge, the attractiveness of China may decline. The participation of these countries in the AIIB is likely to be limited.

Conclusion

These analyses show that countries in Asia and Oceania, in general, have taken a positive and optimistic view of the emergence of the AIIB. They also demonstrate strong interest in greater cooperation with the bank. However, differences of geopolitical and geo-economic emphasis have led them to adopt distinct approaches resulting in different outcomes. The AIIB is seen as a complementary institution helping to fuel enduring economic growth by almost all countries in the region. However, India is the most alert to the trajectory of the AIIB and is seeking a stronger role to prevent the bank from becoming an instrument of Chinese power. Middle-sized powers, like Indonesia and Kazakhstan, on the contrary, are much less interested in the internal politics of the bank. What they care about most is being in a position to secure more funds to sustain their national economies. The countries of Oceania have very little influence within the bank. The loans or grants they obtain are the product of great power rivalry in the Pacific.

In terms of income per capita, Kazakhstan is wealthy enough to ignore potential funding opportunities from agencies controlled by politically unfriendly Western powers. Therefore, since the arrival on the scene of the BRI and the AIIB, Kazakhstan has stopped pursuing loans from the ADB and the World Bank. Instead, Astana is heavily dependent on China's policy banks and multinational corporations. Indonesia, in contrast, is too lacking in infrastructure to neglect funding from elsewhere. While maintaining the level of loans from traditional agencies, Jakarta is also engaging significantly in both the AIIB and the BRI. The latter's problematic outcomes in other places have not curtailed its interest. The perception of the Pacific Island countries could be quite similar. Although India resembles Indonesia in that it maintains its cooperation with the ADB and the World Bank, India sees the AIIB as different from the BRI. The opaqueness and hidden strategic ambitions inherent in the BRI have deterred India from participation in that project. Jakarta, on the other hand, has embraced the BRI because of its willingness to invest in coal-fired energy generation, whereas New Delhi has rejected it due to its lack of compliance with international and domestic norms and policies. The AIIB's multilateral governing structure and its compliance with best practice have convinced New Delhi that the bank has sufficient external restraints. The AIIB's acceptance of consultation, democracy and transparency has also reassured democratic India that its contribution and support will be able to stop the AIIB from evolving into an instrument of Chinese power that might threaten India's national interests and security.

Notes

1 Here, I include Hong Kong, Macau and Taiwan. Although Russia is classified as a European country by the UN, the AIIB classes it as a regional member.
2 One of them, the Egypt Round II Solar PV Feed-in Tariffs Program involves 11 photovoltaic power plants. Here, we class this as one project rather than 11.
3 For more detailed data, please visit Ministry of Commerce and Industry, Government of India at https://dgft.gov.in/more/data-statistics/export-import-data-bank.
4 In terms of GDP in current US$, India was the seventh largest economy in 2018; in terms of GDP based on purchasing power parity (PPP), India ranked third while China surpassed the US and was number one.
5 For the data, please go to SIPRI Military Expenditure Database, Stockholm International Peace Research Institute, www.sipri.org/databases/milex.
6 For the data, please refer to the "China Global Investment Tracker" data compiled by the American Enterprise Institute and the Heritage Foundation.
7 See endnote 6.

6 European participation in the AIIB

The Articles of Agreement of the Asian Infrastructure Investment Bank (AIIB), were signed in June 2015. This important achievement in China's global financial diplomacy was endorsed by 57 founding members of the AIIB from around the world, including 14 European countries. It is interesting to ask why, despite strong political pressure on its traditional allies from Washington, half of all European Union (EU) members, plus Iceland, Norway and Switzerland, actively pursued founder membership. The United States is worried that the AIIB will not follow best practice in international development finance and that it will undermine the influence of international financial institutions controlled by the West, including the World Bank and the Asian Development Bank (ADB). Since European countries remain powerful in those institutions, the fact that at least some of them are enthusiastic about joining the AIIB seems even more puzzling. In fact, after the AIIB started to operate, another six EU countries became members or prospective members by the end of 2019. Furthermore, the AIIB's main goal is financing infrastructure development in Asia, which is the engine behind China's Belt and Road Initiative (BRI) that seeks economic cooperation along the Silk Road economic belt through Central Asia and the "maritime Silk Road." Some see the AIIB and the BRI as part of China's efforts to restore its faltering economic momentum. Given China's ever-increasing wealth, knowledge, experience and capacity for investing in Asia, it is uncertain how the European countries can compete with Beijing for economic gain. However, if we assume that the AIIB will bring Europe extensive economic benefits, why is it that half of the EU member states have turned their backs on it in the beginning?

Here, I argue that both strategic and economic factors are important in explaining the various European countries' initial policies on joining the AIIB as founding members. The strategic factors involve the three dyadic relationships that constitute a strategic triangle between one particular European country, the US and China, as well as the alliance security dilemma between the first two. If the level of alliance security dilemma is high and China's strategic importance becomes higher, the European country will be less likely to respond to pressure from Washington and more likely to join the AIIB. If the European country in question sees economic potential in Asian markets, that is another reason why it may be willing to finance the new bank. The countries that are most likely to join the AIIB are those for which both of these factors are strong, and countries least likely to join are those for which both factors are weak. Countries which are strongly influenced by only one of these factors will likely be hesitant about joining. In this chapter, I use a mixed method that includes both quantitative and qualitative approaches to test this main argument. For the quantitative approach, I first estimate the probability of becoming an AIIB founder member for 31 European countries. Based on the predictions of the statistical model, I select three representative countries for in-depth case studies. Each case represents either a high, medium or low chance of joining the AIIB in the first place. Readers should note that this chapter will focus on strategic and economic circumstances confronted by the European countries before June 2015, when the bank was formally established. Furthermore, not all European countries have applied for project loans by the end of 2019. Compared with regional members, Europe's situation and its role in the AIIB are more interesting to investigate before 2015. As a result, this chapter will only discuss the development after 2015 when necessary.

In the rest of the chapter, I first discuss recent debates regarding Europe's seeming enthusiasm for this China-led development bank, and on the basis of this discussion, I propose an analytical framework. In Section 3, I present the research design and results of the quantitative analysis, while Section 4 consists of three in-depth case studies. This is followed by a conclusion in which I suggest the implications of the findings.

Explaining Europe's reactions to the AIIB

The question is, why has the AIIB been welcomed by many EU countries while it is regarded with strong suspicion by Washington? Fourteen of the 28 EU states became founding members of the bank in 2015, including powerful states like the UK, France and Germany, as well as smaller states such as Denmark, Luxembourg and Malta. There is apparently no EU-wide consensus on the AIIB. Although many explanations have been put forward, a more systematic, comprehensive and convincing analytical framework to account for the different attitudes among EU members is needed. Among the existing explanations, three lines of argument can be identified.

First, forming and joining an international institution can provide legal liability, reduce transaction costs, reduce uncertainty and improve information (Keohane, 1984). Cross-border financing can generate huge costs for investors who lack knowledge and experience of local administrative, legal and social frameworks. Joining the AIIB may provide a solution for rational European countries seeking a share in Asia's potential economic prosperity. It may not only allow them to acquire useful information through regular meetings and deliberations with local partners and to benefit from decreasing costs as they learn from experience, but also give them access to Asia's investment markets through legal contracts with AIIB borrowers backed by the AIIB. European members of the AIIB can expect to enjoy more certain economic opportunities. In addition, involvement in the AIIB's infrastructure projects will lead to stronger economic ties with Asian states, thus creating more export opportunities for European countries (Ferdinand, 2016, pp. 954–955). In general, there are economic incentives for countries seeking a share in Asia's economic future to join the AIIB, participating its projects and engaging in the region as early as possible.

The second explanation is based on the realist perspective that international institutions seldom work. When they do work, they merely reflect the logic of power distribution politics. The most powerful states create institutions in order to increase their relative power (Mearsheimer, 1994). Thus, even though the AIIB can alleviate problems in cross-national exchanges, it cannot address the fundamental problem of fear in an anarchic world. It is seen by the great powers that have a big stake in Asia and the global financial system as an instrument for enhancing and expanding China's economic and political power in the region. This is the view of the US and Japan in particular (Dyer & Parker, 2015; Lam, 2014, pp. 131–133; Sobolewski & Lange, 2015). In Europe, states that share US concerns over the AIIB's development are more likely to follow Washington's lead and turn their backs on the AIIB. In a nutshell, the nature of the strategic triangle between the US, China and a particular European country will determine how far that country's attitude to the rise of China corresponds with that of the US and, as a result, will influence that country's decision whether or not to join the AIIB.

According to the third explanation, international organizations (IOs) can work to address both interests and power through formal and informal governance. When a powerful state tries to promote an agenda that requires support (formal votes) from other members of the IO and, at the same time, its outside options increase, other members will vote in favor of the powerful state's agenda to prevent it from exiting the IO. In return, the powerful state may give up a certain degree of formal voting power in exchange for deference (informal influence) from other members. While the powerful state achieves its objective and the IO's legitimacy is maintained, others stay in the IO and increase their formal control (Stone, 2011). Conflicts between interest and power can be resolved through this kind of bargaining. China's initial undertaking (subsequently reneged upon) that it would forgo veto power in the AIIB in exchange for Europe's participation can be a vivid example of this behavior (Wei & Davis, 2015). Powerful European countries join the AIIB in the expectation that they will be able to promote a reform agenda from within and make sure that the bank adopts best practice in international development finance (Renard, 2015a, pp. 5–6). By acting as a powerful collective financier, European members can achieve reform through informal influence or by gaining more voting shares in the future. Even if China eventually becomes the single most powerful member of the AIIB, the success of the bank and the BRI will hinge on the active participation and cooperation of its partners (Ferdinand, 2016, p. 956). Thus, the European countries may indeed be able to exert a certain degree of informal influence on China's behavior. This is probably their most convincing excuse for ignoring Washington's advice.

These three explanations involve the factors of economic interests and strategic position. It appears that a more convincing analytical framework would be one that adopts an eclectic approach consisting of both liberalist and realist factors. Such an approach can be more useful for intertwined reality and encourage communication across theoretical boundaries (Katzenstein & Sil, 2008; Snyder, 2004). This chapter thus argues that the choice made by European countries depends on their perceived stake in the Asian market and the nature of their triangular strategic relationship with China and the US. In terms of economic interests, if a European country is highly dependent on Asian trade and investment and if it expects to benefit from this more in the future, it is likely to join the AIIB not only for profit reasons but also because of the institutional benefits membership brings.

Regarding the strategic factor, I use Dittmer's strategic triangle theory and assume that there is relative amity between the European country and the US while there is relative enmity between that country and China. Given that U.S-China relations remain in stalemate, such strategic triangle forms a "stable marriage" relationship. China, as an outcast under this scenario, is strongly motivated to improve its strategic relations with European countries and to try to transform the stable marriage into a "romantic triangle," which leads to amity between the European country and China while the other two dyadic relationships remain unchanged (Dittmer, 1981). European countries will then replace the US as the pivot, which is the most advantageous position in all kinds of triangles. In fact, some European countries may accept China's goodwill due to their alliance security dilemma with Washington. Snyder (1997, pp. 180–192) argues that when confronting a common adversary, states seek strong commitment in the alliance for fear of abandonment by others. However, strong commitment also creates an entrapment situation that drags disinterested states into unnecessary conflicts involving a certain ally. Therefore, if common security stakes become ambiguous among the allies while the fear of entrapment heightens, the allies may move away from the alliance and act more circumspectly to the original adversary. After the end of the Cold War, the 2003 US invasion of Iraq and the US pivot to Asia, Washington has played down the importance of the security agenda in Europe, which may alarm Europe for fear of potential abandonment by the US. In addition, some European countries do not share US security priorities and fear being entrapped in Washington's own battlefield. A situation like this would make any rational European country less sensitive to the pressure from the US and more responsive to China's wooing.

Combining the two factors – interest and strategic position – this chapter argues that a European country is more likely to join the AIIB as a founding member in the first place if its economic interests in Asia are substantial and its strategic relations with China are becoming more cordial. If both of these factors are absent, the country will have little reason to risk having its strategic relations with Washington downgraded by joining the bank. If only one factor is present, the country may not be so enthusiastic and may base its decision on other objective factors, such as its financial situation. One should note that this chapter does not assume that either of these factors has an overriding influence. They complement each other.

Probability of becoming an AIIB founding member

To assess the factors that might cause European countries to choose to join the AIIB as founding members, I first provide quantitative evidence to test whether strategic position and the prospect of economic benefits might affect a European country's decision to join the AIIB. The dependent variable is a dummy variable that indicates whether a particular European country became a founder member of the AIIB. Here I include 28 EU members and three non-EU European founder members of the AIIB.

For the explanatory variable in terms of strategic factor, I use a dummy variable to represent whether a particular European country had a strategic partnership with China before it signed the AIIB Articles of Agreement. Although a strategic partnership is not the same as a formal alliance, it does indicate that the country in question agrees to pursue a stable, long-term cooperative relationship in the economic, scientific, technological, political and cultural fields (Snyder, 2009, pp. 499–501). This indicator thus gives us a broad picture of which European countries are currently developing such positive long-term strategic relationships with China. According to Feng and Huang (2014, p. 18), ten EU member states have secure strategic partnerships with China. In addition, the distance between individual European countries and the US is a critical strategic factor, thus I use a political affinity score that measures dyadic voting similarity in the UN General Assembly between the US and that country (Voeten, Strezhnev, & Bailey, 2016). This reflects the degree of agreement on global affairs between any two countries in the world. A higher score suggests a closer relationship made possible by sharing more common interests. In theory, these two variables present a broad picture of the strategic triangle that exists between any given European country, the US and China.

The potential material benefits provided by the AIIB are another important incentive for becoming a founding member. I measure this by the level of each European country's economic dependence on China alone, Southeast Asia, South Asia, Central Asia and all of those regions together. For European countries, these regions are potential export markets and direct investment destinations highlighted by the Chinese government. By the end of 2019, in fact, 59 out of 62, or 95%, ongoing projects are located in Asia. To test the economic factors involved, I use the volume of each European country's foreign direct investment (FDI) stock in those regions and the total volume of its exports to those regions. Recognizing that the size of the country might have a positive association with FDI stock and export volume, I use GDP as a control variable.[1] Another plausible suggestion is that European countries experiencing fiscal difficulties cannot afford to subscribe to the AIIB's initial shares; therefore, they are unlikely to be interested in joining the bank (Renard, 2015b). I use GNI per capita and government debt to GDP ratio to control for this factor.[2] Lastly, some argue that countries with a high level of governance at home are likely and keen to bring these standards to the international arena. I do not use the World Bank's Worldwide Governance Indicators (Kaufmann, Kraay, & Mastruzzi, 2010). Instead, I use GNI per capita as a proxy due to its strong and positive correlation with the World Bank's indicators (Pearson's Correlation Coefficient = 0.8768). All variables come from 2014 data, which is one year before the birth of the AIIB. Table 6.1 below summarizes all variables.

I use probit analysis to estimate the likelihood of European countries joining the AIIB as founder members. All models use robust standard errors. In Table 6.2, Models 1–4 show that, if a European country has a strategic partnership with China, has a lower level of political affinity with the US or has larger direct investments in most of Asia, that country is more likely to have joined the AIIB as a founding member. The dyadic political affinity index of European countries and the US is strongly and negatively correlated with China's dyad (Pearson's Correlation Coefficient = –0.9755), which suggests that those countries that have fewer interests with the US in global affairs, have more perspectives in common with China. In terms of strategic interests, European founder members of the AIIB may already have moved away from their traditional strategic ally, the US, and become closer to China. If the previous China-Europe-US strategic triangle can be conceptualized as a stable marriage, in which the US and Europe were close and staunch allies and both hostile to China, it is likely that the structure has now changed to a "romantic triangle," in which Europe may evolve to become a pivotal player enjoying positive relations with both of the other parties (Dittmer, 1981). If such a change is indeed happening, Europe and China will gain while the US will lose. A similar conclusion can also be drawn from Model 7.

All the models take into consideration economic incentives. Ceteris paribus, as Models 1–4 and 7 show, European countries that have invested more in the AIIB's potential borrowers in Asia, China, Southeast Asia and South Asia as well as those

Table 6.1 Summary statistics of variables

Variable	N	Mean	St. Dev.	Min	Max
AIIB membership	31	0.548	0.506	0	1
strategic partnership	31	0.323	0.475	0	1
political affinity	31	0.155	0.078	0.040	0.434
FDI stock in Asia	31	1.325	2.317	0	9.449
FDI stock in China	31	0.505	1.019	0	5.083
FDI stock in Southeast Asia	31	0.617	1.125	0	4.096
FDI stock in South Asia	31	0.188	0.395	0	1.775
FDI stock in Central Asia	31	0.015	0.045	0	0.237
Exports to Asia	31	1.472	2.900	0.007	14.692
Exports to China	31	0.772	1.828	0.003	9.920
Exports to Southeast Asia	31	0.398	0.683	0.002	2.989
Exports to South Asia	31	0.257	0.503	0.000	2.177
Exports to Central Asia	31	0.045	0.070	0.000	0.357
Debt/GDP ratio	31	0.704	0.372	0.097	1.769
GDP (million US$, log)	31	12.285	1.607	9.174	15.168
GNI (log)	31	10.442	0.353	9.732	11.114

Note: FDI and export volume are US$10 billion.

Table 6.2 Probability of becoming an AIIB founding member (FDI)

	(1)	*(2)*	*(3)*	*(4)*	*(5)*
	AIIB	AIIB	AIIB	AIIB	AIIB
Strategic Partnership (CN)	3.217***	3.186**	2.812**	2.443*	1.699
	(1.143)	(1.534)	(1.431)	(1.310)	(1.403)
Political Affinity (US)	−19.91***	−14.23**	−20.88***	−18.93**	−3.873
	(7.583)	(6.536)	(8.069)	(7.870)	(4.173)
FDI Stock in Asia	2.008***				
	(0.751)				
FDI Stock in China		5.153***			
		(1.636)			
FDI Stock in SE Asia			2.997***		
			(1.007)		
FDI Stock in South Asia				9.673**	
				(4.085)	
FDI Stock in Central Asia					18.92
					(12.22)
Debt/GDP	−2.486**	−2.476**	−2.408**	−2.333**	−1.380
	(1.080)	(1.197)	(1.158)	(1.141)	(0.969)
GDP	−0.443	−0.481	−0.0971	−0.118	0.00869
	(0.334)	(0.351)	(0.291)	(0.312)	(0.315)
GNI per capita	1.882	2.344*	2.098	2.397*	3.394**
	(1.414)	(1.360)	(1.505)	(1.430)	(1.540)
N	31	31	31	31	31

Note:

1 Standard errors in parentheses.
2 * $p < 0.10$, ** $p < 0.05$, *** $p < 0.01$
3 All models pass the Wald chi-square test.
4 FDI stock is in US$10 billion.

which export more to China, are more likely to join the AIIB. When we compare the effects of potential markets for direct investments and those for exports, the former seems to be more substantial. In Table 6.3, only the item "exports to China" in Model 7 has some effect. Exports to other regions not only have no significant association with the probability of joining the AIIB but also do away with strategic factor. As a whole, the evidence suggests that economic incentives stem more from the AIIB's potential investments than from the region's export markets, with the exception of China. Of those investment destinations, China, Southeast Asia and South Asia receive more attention from European countries than Central Asia.

Another interesting finding is that rich (high GNI per capita) or financially healthy (low government debt/GDP ratio) European countries have a higher probability of subscribing to AIIB shares. For a rich country, financial difficulties may abate its enthusiasm for the bank. Lastly, can the Europeans influence the AIIB from within? Although a positive effect of GNI per capita on participating in the AIIB can be identified, suggesting that the AIIB members from Europe adopt higher governance quality at home and are therefore likely to bring financial best

Table 6.3 Probability of becoming an AIIB founding member (Exports)

	(6)	(7)	(8)	(9)	(10)
	AIIB	AIIB	AIIB	AIIB	AIIB
Strategic Partnership (CN)	2.303	2.513*	2.124	1.494	1.827
	(1.418)	(1.380)	(1.368)	(1.356)	(1.394)
Political Affinity (USA)	−11.33*	−16.49**	−12.69**	−4.080	−6.152
	(6.138)	(6.684)	(5.797)	(3.470)	(3.873)
Exports to Asia	0.708				
	(0.473)				
Exports to China		2.385***			
		(0.902)			
Exports to SE Asia			3.135*		
			(1.616)		
Exports to South Asia				−0.321	
				(0.779)	
Exports to Central Asia					13.56
					(8.436)
Debt/GDP	−2.031*	−2.267**	−1.901*	−1.288	−1.144
	(1.106)	(1.126)	(1.035)	(0.929)	(0.923)
GDP	−0.152	−0.267	−0.185	0.173	−0.0813
	(0.325)	(0.310)	(0.318)	(0.317)	(0.329)
GNI per capita	2.621*	2.350*	2.408*	3.302**	3.536**
	(1.446)	(1.333)	(1.327)	(1.661)	(1.559)
N	31	31	31	31	31

Note:

1 Standard errors in parentheses.
2 * $p < 0.10$, ** $p < 0.05$, *** $p < 0.01$
3 All models pass the Wald chi-square test.
4 Export volume is in US$10 billion.

practices to the AIIB, the 17 European members together only control 22.09% of the votes (Chen, 2016). They probably do not have sufficient influence to push through governance reforms (Maher, 2016). According to one French government source, "governance (issues) were unresolved, but it was important for the Europeans to show an interest from the outset . . . we'll see how it goes" (Taylor & James, 2015). Even if the European countries try to bring reform plans to the AIIB bargaining table, the chance of success appears to depend less on Europe's but more on China's goodwill.

Optimistically, let's assume European countries have a certain level of capability to bring the bank's financial governance structure into line with global standards and restrain China's financial ambitions. The scenario will be based on the assumption that countries with a high level of governance at home are likely to bring these standards to the international arena. GNI per capita is a good proxy for a country's governance level as it is strongly and positively correlated with the World Bank's Worldwide Governance Indicators (Pearson's Correlation Coefficient = 0.8768).[3] Moreover, in Figure 6.1, a more direct scatter plot is used

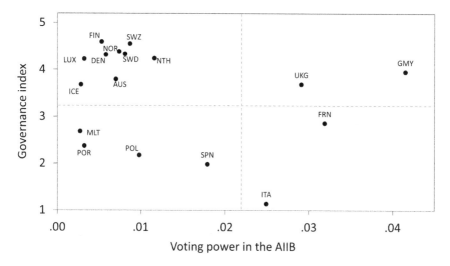

Figure 6.1 European countries' governance level and voting power in the AIIB

to show the relationship between the World Banks's Worldwide Governance Indi-cators and the voting power of each European AIIB member. The two dashed lines represent the average of the highest and lowest values of both indicators respectively. I assume that countries with a high level of governance at home are more likely to bring those standards to the international arena. Of the 11 countries with governance levels above the average, only two (the UK and Germany), or 18.2%, have the power to push for a higher governance level in the AIIB. But the countries with the highest governance levels that would be most likely to push for governance reform are clustered in the second quadrant, indicating that they have too little voting power to have a meaningful influence on the AIIB.

Finally, Table 6.4 displays the predicted probabilities of joining the AIIB as founding members using Model 1, which includes the variable of European coun-tries' FDI stocks in the AIIB's potential investment destinations. This economic indicator might be the most relevant for measuring economic incentives for join-ing the AIIB. The model predicts that 14 European countries have a high probabil-ity of joining the AIIB as founding members, whereas 13 of them actually joined as founders. Ireland, the only non-founding member in this group, nonetheless became a formal non-regional AIIB member on October 23, 2017. Three of the four countries with a medium level of probability actually joined. Belgium, the only non-founding member in this group, applied for the membership and was approved by the AIIB Board of Governors on March 23, 2017. Belgium became a formal member of the bank on July 10, 2019 after completing domestic ratifica-tion and initial capital subscription, which took the country more than two years. Domestic attitudes toward the AIIB seem to be divided. Of the 13 countries with a low predicted probability of joining, only Portugal joined the AIIB as a founding

Table 6.4 Predicted probability of becoming an AIIB founding member

High (71%~100%)		Medium (31%~70%)		Low (0%~30%)	
Country	*FM*	*Country*	*FM*	*Country*	*FM*
Austria	O	Belgium	△	Bulgaria	X
Denmark	O	Finland	O	Croatia	△
France	O	Iceland	O	Cyprus	X
Germany	O	Poland	O	Czech Rep.	X
Ireland	△			Estonia	X
Italy	O			Greece	△
Luxembourg	O			Hungary	△
Malta	O			Latvia	X
Netherlands	O			Lithuania	X
Norway	O			Portugal	O
Spain	O			Romania	△
Sweden	O			Slovakia	X
Switzerland	O			Slovenia	X
UK	O				
92.9% (13/14)		75% (3/4)		7.7% (1/13)	

Note:

1 This prediction adopts Model 1 in Table 6.2.
2 "O", "△" and "X" refer to founding membership, normal membership acquired from 2016–2019 and non-member, respectively.

member. However, another four countries in this category applied for membership after 2017. Findings suggest that as the AIIB evolves into an organization that tries to follow the best practices as well as shows little evidence toward serving China's geopolitical purposes, European countries that were originally skeptical may start to change their thoughts.

Recognizing the drawback of including only a small number of samples in probit estimations, I conduct three in-depth case studies in the following section. Cases are selected in view of the predictions in Table 6.4. I have selected Germany, Belgium and Romania as cases which differ in their circumstances and their subsequent decisions as to whether or not to join the AIIB. One has a high probability of joining as a founding member based on strategic and economic factors, and the other two have medium and low probability, respectively.

Germany: romantic and rational encounter

During the visit of Premier Wen Jiabao of China to Germany in 2004, the two countries issued a joint declaration on the establishment of a partnership of global responsibility within the framework of the 2003 Sino-European comprehensive strategic partnership. The two governments declared their intention to consult more closely on worldwide issues (*China Daily*, 2004). Ten years later, when President Xi Jinping visited Germany in March 2014, he and Chancellor Angela

Merkel declared their intention to expand this relationship into a comprehensive strategic partnership that emphasized their common interests and to hold regular consultations on global political and security issues (The Federal Government of Germany, 2014). Xi suggested that the two sides would become not only significant economic partners but also trusted partners in political and strategic matters (*Global Times*, 2014). As Germany's relations with China moved forward, its relations with the US seemed to falter. Germany's foreign minister, Frank-Walter Steinmeier, recently noted how Germany's partnership with the US used to be an important element of its foreign policy but "as the United States and the EU have stumbled, Germany has held its ground and emerged as a major power" (Steinmeier, 2016, pp. 110–111). Warmer strategic relations with China do not necessarily mean alienating Germany's traditional ally, the US, but should this happen, the China-Germany-US strategic triangle would change from a stable marriage structure into a romantic triangle that favors both Germany and China at the expense of the US. While Germany's position would improve as it evolves from being a partner to being a pivot, and China would improve its position by becoming a wing instead of an outcast, the US would be demoted from a partner to a wing.

There are at least three areas of divergence in perception and behavior between Germany and the US that might be increasing transatlantic differences. First, in terms of global strategic issues, Germany, together with most EU members, has long emphasized a UN-led multilateralism (Steinmeier, 2016, p. 110), emphasizing constant deliberation and adherence to international law or norms. These countries prioritize solving problems through international organizations and global governance (Shambaugh, 2005, p. 9). The unilateral decision by the US to invade Iraq in 2003 made Europe deeply suspicious of Washington. The German chancellor of the time, Gerhard Schröder, highlighted the contrast between Europe's multilateral approach and the Bush administration's unilateralism by forming a coalition against the Iraq war (Szabo, 2009, p. 24). In addition, both China and Germany believed that, under a multilateral global structure, they should help develop other important countries or regional institutions, such as the Association of Southeast Asian Nations (ASEAN) and the Shanghai Cooperation Organization. The latter institution has eight full members, seven of which are non-democracies. Compared to Washington's hostile attitude to China-led regional institutions (Feigenbaum, 2011), including the AIIB, Germany seeks to develop mutual trust and multilateral engagement on pressing global issues (Szabo, 2009).

The second area of perceptual difference between Germany and the US arises because Berlin's perception of military power and its deployment is different from that of Washington. The US has maintained substantial overseas military bases, many of them in Asia. In contrast, Germany is reluctant to engage in military deployment overseas, although it did deploy its forces in Kosovo and Afghanistan to protect civilian lives. The German government, at least in the short term, is unlikely to rely solely on military means to resolve conflicts. Rather, it will emphasize institution building. In the words of Germany's foreign minister, Frank-Walter

Steinmeier, "We [Germans] choose Recht [law] over Macht [power]" (Steinmeier, 2016, p. 110). Berlin's reluctance to use force resonates with Beijing's emphasis on non-interference in its foreign policy (Kundnani & Parello-Plesner, 2012, p. 7). Whereas Washington sees Taiwan as a valuable strategic asset in Asia and is influenced by a strong pro-Taiwan lobby, Germany's adherence to non-interference and the "one-China" policy means that it is unlikely to come into strategic conflict with China over East Asian affairs, which makes a Germany-China strategic partnership less problematic (Shambaugh, 2005, pp. 20–21). Without any visible geopolitical ambitions, Germany can easily accept and cooperate with China in the AIIB, which is seen by Washington as a tool for extending Beijing's geopolitical influence in the region.

Transatlantic strategic contradictions increased still further in 2004 when Chancellor Schröder was expected to propose lifting the military embargo on China imposed as a result of the 1989 Tiananmen massacre. In return, Germany sought China's support in its effort to gain a permanent seat on the UN Security Council (*Der Spiegel*, 2004). Although this issue remains controversial in Germany and is not strongly supported by the current chancellor, Angela Merkel (*The Economist*, 2010), the ongoing development of the Germany-China strategic partnership will lead to a higher level of political trust and increase the chances of the embargo being lifted. Should this happen while US-China relations remain tense, it may send a strong signal to Washington that Berlin is determined to separate itself from Washington strategically.

The third area of difference between the US and Germany concerns the way each deals with the issue of human rights in China. While the US tends to publicly criticize China's poor human rights record, the German government keeps a relatively low profile. Instead of seeking punishment for China, Germany pushes for incremental reform through constant communication in private between officials on the two sides. In 1992, shortly after the unification of Germany, Foreign Minister Klaus Kinkel visited China seeking economic partnership and support for UN reform. Lured by the prospect of promoting Germany's material interests, Kinkel said that bilateral relations could return to normal and would no longer be dependent on an improvement in China's human rights (Möller, 1996, pp. 717–719). When Angela Merkel infuriated China by receiving the Dalai Lama, Foreign Minister Steinmeier sent the Chinese government a confidential letter stressing that Germany recognized that Tibet was a part of China (Kundnani & Parello-Plesner, 2012, pp. 3–4). So, although Berlin sides with Washington in promoting human rights, the Germans have adopted a subtler and more patient approach, which is more acceptable to China.

These three major areas of difference between Germany and the US are reflected in their voting record in the UN General Assembly (see Figure 6.2). In the voting similarity index 0 represents the two countries voting differently and 1 represents voting the same. Since the General Assembly votes on various pressing global issues, the index provides a reflection of the degree of similarity in two governments' perceptions of global affairs. On most occasions since 1991, Germany has agreed with China on global issues more often than it has with the US. This divide

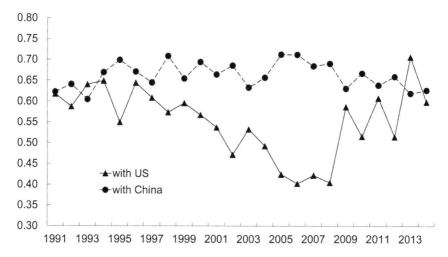

Figure 6.2 Germany-China and Germany-US UNGA voting similarity index

increased in 2003 when the US invaded Iraq. Although, in 2013, Germany's voting was more in line with that of the US than it was with China, the general pattern seems to be more favorable to China. In a Gallup worldwide poll conducted in 2014, the approval rate among Germans for the US leadership was 44% and the disapproval rate was 46%. This put Germany at the lower end of the scale with regard to approval of the US government among forty European countries and suggests that, a year before the establishment of the AIIB, German society was quite divided in its opinion of US global leadership (*Gallup*, 2015, p. 8).

In the absence of significant strategic differences, Germany had a positive attitude toward joining a China-led international financial institution and was almost without any geopolitical concerns (Federal Ministry of Finance, Germany, 2015). So, the German government perceived joining the AIIB purely in terms of the promising economic opportunities it offered. While China needs sophisticated German machinery and technology to take its domestic economic growth to another level, Germany needs more markets for its products and investment opportunities; China's enormous market has the potential to satisfy this need (Kundnani & Parello-Plesner, 2012, p. 2; Steinmeier, 2016, p. 108). As a matter of fact, before unification, the Federal Republic of Germany (FRG) was China's most important trade and investment partner in Europe. During the 1980s, more than half of China's technology imports came from the FRG. China was also the third-largest recipient of German government development aid in the 1990s (Möller, 1996, pp. 712–715). In 2014, German exports accounted for about 45.6% of total EU exports to China, and Germany's FDI stock in 2014 accounted for about 36.4% of total EU FDI stock. Germany is also the largest exporter among EU countries to Southeast Asia (28.6%), South Asia (24.8%) and Central Asia (26.4%) as well as being a leading European, direct investor in Southeast Asia

(19.3%), South Asia (37.0%) and Central Asia (9.8%). The economic potential of these export and investment markets is closely connected to the success of the AIIB. China's export and investment markets alone are already too large to allow Germany to stay on the sidelines (Higgins & Sangermarch, 2015).

As well as being economically complementary, Germany and China share a number of economic characteristics. As Wolf (2010) has noted, both China and Germany are the world's largest manufacturing exporters; they have accumulated massive surpluses of savings over investments and have huge trade surpluses. Both believe that the countries that import their products should keep buying but should also call a halt to irresponsible borrowing. As a result, they pursue a deflationary macroeconomic policy and resist attempts to correct the problem of global economic imbalance. This alignment on the opposite side to Washington reached its peak after the global financial crisis of the late 2000s. Both Beijing and Berlin were apprehensive of using quantitative easing to resolve the crisis. At the G20 meeting in 2010, the two countries joined in their opposition to Washington's plan to curb current account surpluses (Kundnani & Parello-Plesner, 2012, p. 6). In its external economic relations, Germany resembles China more than it does the US, and this may have helped create more opportunities for Berlin-Beijing bilateral cooperation.

In these circumstances, it is no wonder that Germany saw, in membership of the AIIB, an opportunity to reap lucrative economic rewards, while at the same time helping to improve living standards in emerging economies, shaping a more multilateral global system and encouraging China to adopt global standards. In this way, China can be a responsible stakeholder rather than a potential challenger. When Germany's finance minister, Wolfgang Schäuble, first mentioned that Germany intended to join the AIIB, he said, "We want to contribute our long-standing experience with international financial institutions to the creation of the new bank by setting high standards and helping the bank to get a high international reputation" (Thomas & Hutzler, 2015). In September 2015, the German cabinet approved draft legislation for Germany to join the bank and make a contribution of US$4.5 billion to the bank's total capital of US$100 billion. That gives Germany a voting share of 4.15%, which is the fourth largest among all members and the largest among non-regional members. Germany's activism and enthusiasm for the AIIB were underlined when Chancellor Merkel urged Tokyo to join the bank during a telephone conversation with Prime Minister Shinzo Abe (*The Japan Times*, 2015).

Being the EU country with the greatest voting power in the AIIB, Germany is the only such country with the potential to hold either the executive director or alternate executive director positions. Since the end of 2019, Nikolai Putscher has been an alternate executive director based at the German embassy in Beijing, even though the AIIB's board is non-resident (Hirsch et al., 2019). Among the senior management team, German-born Joachim von Amsberg has served as the vice president for policy and strategy since the bank began to operate in January 2016. In Amsberg's opinion, the original suspicions about the AIIB's geopolitical ambitions have "given way to much positive comment in the media and in the general discussion." The bank has also improved its relationship with the World Bank and the ADB, as well as demonstrating its complementarity (Valero, 2018). Another German national, Martin Kimmig, has also served in the senior management team as the chief risk officer since 2016.

Having been involved with the AIIB for a few years, Germany appears to be satisfied with the bank's trajectory. Despite domestic concerns that AIIB projects could have an adverse environmental and social impact in the recipient countries, there is no apparent geo-strategic apprehension about the AIIB. Instead, the German government is seeking to enhance its level of participation in order to check China's influence, which might become too strong due to the AIIB's non-resident board design. With this in mind, Germany based its executive director at the German Embassy in Beijing in order to maintain close contact with the bank (Stanzel, 2017). In the eyes of the German government, the standards the AIIB has adhered to are comparable with those of the World Bank. The bank has had a successful start and is succeeding at integrating itself into the international financial architecture, manifested by its attracting more than one hundred members, as well as receiving positive recognition by the United Nations, other IFIs and international rating agencies (Federal Ministry of Finance, Germany, 2019).

To summarize, given the two countries' closer bilateral strategic partnership and convergent economic interests, it is not surprising that Germany feels quite comfortable about joining this new China-led IFI. Nevertheless, Germany fully understands that the AIIB is a young institution which may be subject to change given the rapid development of global politics. As a result, Germany needs to pay close attention to the bank and ensure that it stays on the right trajectory.

Belgium: enthusiastic but hesitant

Like its fellow members of the EU, Belgium is a staunch strategic ally of the United States that is in strategic circumstances similar to those of Germany. It prefers to use multilateral channels and emphasizes the rule of law where global strategic issues are concerned. For example, Belgium was one of the harshest critics of the Iraq war of 2003 and it came into conflict with the US when it passed a law allowing war crimes to be tried in Belgium regardless of where in the world they had been committed. Such a law could have seen top US military personnel, such as the commander of US forces in Iraq, put on trial in a Belgian war crimes court. In retaliation, the then US defense secretary, Donald Rumsfeld, threatened to suspend Washington's promised €400 million financial support for a new NATO headquarters in Brussels (Black & MacAskill, 2003). After 2003, the gap between Belgium and the US on global issues widened (see Figure 6.3). Belgium cut its military spending by 17.6% between 2008 and 2014; its military spending as a proportion of GDP is 1.1%, one of the lowest among the members of NATO which has a spending target of 2% of GDP.[4]

Belgium's passive defense policy was criticized by Denise Bauer, the US ambassador in Belgium, in an opinion piece she published in the local paper *De Standaard* (*Flanders News*, 2015). Responding to criticism from its transatlantic

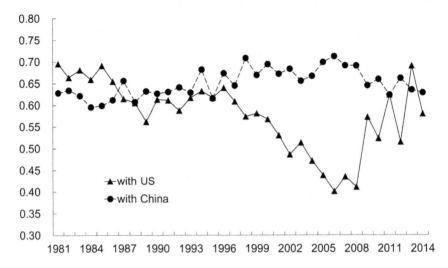

Figure 6.3 Belgium-China and Belgium-US UNGA voting similarity index

partner, the Belgian defense minister, Steven Vandeput, argued that priority should be given to increasing defense spending if the country was to remain a credible military partner of the United States. As the host country of both the EU and NATO, Vandeput said, he would expect Brussels to play the role of a loyal and reliable partner (Banks, 2015). As the headquarters of two of the world's most important strategic international organizations, Brussels might be under more pressure to maintain good relations with Washington as part of their joint effort to tackle security concerns arising from Islamic State of Iraq and Syria (ISIS), and a more aggressive Russia and assertive China. Responding to the question "What or who do you see as the biggest threat to global stability – Russia, China or maybe climate change?" Vandeput answered, "The combination of several threats at the same time will be the main challenge," and he refused to prioritize one above the others (Banks, 2015). In addition, smaller EU member states such as Belgium cannot afford to confront the US directly, unlike their bigger neighbors, such as France, Germany or the UK (Renard, 2015b).[5] However, this argument is not supported by the results of multivariate probit analysis of 31 countries. But, if we regress AIIB membership only on the size of country, as shown in Table 6.5, countries with bigger economies and larger military budgets have a higher likelihood of joining the AIIB.

Compared with Germany, a country that takes a more sanguine view of Russia and China on account of their enormous economic potential and thus downplays sensitive issues such as human rights and democratization (Szabo, 2009, p. 26), Belgium keeps a more vigilant eye on strategic issues concerning these emerging powers. The fact that 64% of Belgians approve of US global leadership and only 27% disapprove – compared to the two percentage point difference in approval

Table 6.5 The effects of GDP and military spending on joining the AIIB in Europe

	(1)	*(2)*
	AIIB	AIIB
GDP (log)	0.455**	
	(0.193)	
Military Spending (log)		0.268*
		(0.161)
N	31	31

Note:

1 Numbers in parentheses are robust standard errors.
2 * $p < 0.10$, ** $p < 0.05$, *** $p < 0.01$.

and disapproval rates among Germans – indicates that Belgians in general have a very positive view of the United States' global role (*Gallup*, 2015, p. 8).

Although Belgium and China upgraded their bilateral relationship to one of all-round partnership and cooperation in 2014, it was not yet a strategic partnership with institutionalized mechanisms and regular visits and consultations concerning strategic issues. Chancellor Merkel has visited China each year since the two countries established their comprehensive strategic partnership in 2014. Since 2002, however, there have only been two visits of a Belgian prime minister to Beijing – Guy Verhofstadt in 2002 and Elio Di Rupo in 2013. Although Belgium's perception of global and regional strategic issues is quite similar to that of Germany, there is a slight but noticeable difference between the two countries' relationships with the US and China. In their strategic triangle, Brussels and Washington still have a quite stable "marriage" which is not yet threatened by China. While Washington is sending a clear signal that it distrusts the China-led AIIB while China is playing a more open role, it is rational for Belgium to be more cautious for fear of harming the Brussels-Washington alliance.

Among the EU member states, Belgium is probably the most reliant on external trade. Its exports to GDP ratio was 88.8% in 2014, which is the highest among the 28 EU members. Belgium has long defined itself as a trading state whose foreign policy is designed to serve its global trade relations (Breuning, 2016, pp. 72–75). Despite this, Belgium's exports to and FDI in Asia only account for a small portion of its total exports and investment. For example, in 2014, its exports to China, Southeast Asia, South Asia and Central Asia as a whole accounted for only 5.9% of its total exports, and its FDI in these areas accounted for a mere 1.5% of its total FDI. Only 4.5% of EU exports to China and 3.7% of EU FDI come from Belgium. Other Asian regions receive even less. The markets of those Asian regions linked to the AIIB, though they may be promising, have yet to become significant for Belgium.

Belgium generally follows the logic of the trading state. Any changes in the country's external economic policy that negatively affect domestic exporters often meet with strong opposition from the parliament. For example, when the federal government wanted to end the policy of tying development aid to trade in the mid-1990s, it encountered strong domestic opposition and was forced to abandon the plan. The government had failed to link this reform with the idea of a trading state, although the two were not necessarily incompatible (Breuning, 2016). Whether AIIB-funded infrastructure projects would be tied to bank members' exports is an important issue for a trading state like Belgium. In the probit analysis above, level of exports is not strongly correlated with a European country's likelihood of joining the AIIB. This result suggests that, although some countries have developed their trade relations with China to a certain level and have strong interests in that area, the export opportunities provided by the AIIB are by no means clear, while investment in infrastructure does not guarantee extensive export markets. In addition, Belgium remains weak in infrastructure exports. According to a report produced by the ADB, in the period 2010–2020, the most vital areas in which infrastructure is required in Asia are energy (electricity), telecommunications, transport and water and sanitation, with a total value of about US$8 trillion (Asian Development Bank Institute, 2009, p. 167). According to OECD data, only 6.4% (US$58 billion) of Belgium's FDI stock went to those sectors in 2012. Using FDI flow in 2012, the number amounts to US$2.3 billion, which is merely 0.03% of the ADB's estimation. In that year, the manufacturing and service sectors accounted for 91.6% of Belgium's total outward FDI stock. Belgium may not be in an ideal position to compete for infrastructure investment competition in Asia. Due to the fact that only a tiny percentage of its FDI is in Asia, as well as its having next to no involvement in infrastructure investment, becoming a founder member of the AIIB would have been a "nice to have" option for Belgium, but it is far from being a necessity.

Another important factor underlying EU member states' decisions whether or not to join the AIIB is their domestic financial situation. Belgium's government debt to GDP ratio is 108.9%, which is the fifth largest in the EU after Greece, Italy, Portugal and Cyprus. Of these five highly-indebted countries, only Italy and Portugal became founding members of the AIIB. Italy is one of China's most important economic partners in Europe, but Portugal's reasons for joining are less clear. In the quantitative model, Portugal is the only country in the category of lowest probability (0–30%) that actually became joined the bank. In Belgium's case, several sources mention that, while weighing up the costs and benefits of joining, domestic financial situation is not an important factor (Fu, 2015; Renard, 2015b). Another factor that is missing from the quantitative model is Belgium's federal system with its three highly autonomous regions. Each region has its own autonomous foreign policy and minister of international trade, which makes it difficult for the country to operate a unified external economic policy (Deschouwer, 2012, pp. 238–239). This is especially true during periods of financial difficulty.

As a consequence, Belgium decided to postpone its decision on joining the AIIB in the beginning. This may have been acceptable to both Washington and Beijing, and economically and financially rational as far as the Belgian government was concerned, but others were not of that opinion. For example, the former prime minister of Belgium, Elio Di Rupo, publicly expressed his shock that Belgium did not apply to join (Fu, 2015). Interestingly, right after the application deadline, the Belgian council of ministers gave the green light to finance minister Johan Van Overtveldt's proposal to join the bank and said that they would aim to complete the admission procedures by the beginning of 2016. Van Overtveldt argued that joining the AIIB "will promote the Belgian and European economy through increasing trade relations with these countries."[6] In the opinion of the secretary of state for foreign trade, Pieter De Crem, joining the AIIB would "give us much easier access to the Chinese economy, and that's a good thing for our businesses" (Paelinck, 2015). These two statements indicate that Belgium has acted like a typical trading state where membership in the AIIB is concerned, giving higher priority to finding export markets than to investing in the bank's prioritized infrastructure projects.

Belgium's conservative attitude toward the AIIB did not last long. It submitted a membership application in January 2017 which was approved in March that year. It took more than two years for Belgium to complete the membership process, and it became a full member on July 10, 2019. Belgium subscribed 2,846 shares in the AIIB and is paying US$56.9 million in five equal annual tranches. This gives Belgium a voting power of 0.4112%. Although the Belgian government embraced the AIIB, the federal parliament was less enthusiastic. According to the official minutes, members of parliament questioned senior government officials regarding their concerns about joining the AIIB. These concerns included whether the AIIB would bring any real benefit to Belgium's domestic economy; whether the bank would respect transparency, environmental and social standards; whether the Belgian government would have any influence over loan decisions; and whether the AIIB would have a negative impact on traditional actors in the region, such as the World Bank and the ADB. Nevertheless, the parliament did not obstruct the government's pursuit of AIIB membership. Deputy Prime Minister Kris Peeters believed that

> The AIIB has the ambition to set the example for other development banks in China and abroad by adopting sound global standards with respect to economic viability, fiscal sustainability, climate and environment-friendliness and social sustainability . . . AIIB is actively seeking partnership with other multilateral banks such as the Asian Development Bank, the World Bank and the European Investment Bank.
>
> (Zheng & Pan, 2017)

To summarize, as a small trading state, Belgium's strategic ambiguity with regard to both Washington and Beijing has persuaded it to pay more attention to the United States' hostility toward the AIIB, as well as to place more emphasis on its export interests than on the bank's investment opportunities. Belgium is only moderately reliant on Asian markets at the moment; joining the AIIB in the first place was not an urgent issue for the government – it also depended on other pressing issues, such as the country's financial situation. Belgium is the only country in continental Western Europe that has not joined the AIIB as one of the founding members, even though the incentives for participation remained high.

Not surprisingly, the country joined the bank as the second-round member in 2017 and obtained full membership in 2019.

Romania: show me the money

Although Romania and China do not have a bilateral strategic relationship, their two presidents, Ion Iliescu and Hu Jintao, agreed to build a "full-range cooperative partnership" during a meeting in Bucharest in 2004. This non-strategic partnership was mainly concerned with increasing the number of official visits between the two sides, as well as enhancing cultural, touristic and economic cooperation (*People's Daily*, 2004). Despite the efforts of the former Romanian prime minister, Victor Ponta, to establish a strategic partnership in 2013, no such plan has been realized. Bilateral cooperation still consists mostly of exploring economic opportunities (Besliu, 2014). According to information from the PRC's foreign ministry, the Romanian president has only visited China once since 2006.

Romania may have more strategic interests in common with the United States than it does with China. Romania was one of the few countries that supported the Iraq war and committed to stationing troops in Iraq. The then president, Traian Băsescu, saw the US as an essential strategic ally. In the words of Romania's then foreign minister, Mihai Răzvan Ungureanu, in 2006, "Our countries have been strengthened through our cooperation in facing emerging security threats and advancing freedom and democracy in our immediate neighborhood and beyond" (American Cultural Center, Bucharest, Romania, 2006, pp. 21–26).

Romania currently shares another security concern with the US regarding Russia's increasingly aggressive behavior in its neighborhood, including its actions in Ukraine and Moldova (Transnistria). In 2015, the Romanian government committed to increase its defense spending over the next ten years (DeGhett, 2015). In addition, Bucharest has appealed to the US and NATO to enhance their military deployments in the Black Sea. In May 2016, Washington and Bucharest together presented the deployment of an anti-missile defense system based in Romania to protect NATO members. Russia regarded this as a threat to its security (Rodina, 2016). As China is seeking a closer relationship with Russia, increasing Romania-US military cooperation is likely to raise China's suspicions (Long, 2014). At the societal level, 50% of Romanian respondents expressed approval of US global leadership in a 2014 poll and only 16% expressed disapproval, meaning that Romania was ranked seventh among 40 European countries in terms of public approval of the US (*Gallup*, 2015, p. 8). Only three other countries had a lower disapproval rating, which suggests that the Romanian people are quite willing to follow in Washington's footsteps in terms of global affairs. Since Romania has such a strong strategic relationship with the US, it is likely that US opposition to the AIIB would be a strong factor dissuading Bucharest from joining the bank.

Although Romania and China have continued to explore mutually beneficial economic opportunities, the actual level of economic exchanges between the two countries remains trivial. This fact is also reflected in Romania's less than enthusiastic attitude toward a China-led "16 + 1 Strategic Cooperation Framework," a platform for greater cooperation between China and Central Eastern Europe. Oehler-Şincai (2016) argues that, due to its unfavorable investment environment and domestic political situation, the 16+1 framework hardly brings in any tangible benefits. According to UNCTAD data, in 2014, Romania's exports to China, Southeast Asia, South Asia and Central Asia amounted to only 2.3% of its total global exports, while exports to China alone accounted for a mere 1.1%. Romania has a trade deficit with China and its trade dependency on China is low. In addition, in 2014 Romania had no investments in China. In that year also, Romania accounted for only 0.3% of total EU exports to China, 0.2% of exports to Southeast Asia, 0.8% of exports to South Asia and 1.0% of exports to Central Asia, and it was at the bottom of the table in terms of EU exports to these regions. Probably the only encouraging sign is Romania's 8.6% share of the EU's FDI stock in Kazakhstan.

Other than that, current bilateral economic relations are weighted heavily in favor of the Chinese side. Romania looks more like a potential target for Beijing's global trade and investment aimed at satisfying the expansion ambitions of its multinational corporations. Romania's ambassador to China, Doru Costea, took a realistic view of this situation when he noted in 2015 that "Chinese capital is found in Europe mostly through its involvement in mergers and acquisitions . . . our projects are usually in the green field or brown field category; as a consequence, the two parties are also involved in a mutual process of learning the rules and the procedures that need to be complied with in these cases" (Stanciu, 2015).

From this perspective and based on previous experience, it is clear that China-led inward investment projects have not provided any pertinent support to Romania. Moreover, Romania is aware that many of the investment projects promised by China have not yet materialized. Domestic political issues, such as corruption, frequent changes of government, bureaucratic inefficiency and red tape, further thwart the fulfillment of Chinese investments (Popescu & Brînză, 2018). As a result, Romania could not see that China would bring it any real benefits and this reduced Bucharest's enthusiasm for participating in China-led projects. All these issues indicated that Romania could not fulfill most of the conditions necessary for AIIB membership by mid-2015. Indeed, the country did not become a founding member of the bank.

Since the birth of the AIIB, the strategic situation between Romania and China has gradually changed. In July 2016, the EU expressed its commitment to a comprehensive strategic partnership with China in the EU-China 2020 Strategic Agenda for Cooperation. This document identified important opportunities for cooperation with China, particularly in the creation of jobs and promotion of growth in the European Union. The EU-China Connectivity Platform was established to improve transport, services and infrastructure links between Europe and Asia (Council of the European Union, 2016). The EU's positive attitude toward China encouraged individual member states to themselves collaborate further with the Chinese. In mid-2016, the Romanian government started discussions regarding the conditions for joining the AIIB. Rather than subscribing shares in the bank and financing development in Asia, the country actually needs the AIIB's financial resources to upgrade its own infrastructure (Suokas, 2016). According to the World Economic Forum's *Global Competitiveness Report 2015–2016*, Romania ranked 86th out of 140 countries worldwide in terms of extent and efficiency of its infrastructure in 2014 and is below the average of emerging and developing Europe (Schwab, 2015, p. 308). Worse, Romania has the second lowest GNI per capita in the EU, just above Bulgaria. Thus, Romania began to consider the possibility of joining the AIIB as a prospective borrower. Although the quantitative findings suggest that wealthier European countries (with higher GNI per capita) are more likely to join the AIIB because they have the financial resources to fulfill its capital requirements, less wealthy European countries were increasingly interested in exploring financial assistance from the AIIB, especially when the bank seemed to be strategically harmless.

In August 2016, the Romanian Ministry of Public Finance under Prime Minister Dacian Cioloş, in office from November 2015 to January 2017, wrote to the AIIB expressing interest in membership (Bernovici, 2016). Romania's application was approved by the AIIB on May 13, 2017. After completing the necessary procedures, the country became a full member on December 28, 2018. It has subscribed to 1,530 shares in the AIIB and will pay US$30.6 million in five equal annual tranches. Its voting power is 0.2950%. The Romanian government sees AIIB membership as giving the country "the opportunity to get funding for infrastructure projects and to boost its economic development" (Banila, 2017). The Romanian Foreign Ministry announced that joining the bank will provide "Romanian companies the opportunity to access the Bank's financial mechanisms to diversify cooperation with Asian partners in areas such as energy, urban development, transport, information technology and agriculture." (Ministry of Foreign Affairs, Romania, 2016).

From this close examination of the case of Romania, it appears that the country meets few of the conditions necessary for becoming a founding member of the AIIB when the bank was created in the first place. Strategically, Bucharest cannot afford to downgrade its security cooperation with Washington in view of its need to defend itself against Russia; economically, Romania is only minimally involved in the Asian market; financially, the country needs investment in sectors that may be beyond the scope of the China-led AIIB and is in no position to finance a bank that offers it only uncertain opportunities. As a result, Romania did not apply to become a founding member of the AIIB, and the decision whether or not to join has been put on hold. However, as the strategic situation became more favorable after 2016, and as the AIIB evolves into a development bank that looks harmless, Romania decided to apply for AIIB membership and pursue the potential loan and investment opportunities.

Conclusion

This chapter seeks to provide an eclectic explanatory framework for why some European countries have decided to become the founding members of the AIIB as at a time when their important traditional strategic ally, the United States, was urging them to think twice before doing so. This chapter argues that the decision depends on the European country's strategic situation, as well as its level of economic dependence on and perception of opportunities in Asia. Ceteris paribus, those countries that share less common strategic interests with the US, have already established a strategic partnership with China and are extensively engaged in Asian markets are the most likely to join the China-led bank; the countries that do not fulfill those conditions are the least likely to join. The finding also shows that wealthier or financially healthier European countries have more interest in becoming founder members of the AIIB. Probit analysis and three in-depth case studies offer initial evidence to support this analytical framework.

The findings also offer several suggestions for strengthening the AIIB. First, for the bank to recruit more European members or obtain more support from Europe, China will have to strengthen its strategic ties with those countries that have yet to submit applications to join. Specifically, Beijing has to address Europe's common strategic concerns, such as Russia's increasingly aggressive regional ambitions, unrest in the Middle East and the rise of ISIS. At the moment, Washington stands closer to Europe on all of these issues, something which will enhance its already strong political influence there. In this regard, China has done a fairly good job of drawing another six EU countries into the AIIB since 2016. Second, China has to put more emphasis on opportunities for trade rather than investment in infrastructure, because it seems that European countries focus more on the export opportunities that could arise from AIIB projects. Most of the countries are capable and competitive enough, and have the financial resources, to bid for infrastructure investment projects in Asia and Asia-Europe corridor. Third, although the AIIB's governance standards are at least partly in line with those of the IMF and the ADB, it remains uncertain whether the bank will be monitored to ensure that it actually follows best practice. In exchange for US acquiescence, Europe has promised to keep a close eye on the AIIB's operations and push for more reforms. Should the AIIB, in practice, become an irresponsible lender and if its projects prove to be detrimental to the environment and the interests of the destination countries (Simonov, 2016), Europe may withdraw its support.

Finally, although most European countries have welcomed the creation of the AIIB, the EU itself began to treat China as a systemic rival that is promoting an alternative model of governance. In response, the EU intends to strengthen the security of its critical infrastructure and technological base, especially concerning Chinese investment in standard-setting and the supply of critical equipment which might pose a risk to the EU's security (European Commission, 2019). This move will not only affect individual European countries' China policies, but may also lead to discord between countries in different strategic situations (Berkofsky, 2019). If the AIIB starts to deviate from its current compliance with EU-recognized best practice and implements policies "with Chinese characteristics" that are not acceptable to the EU, the bank will lose its popularity in Europe.

Notes

1 Data on export volume, FDI stock and GDP are all for 2014 and are taken from UN Comtrade Database (http://comtrade.un.org/data/), UNCTAD's bilateral FDI statistics

(http://unctad.org/en/Pages/DIAE/FDI%20Statistics/FDI-Statistics-Bilateral.aspx) and the World Bank (http://data.worldbank.org/), respectively.

2 GNI per capita data comes from the World Bank and is based on purchasing power parity in 2014; government/GDP ratio comes from Trading Economics, which can be accessed at www.tradingeconomics.com/country-list/government-debt-to-gdp.

3 The World Bank's Worldwide Governance Indicators consist of six dimensions: voice and accountability, political stability and absence of violence/terrorism, government effectiveness, regulatory quality, rule of law and control of corruption (Kaufmann, Kraay, & Mastruzzi, 2010). I used factor analysis to locate a latent variable for governance level but did not add it to the model due to its extremely high correlation with GNI per capita.

4 Data come from Stockholm International Peace Research Institute and can be accessed at www.sipri.org/databases/milex.

5 This argument is based on the author's interviews with Belgium-based international relations scholars.

6 This comes from a press release published on Van Overtveldt's personal website. It can be accessed at http://vanovertveldt.belgium.be/en/government-gives-green-light-accession-asian-infrastructure-investment-bank.

7   Countries shunning the AIIB

The previous chapter argued that the decision of European countries to join the AIIB is based on a tradeoff between strategic and economic calculations. Countries with deep strategic concerns or limited economic opportunities have generally chosen not to participate in the AIIB. This chapter will focus on countries, especially regional powers, that share similar concerns. Nevertheless, this chapter differs in that these countries possess greater strategic concerns than their European counterparts. The power competition between these countries and China is an ongoing issue. In addition, all of these countries are developed countries with advanced national infrastructures. They do not need external funding agencies such as the AIIB to help their economic development. Instead, they are important global exporters of capital, expertise and experience in development finance. Some of them are currently engaging in heated global financial competition with China. Although the US is not eligible to become a regional AIIB member, it has had a strong presence in Asia since World War II. Japan has been a firm ally of the US economically and militarily and has assisted the US in responding to the region's changing power distribution. As an informal middle-power partner of both Japan and the US, Taiwan is forced to confront China's threat to its national survival. Therefore, great vigilance is needed when initiating China-related policies in these three countries. In general, these three countries have important but slightly different strategic concerns regarding the emergence of the AIIB, and their expected economic interests are unclear. As a result, all of them have avoided involvement with the AIIB since the bank was founded.

As for the rest of this chapter, the next section will discuss the dimensions of the strategic concerns involved in more detail, particularly changes in the power distribution structure. Empirical analyses will follow, linking the economic and strategic aspects to the decision of the US, Japan and Taiwan not to participate in the AIIB. The last section concludes the chapter.

Imminent strategic concerns and ambiguous economic interests

Instead of considering the trade-off between strategic concerns and potential economic benefits as their European counterparts have, China's main geopolitical competitors in the region perceive the China-led international institution as a potential threat. Even though joining the AIIB may not necessarily result in economic harm, China's rivals have been very circumspect about their interactions with China and the Beijing-led AIIB. In addition, most of them are developed and wealthy countries. Rather than being borrowers, they usually play the role of creditors in the region. They do not need financial assistance from China and can afford to ignore any possible gains that might result from their involvement with China. Moreover, these countries have been engaging in the region for a long time and have already created tight interdependent relationships with their regional counterparts. They have secured access channels to pursue their own interests in the region without the need for cooperation with China. As a result, the creation of the AIIB brings more strategic threats than opportunities to these countries.

The perception of such a threat may come from three dimensions. The first dimension pertains to the change in international structures. The concern here results from a fear that the emergence of the AIIB will further China's relative power globally at the expense of other regional players. The AIIB will become Beijing's financial instrument to fulfill its political agenda in the global arena. The AIIB can help China improve its relative power through both internal and external balancing strategies. Internally, exporting excessive factors of production will continue to drive the growth of China's large state-owned enterprises (SOEs), which constitute an important source of domestic economic growth (Xing, 2016). Searching additional investment markets for SOEs allows China to continue to accumulate wealth rapidly to sustain the momentum of its economic growth and subsequently advance its military capabilities. Externally, China can use financial incentives to undermine established alliances and create new alliances in its favor. In addition, exporting infrastructure can be beneficial for better aligning other countries' standards and governance with China. Should the AIIB emerge as the most attractive international financial institution (IFI) in the region, traditional great powers, such as the US and Japan as well as the US hub-and-spoke system, may lose influence in the region. Even though China and the AIIB have not yet demonstrated a fervent ambition to change the international system, these other great powers suspect that the evolution of the AIIB will fuel China's national capability and confidence. If the aforementioned powers do not check the AIIB now, it will be hard to restrain the bank and China's ambition in the future. This kind of thinking does not hold that participating in the AIIB will prevent the bank from going astray. In contrast, as long as the AIIB allows China to accumulate sufficient momentum and arrange its regional geopolitical deployment freely, the profits from changing the international system will soon exceed the costs. Therefore, the AIIB should be contained at the beginning before China becomes intractable.

The second dimension relates to the effect on the international financial system and governance. For Western powers, if the AIIB emerges further, the Bretton Woods system the West built and controls will confront the challenges that arise. Although the findings in previous chapters suggest that the AIIB does not majorly impact the leading financial institutions, other great powers may fear that tolerance of the bank will lead to changes in the distribution of power in the international financial system that would be beneficial for China and the AIIB. The established best practices will gradually be substituted by China's way of governance. Western powers worry that if this situation happens, the quality of development financing will deteriorate and financial power may start shifting to China. In addition, a "race to the bottom" will follow shortly thereafter. Unlike the World Bank and the ADB, the AIIB is likely to ignore the best practices in regional infrastructure projects. To compete with the AIIB, other international financial institutions may also lower their development finance standards. The outcome will become harmful not only to the current system but also to the environment and the society within the debtors' countries. Due to such concerns, although non-AIIB participants recognize the insufficiency of funding for regional infrastructure, they place greater emphasis on increasing their financial commitments than on relying on China's generous donations. To them, permitting the emergence of the AIIB would jeopardize the more acceptable international financial system.

The third dimension relates to national security; the threat comes from the perception of the AIIB as an instrument of power for China. The AIIB may provide loans for infrastructure projects in strategic locations, especially in countries that are financially too fragile to pay back outstanding debts. Thus, the debt may turn into a debt-for-equity swap, which would allow Beijing to take control of strategic locations (Parker & Chefitz, 2018). Other great powers' overseas strategic deployments may be affected by China's ambitious regional engagement. In addition, the AIIB may become China's financial arm used for rewarding its political and diplomatic allies. Past studies have shown that the World Bank and the ADB have been susceptible to the political influence of their major shareholders (Dreher, Sturm, & Vreeland, 2009; Lim & Vreeland, 2013). The AIIB may be no less predisposed to political manipulation because China's voting power in the bank is greater than that of the US and Japan in the World Bank and the ADB. China can finance more loans or bankrolls with more favorable terms in exchange for debtors' cooperation on occasions of international concern. As a consequence, the AIIB may result in a closer strategic relationship between China and the bank's borrowers at the expense of other great powers' interests. Moreover, bank participants may unconsciously be involved in complex strategic interactions that will ultimately harm their national interests. In the case of Taiwan (Taiwan and ROC will be used interchangeably), joining the bank would result in sovereignty costs and demote Taiwan's international status. Beijing and Taipei disagree on the membership name to be used. Taiwan is not allowed to participate under the name Taiwan, given its sovereignty implications. In other cases, countries will have to disclose the substantial economic and financial data that is required for applying for AIIB membership. International creditors of the AIIB will need enough data and information to evaluate each country's national repayment capacity. However, this may be unacceptable to totalitarian countries, where it may endanger a dictator's political survival. For dictators, the political costs incurred by revealing the national situation can be much higher than the possible economic opportunities. North Korea is such a case (Babson, 2015). The abovementioned political, diplomatic and sovereign costs have divergent effects on different non-participants of the bank, who, in general, fear that participation in the AIIB will help fuel China's geopolitical ambitions that are detrimental to their own national interests.

By the end of 2019, 17 out of 67 countries in the Asia and Oceania regions remained non-AIIB members. Of those non-participants, the Solomon Islands, Micronesia, Palau, Kiribati, the Marshall Islands, Nauru and Tuvalu are Oceanian microstates located in the Pacific Ocean. Most of them have not joined the bank because of their diplomatic relations with Taiwan. Bhutan, Iraq, Macau, North Korea, Palestine, Syria, Turkmenistan and Yemen are eight prospective AIIB regional members that have not joined the AIIB because of domestic political considerations – they are either too financially fragile to provide the necessary capital shares, too politically chaotic to engage in external affairs or too externally disinterested to participate in international affairs. Despite not joining the AIIB, they do not tightly associate the emergence of the AIIB with China's geopolitical ambition. The remaining two non-AIIB members in the region are Japan and Taiwan. These two countries, along with the US, are the most worried about the looming strategic threats caused by the AIIB. Despite Beijing's constant requests to Japan and the US to join the bank when it began, Washington and Tokyo refused to apply for founding membership. Even though both of these governments sometimes claim to perceive the AIIB positively, they remained non-members at the end of 2019. Their decisions come from the strong sense of changes in power distribution.

Table 7.1 illustrates that since 2000, China has grown a great deal both economically and militarily. In terms of national capability, China has surpassed Japan to become the most powerful country in the region. The power gap between the two has started to widen since the late 2000s. Without external support from Washington, Tokyo is not powerful enough to compete with Beijing if conflicts occur. From a macro perspective, China and the US are compatible rivals, and the former's GDP can be expected to surpass the latter's soon. In the military realm, the US remains a global hegemon, but not all of its military deployments are focused in the Asia-Pacific region. Consequently, Washington should logically be alert to

Table 7.1 Comparing power dimensions of China, Japan and the US

Year	Country	2000	2005	2010	2015	2018
GDP	China	1,211	2,286	6,087	11,016	13,608
(US$ billion)	Japan	4,888	4,755	5,700	4,390	4,971
	US	10,252	13,037	14,992	18,219	20,544
Military budget	China	41	77	138	204	239
(US$ billion)	Japan	44	45	45	46	45
	US	430	632	785	617	634
Total reserves	China	172	831	2,914	3,405	3,168
(US$ billion)	Japan	362	847	1,105	1,233	1,271
	US	128	188	489	384	450

Note: Data comes from the World Bank and SIPRI.

Beijing's surging military power. As a result, China's global engagement in the form of the AIIB, for example, should be dealt with carefully. In addition, both Tokyo and Washington control the most important development finance agency in the region, the ADB. They have reason to worry that the growth of the AIIB could undermine the ADB's influence in the region. Taiwan is another country that has paid close attention to strategic issues when considering whether to join the bank. Beijing attempted to undermine Taiwan's sovereignty by placing unacceptable conditions on Taipei. If Taiwan agrees to China's membership requirements, its sovereignty will be eroded. As a consequence, China's ulterior strategic agenda behind inviting Taiwan to the AIIB is a major obstacle for Taiwan's choice to join the bank.

Next, I will present three cases specific to countries that face imminent strategic concerns regarding the AIIB. They are the US, Japan and Taiwan. Although at some point in time, each of these countries thought about applying for membership, they each chose to refrain from joining the AIIB.

United States: a looming threat ahead

Given the dominant global status of the United States, obtaining Washington's endorsement for the AIIB would boost the bank's reputation and influence. China's aspiration for great financial power could be achieved with participation from the US (Yang, 2016). As a new and inexperienced bank in the field of development finance, the AIIB would be able to gain expertise and learn techniques from Washington if the US were to participate. The provision of initial capital from the US for the AIIB could also alleviate China's financial burden. For these reasons, Beijing and the AIIB initially invited the US to become one of the founding members. In an interview with the *Wall Street Journal* in 2015, Chinese President Xi Jinping said, "In addition to Asian countries, countries outside Asia such as Germany, France and the UK have also joined the AIIB. China welcomes the US to join the AIIB. This has been our position from the very outset" (Bermingham, 2015).

The US declined to join the bank and was criticized domestically for neglecting the benefits that could follow from obtaining membership. Some US scholars pointed out the potential economic disadvantages of not joining the AIIB, which include losing economic leverage in the region, undermining American business interests in China, and missing economic opportunities to partner with China (Chakravorti, 2015). Leaving economic calculations aside, US participation in the AIIB could reassure the bank's integration into the liberal international order. If the US joined the bank, it could shape a better future for the bank (Lipscy, 2015b). Given these expected benefits, it would be logical for Washington to embrace the AIIB. Indeed, the economic relationship between the US and the Asia-Pacific region has improved significantly since the 1990s. According to official US data (see note to Table 7.2), when the AIIB began operations in 2016, the total volume of US trade and outward investment to the region increased to nearly five times what it had been in 1990. Foreign aid to the region grew almost six-fold during the same period. As for economic opportunities, the White House should have given the green light for cooperation with China in the AIIB to capitalize on and further cultivate regional infrastructure projects. Washington should work with the AIIB to develop previously unreached markets.

Can we find a strong correlation between US economic growth and economic engagements in the Asia-Pacific region? Table 7.2 demonstrates the initial statistical results of possible associations using official US data from 1990 to 2016; in effect, there has been no obvious correlation. Ironically, by neglecting the statistical significance, one can see that greater economic relationships in trade, FDI and foreign aid have been negatively associated with US domestic economic growth. One can only find a positive association between the US trade balance with the region and its economic growth. Conservatively speaking, according to Table 7.2, joining the AIIB could allow more US products and services to be exported to the Asia-Pacific region, thereby contributing to the US trade balance and subsequently benefiting the country's economic growth. However, the expected benefits might not be critical enough for the US to disregard the negative strategic effects associated with such a move. In addition, the US does not need the AIIB to cultivate economic objectives. As the most powerful country among the region's influential IFIs, the ADB and the World Bank, the US possesses enough leverage for strategic maneuvering.

Given the uncertainty of the economic opportunities brought about by AIIB membership, the most worrying situation facing the US is the change in the distribution of power in the region and its subsequent impact on Sino-US competition in the region. Henry Paulson Jr., who was the chairman and CEO of Goldman Sachs and US Secretary of the Treasury in the George W. Bush administration and maintains a close relationship with senior Chinese officials and elites, has witnessed China's economic reform and strives to promote a cooperative Sino-US relationship that upholds the global order. Observing the creation of the New Development Bank by China and other BRICS countries, he commented that "we

Table 7.2 Correlations between US GDP growth and its economic engagement in the Asia-Pacific region

	Economic growth
Import from the Asia-Pacific	−0.2562
Export to the Asia-Pacific	−0.2608
Total trade with the Asia-Pacific	−0.2591
Trade balance with the Asia-Pacific	0.2432
Outward FDI to the Asia-Pacific	−0.0606
Outward FDI stock to the Asia-Pacific	−0.2953
Foreign aid to the Asia-Pacific	−0.3905*

Notes:

1 Economic growth data comes from the World Bank; Trade data comes from US Census Bureau; FDI data comes from US Bureau of Economic Analysis; foreign aid data comes from USAID Data Services.
2 * represents .05 significance level of correlation coefficients.

should have no illusions that China will simply accept this system in its exact form forever. Indeed, China has been testing alternatives" (Henry M. Paulson, 2015, p. 394). Nevertheless, he responded "That's bullshit" when he was asked to make a comment regarding the idea that the emergence of the AIIB would cost the US its role as the underwriter of the global economic system (Udland, 2015).

In 2014, when China was gathering regional support for creating the AIIB, the White House viewed the creation of the AIIB as a deliberate action to undercut the World Bank and the ADB. Washington made strong efforts to persuade its close allies to avoid the project (Perlez & Cochrane, 2013). They worried that China was about to reconfigure the regional order in Asia. Confronted with China's attempt to claim a dominant status in terms of economic and military power, a senior US official at the State Department, Robert Wang, confirmed this worry at the annual Asia-Pacific Economic Cooperation summit, saying, "China in a leadership role? That's not a small message . . . [for China] it's pride. We've arrived. That has a message. Next time you deal with them, you remember it" (Page, 2014). Unlike European countries that are not the most influential global powers or great powers in the Asia-Pacific region, the US, under the Obama administration, appeared to worry most about the possibility of a power transition following the creation of the AIIB. Washington cannot afford to help the AIIB grow further.

In September 2014, the AIIB Secretary-General of the Multilateral Interim Secretariat and the first AIIB President, Jin Liqun, was undeterred by the US distancing itself from the bank. He paid a visit to senior White House national security officials and tried to soften Washington's tough stance. According to a news report, when Jin encouraged Washington to join the bank in an ombudsman function to help with transparency, Evan Medeiros, the National Security Council's senior adviser on China, replied, "I am not going to buy the cake you have cooked." Nonetheless, Jin replied in a friendly manner, saying, "You are always welcome into the kitchen to help with the baking" (Perlez, 2015). Although Washington remained steadfast, the circumstances looked gloomier when a number of European allies decided to join the bank. Given the relative decline of the US' regional economic governance, some have interpreted the creation of the AIIB as China's soft-balancing strategy that aims to geo-strategically entice involved countries away from the US (Chan, 2017). A senior US administration official observed the change in the strategic structure and commented that "we are wary about a trend toward constant accommodation of China, which is not the best way to engage a rising power" (Dyer & Parker, 2015).

There is concern that the AIIB will become an instrument of foreign policy for China, especially if the country can claim veto power in the AIIB to enable diplomatic maneuvering and amass power. One might argue that the US can negotiate for greater voting power if it joins the bank (Balachandran, 2017), but the US can only gain a satisfactory share if there is a massive increase in authorized capital stock, which requires a supermajority (75%) of votes from the AIIB Board of Governors. In other words, China can singly veto this agenda. Based on the author's calculation, if Beijing does not voluntarily release a large portion of its subscribed shares, the power distribution of the AIIB will not see a significant change. China will still control just over 25% of the voting share even if the number of members expands to 200. In addition, AIIB's institutional design excludes representative of non-regional member states from acting as the bank's president. As a non-regional member, the US will never take the helm of the bank. Furthermore, the accommodation of the AIIB may further embolden China's regional ambitions and threaten US strategic interests in the Asia-Pacific region. The established development finance arrangements shaped by the US-led ADB and the World Bank would also be at risk – and not only in terms of infrastructure development; there is also anxiety about possible damage to the current world trade system. In a US House of Representatives hearing entitled "Advancing US Economic Interests in Asia" held by the Committee on Foreign Affairs on the eve of the establishment of the AIIB in May 2015, the Chairman, Edward Royce, said, "Beijing is making rapid anticompetitive moves that are throwing the world trade system off balance . . . the Asian Infrastructure Investment Bank is designed to shut out the United States . . . Beijing is pressing its neighbors to choose the US or them" (*Advancing US Economic Interests in Asia*, 2015).

One should note that despite the concern over power transitions, the US has not resorted to all-out containment of the AIIB. The containment strategy will only stop China's military advance and will not leave it to other less strategically sensitive and less conflict-prone agendas, such as that of the AIIB (Etzioni, 2016). In addition, acquiescence toward the bank's creation might mitigate China's discontent with the established order and the country's emerging aggressiveness. Furthermore, the participation of its allies inside the AIIB can help Washington more flexibly shape the bank to its favor from the outside. Recognizing that China will hold a dominant position in the AIIB, if the US becomes a member of the bank, this will still not grant the US enough strength to influence the bank. Direct involvement may unexpectedly result in more political and economic liabilities in the future.

It is apparent that the US is worried that the rise of the AIIB will result in a power transition in the Asia-Pacific financial system, but the government has refrained from explicitly criticizing the bank in public. The most identifiable criticism coming from the US government has been about the bank's probable damage to the best practices shaped by the Bretton Woods system and the potential environmental and social impacts brought about by AIIB projects. Although this perspective recognizes the insufficiency of the current financial resources in supporting regional infrastructure building, the more pressing issue is not the level of sufficiency but instead the resulting ramifications for the established financial arrangements. When Washington attempted to dissuade others from joining the bank in 2014, it raised concerns about whether China will ensure that the AIIB follows international standards of governance. Indeed, Western countries were absent in the first few meetings of chief negotiators at the AIIB. The countries shared Washington's concerns when the governance structure of the bank remained unclarified. While not commenting on US interest in joining the bank, Jacob Lew, the US Treasury Secretary during the Obama administration said, "The critical question is do they follow the same kinds of practices that are working to help economies grow and to maintain strong and stable foundations?" (Davis & Sahu, 2014). Jen Psaki, a US State Department spokeswoman expressed the same view, noting that "we [welcome the idea of an infrastructure bank for Asia but we strongly urge that it meet international standards of governance and transparency" (Goh, 2014). During a joint press conference with Prime Minister Shinzo Abe of Japan, President Obama explained the US' absence from the AIIB:

> The [AIIB] projects themselves may not be well designed . . . our simple point to everybody in these conversations around the Asia Infrastructure Bank is let's just make sure that we're running it based on best practices . . . if . . . the Asia Infrastructure Bank . . . is run in a way that ultimately is actually going to lead to good infrastructure and benefit the borrowing countries, then we're all for it . . . but if it's not run well, then it could be a negative thing. And what we don't want to do is just be participating in something and providing cover for an institution that does not end up doing right by its people.
>
> (Obama, 2015)

The most important dimensions of best practices concern transparent and accountable governance, environmental and social safeguards, loan conditions, the structure of debts, human-rights abuses and environmental risks (Etzioni, 2016). An AIIB that moves away from the best practices will be welcome in some developing countries that prefer not to disclose loan information to the public, especially countries with autocratic or corrupt governments. These are also countries demanding a large amount of development finance. To attract those countries, the AIIB might consider lowering the level of best practices enforcement at the expense of those IFIs that are strictly following such rules. In the long term, greater competition may result in institutional change in other IFIs (Lipscy, 2015a). They may start to consider lowering their standards to regain their popularity in the developing world. A race to the bottom in the international financial system looms.

For Washington, the ADB and the World Bank are the most likely targets to be affected. Curtis S. Chin, a former US board member of the ADB worried that the emergence of the AIIB "could shake up other donor banks, forcing them to reduce red tape which often leads to delays in loan disbursements . . . China will need to ensure the bank doesn't focus on getting money out the door with limited concerns about environmental and social impacts" (Davis & Sahu, 2014). Since the US decided not to join the AIIB, it cannot ensure the bank's trajectory from inside the organization. Therefore, it has called for other bank members to provide oversight, depending especially on its Western strategic partners. State Department spokeswoman Jen Psaki mentioned that "it will be important for prospective members of the AIIB to push for the adoption of those same high standards that other international institutions abide by, including strong board oversight and safeguards" (Higgins & Sangermarch, 2015). Treasury Secretary Jack Lew also stated that "I hope before the final commitments are made anyone who lends their name to this organization will make sure that the governance is appropriate" (Sobolewski & Lange, 2015). Explaining the Obama administration's strategy vis-à-vis the AIIB in a US House of Representatives hearing, Daniel Russel, Assistant Secretary of the Bureau of East Asian and Pacific Affairs at the US Department of State, said:

> It is telling that so many major economies held back on a decision to join the AIIB as a founding member until they were satisfied that, number one, the elements in the articles of agreement would be, from their point of view, minimally sufficient to warrant joining, and, second, until they became convinced that, by joining, they would be able to exert influence from within that would help bring the AIIB to a level of governance, of transparency, of standards, of oversight that they consider to be on par with other multilateral development banks.
>
> (The US Rebalance in East Asia: Budget Priorities For FY 2016, 2015)

According to the evidence presented in Chapter 4, the AIIB has so far not deviated significantly from the established international financial arrangements. However, its rise has intensified debates inside the US government regarding institutional reforms in the International Monetary Fund (IMF) and the World Bank. One of the reasons for creating the AIIB can be attributed to China's discontent with its underrepresentation in the Bretton Woods system. The largest steppingstone has come from the US government. In the case of the IMF, an 85% majority of the total voting power is required to approve quota changes, and the US holds just under 17% of the voting shares. In addition, according to regulations governing US participation in the IMF, the US government cannot give a green light to a quota change without congressional approval. Although the Obama administration submitted legislation for Congress's approval to implement IMF reforms, the proposal was rejected several times (*American Journal of International Law*, 2017). Serious debates regarding possible effects resulting from continuous opposition to quota reforms occurred in Congress. Scott Morris, a Senior Fellow at the Center for Global Development who used to serve as the deputy assistant secretary for development finance and debt in the US Treasury Department in the Obama administration, expressed such concerns in a House hearing in October 2015:

> While I very much believe that action on the IMF quota package is critical in its own right, the challenges to US leadership in the MDBs run deeper. If Congress and the Administration are unwilling to address these deeper challenges, then we are likely to see a world in which institutions like the World Bank are eclipsed by new actors like the AIIB, and where the United States finds itself increasingly on the outside looking in . . . It shouldn't be a surprise, then, that the Chinese found so many willing partners when they conceived a new MDB without the United States.
>
> (The Future of the Multilateral Development Banks, 2015)

In December 2015, the US Congress approved changes to the distribution of the voting quota in the IMF that resulted in greater voting power for China (Mayeda,

2015). China's voting power increased from 3.8% to 6.09%, compared to Japan's 6.16%. The arrival on the scene of the AIIB appears to have encouraged the initiation of long-awaited reforms of the international financial system. In the case of IMF quota reforms, the rise of the AIIB has motivated the US to speed up its efforts in reforming the international financial system, which is positive in some ways. However, it also signals the AIIB's potential influence in the system to Washington. It would be problematic for the AIIB to cause the downgrading of best practices in the future.

Lastly, Washington's unspoken worry is the behaviors of its strategic Western partners, many of whom are founding members of the AIIB. Their stances regarding the AIIB call into question the strength of the relationship between the US and its partners. National security issues may arise if Washington cannot secure enough support for its China policy. Anticipating that US allies would share the same concerns regarding the AIIB, Sydney Seiler, the then director for Korea on the US National Security Council, suggested that "even without asking [South] Korea to do so, all countries who have been involved in contributing to and working with the ADB and the World Bank have similar questions" (Chang, 2014). Unlike Japan, South Korea, which is an important military ally of the US, eventually jumped on the AIIB bandwagon and became the fifth largest shareholder of the AIIB, even though it had been quite hesitant in the beginning (Panda, 2015). South Korea, like its Western allies, is a developed country, which means it may be more immune to China's financial lures. However, these countries appear to prefer a more neutral position regarding the AIIB and to find the potential economic opportunities to be more advantageous. In addition, the US' traditional alliance system seemed to be more vulnerable at the time when the AIIB was created. On the one hand, the US' traditional allies tried to avoid becoming trapped between the US and China; on the other hand, the rise of the erratic Donald Trump has subsequently warned these countries of Washington's potential abandonment of them (Snyder, 1997). The strengthening of alliances with other US military allies, such as the Philippines and Thailand, could be even more fragile. These are developing countries that are actively seeking outside infrastructure loans from IFIs such as the AIIB. If, one day, these countries are asked to sacrifice their military or diplomatic relationship with Washington in order to have their proposed projects approved, it will undermine the US' strategic deployment in the region.

In general, at the time when the idea of the AIIB was first proposed and then realized, the US was under the leadership of the Obama administration, which was cautious about the bank. When Donald Trump was elected president of the United States in late 2016, some believed that the Trump administration might have a different view on the AIIB. A senior adviser to Republican President Donald Trump called the Democrat President Obama government's decision to oppose the AIIB a strategic mistake, and he noted that he expected to see a policy shift from then President-Elect Trump (Tarrant, 2016). Although the Trump administration appeared to seek a close relationship with China at the beginning of his term, the Sino-US bilateral economic relationship plunged in early 2018 when a trade war began between the two countries. By the end of 2019, the Trump administration had not agreed to join the AIIB. Instead, the government has remained vigilant in avoiding potential geopolitical effects. Under China's leadership, the AIIB could become China's financial arm to bankroll risky and unprofitable projects in exchange for strategic advantages. Many of these national projects may be rejected by other IFIs. David Malpass, the Under Secretary of the Treasury for International Affairs and later the President of the World Bank, stated the following concern to the US House Financial Services Subcommittee:

> It is worth noting that China has made substantial inroads into the multilateral development banks (MDBs) that are worrisome . . . we are, therefore, working with allies and like-minded countries to guide the MDBs away from what could be viewed as endorsement of China's geopolitical ambitions.
>
> (Malpass, 2018)

Although the US has refrained from stating its outright disapproval of the AIIB, its refusal to join the bank clearly demonstrates that Washington is concerned about the development of the bank regardless of which party is in charge. In addition, the potential benefits of joining the AIIB are unclear, while the US is capable of maneuvering the ADB and the World Bank. The uneasiness created by the AIIB mainly comes from possible changes in the power distribution, infringement upon the established financial order, and breaches in the national security interests in the Asia-Pacific region. The first and last factors have not bothered Washington's traditional allies, but the US itself is concerned with all these issues. As a result, the US continues to remain vigilant about the future direction of the AIIB. If the bank stays on its current path, the US may not interfere with it. However, if the bank runs counter to US interests in those three areas, disagreements between Washington and its allies can be expected to escalate.

Japan: stand with the patron

Japan is a developed country with one of the most advanced economic and social conditions in the world. According to the Global Competitiveness Report 2016–2017, Japan's overall infrastructure performance ranked sixth out of 138 surveyed countries and economies. The country also ranked first in railroad transportation quality (Schwab, 2016). Judging from the macroeconomic statistics, Japan was the second largest economy in the world until China surpassed it in 2010. In international trade, Japan enjoyed trade surpluses starting in the 1980s through until 2010 and accumulated massive amounts of national wealth. According to IMF data, Japan's official reserve assets amounted to US$1.37 trillion at the end of 2019, which places it second in the world. This was also the time when Japan started to significantly increase its official development assistance (ODA). Japan was one of the first two Asian countries accepted as a member of the Organisation for Economic Co-operation and Development (OECD) in the 1960s, which normally admitted high-income members committed to democracy and the market economy. Japan has been economically, financially and industrially viable in its national economic development.

In fact, Japan exported its production, capital and technology to developing countries around the world to help with economic development in those countries. In 1957, Japanese Prime Minister Nobusuke Kishi announced that Tokyo intended to sponsor the establishment of a regional development fund to provide long-term, low-interest loans to developing countries in Asia. Although confronted with suspicion in the region, this proposal later successfully developed into the Asian Development Bank. The ADB was controlled by its top two capital subscribing members, Japan and the US, which together controlled more than 25% of the voting power, making them capable of vetoing important proposals regarding institutional change in the bank. Although Japan hoped to host the bank, prospective members chose Manila as the headquarters after multiple rounds of voting. Since the ADB was established in 1966, the ten presidents have all been Japanese nationals. This Japan-led multilateral bank has allowed Tokyo to create deep and positive connections with economic and social development in Asia and the Pacific region (McCawley, 2017). In terms of the amount of financial assistance, the ADB is the second largest IFI in the region, only slightly behind the World Bank. From 2011 to 2015, the ABD approved approximately US$75.7 billion worth of loans and grants, while the World Bank committed US$99.8 billion (see Table 4.14 in Chapter 4). According to a survey in Southeast Asia, approximately 65.9% of people in the region are confident that Japan will contribute to global peace, security, prosperity and governance, which outperforms the public perception of four other global powers: China (46.8%), India (52.3%), the European Union (41.3%), and the United States (27.3%) (Tang et al., 2019).

When China, once a capital importer of the ADB, was preparing to establish the AIIB, China actively invited Japan to become a founding member. The AIIB sought to acquire capital, experience and techniques from Japan and the ADB. The media reported in late 2014 that China offered the vice president position to Japan. As it was a dominant player in the ADB, Japan did not accept China's invitation and demonstrated its reluctance to become a junior partner of China (Hamanaka, 2016). As a result, when Japan, which is a developed economy with advanced national infrastructure and a dominant power in the ADB, saw the emergence of the AIIB, it was not as enthusiastic as its regional counterparts about seeking a role in the AIIB.

Aside from the lack of economic incentives, the effect of international politics can account for Tokyo's lukewarm attitude toward the AIIB. During the 1990s, when China started to emerge economically, Japan was considered the potential great power that would become dominant both militarily and economically in the first quarter of the twenty-first century. It would attempt to become a more assertive power and be more independent from US influence. China feared the reemergence of Japan in the region (Christensen, 1999). By the end of 2010s, however, Japan had not turned into as great a power as expected. Japan did not translate its economic power into enormous military capability, nor did it attempt to eliminate Washington's influence or challenge US military predominance in the region. Instead, Tokyo's military development stayed within the confines of its alliance with the US. Unlike Japan's limited military ambition, some believe that

China has emerged as a challenger to the US hegemonic power "in a way that has gone beyond the Japan challenge of an earlier era" (Foot, 2017). After 2015, the challenge China posed became unequivocal, thereby emphasizing the importance of the Japan-US alliance to Tokyo even more. Strategically, the military balance of power in Asia is shifting in China's favor.

Although Japan possesses enough military capability to deny China's ambition to acquire the surrounding disputed territories, it will need to address such security concerns with help from the US (Beckley, 2017). Economically, China surpassed Japan as the most dominant power in the region and created the most interdependent economic relationship with its regional counterparts (Chen, 2014). Under such circumstances, when China tried to establish the AIIB, Japan worried that the bank would emerge as a challenge to US hegemony in the region. Although Japan did not reject regional financial cooperation without US involvement, Tokyo preferred to have exclusive Asian leadership in harmony with the US-led regional system (Hamanaka, 2016). A staunch alliance between the two is be illustrated by a statement by Japan's prime minister that revealed that

> It was important for strategic reasons that Japan stick with the United States even when other allies like Britain and Germany have announced they will join the new bank . . . the United States now knows that Japan is trustworthy.
> (Fackler, 2015)

Given Tokyo's fear of China's ambition, it is necessary for Japan to secure its military and economic alliance in the region to counterbalance China's continuous economic emergence. It is imperative to ensure that supporting China's economic statecraft will not harm Japan's regional economic interests. The AIIB looks formidable to Japan in at least two aspects. First, China alone controls more than 25% of voting power in the AIIB, which makes all other members look trivial. Second, the presidency and the location of the headquarters are both monopolized by Beijing. Japan already lost its chance to host the ADB in Tokyo (Hamanaka, 2016). Moreover, Tokyo has to pay circumspect attention to any effects the emergence of the AIIB might have on the ADB. Japan needs to ensure that the policies of the AIIB will not harm the ADB's influence in the future. Such anxiety was reflected by the remark made by the former ADB president Takehiko Nakao in late 2014. He said, "[Establishment of the AIIB] is understandable because there is a very big financing need in the region." However, Nakao was also curious about issues such as membership, shareholdings, the location of the bank's headquarters and as to who would head the bank (*The Straits Times*, 2014).

If Japan officially supports the AIIB, it may harm Japan's interests in several ways. First, the AIIB can receive higher credit ratings more easily with the endorsement of Japan, which can mask the bank's potential governance problems. Second, according to the institutional design of the voting power structure, Japan will not acquire enough votes to influence the bank, just as would happen with the US. Third, based on the estimates of the Japanese Ministry of Finance, Japanese companies are unlikely to benefit from AIIB projects even if the contract-bidding process is open and transparent. Japanese infrastructure projects are well-known for having high quality but also high costs, which may make them less competitive in the realm of the AIIB. Lastly, elevating the AIIB may dilute the influence of Bretton Woods institutions in the region; consequently, Japan's political influence in the region will diminish (Katada, 2016). Tokyo's concerns in these aspects, added to the fact that Japan and China are in intensive competition regarding the economic statecraft of regional infrastructure financing. Both powers bankrolled developing countries in exchange for policy support. While China started the BRI and the AIIB, Japan tried to revitalize its role as the leading donor. Tokyo touted a $100-billion plan for constructing high-quality infrastructure. The evidence suggests that the emergence of China's financial capability diluted Japan's role as the dominant regional donor. When China engaged in the region financially, loan-receiving countries chose to pragmatically diversify the sources of infrastructure financing to avoid long-term reliance on Japan (Liao & Dang, 2020).

It is interesting to note that, although Japan possesses realistic concerns about the AIIB, the Japanese government has refrained from voicing harsh criticisms of the AIIB, just as the US has done. Some have considered Japan's behavior to be showing limited support and embracing part of the agendas, organizing principles or rules of the challenger (China)-led institution (Kim, 2020, p. 83). Official suspicions concern whether the AIIB will abide by the best practices and whether the AIIB will have adverse environmental and social impacts. In October 2014, when China gathered regional countries to discuss the organization of the AIIB, Tatsuo Yamasaki, Japan's vice finance minister for international affairs, voiced the official concern that "we are asking some questions to Chinese authorities about this AIIB because we need to clarify the structure, or the governors, of this new bank . . . we have not yet had enough information from China" (The Straits Times, 2014). When the AIIB was about to begin forming, Japan's Deputy Prime Minister and Minister of Finance, Taro Aso, said that "there could be a chance that we would go inside and discuss . . . but so far we have not heard any responses." The Chief Cabinet Secretary, Yoshihide Suga, voiced his more skeptical view, saying that "we have a cautious position about participation" (Kajimoto, 2015).

On March 31, 2015, the Japanese government officially announced its decision to refrain from applying for membership in the AIIB. Minister Aso stated that

> Japan would not contemplate joining until the new bank demonstrated that it had strict lending standards, including assessments of the environmental and social impacts of development projects . . . [We] have no choice but to be very cautious about participation.
>
> (Fackler, 2015)

Chief Cabinet Secretary Yoshihide Suga added that "we have not yet received any clear explanation . . . we will continue to push China on the matter in partnership with other countries concerned." Japan's minister for economic and fiscal policy, Akira Amari, echoed this sentiment, arguing that "the AIIB needs to ensure good governance and transparency" (*Nikkei Asian Review*, 2015). Indeed, as regional infrastructure finance was dominated by the World Bank and the ADB before the emergence of the China-led AIIB and BRI, a liberal Bretton Woods financial order can be more easily incorporated into the countries in this region. Regardless of the positive or negative effects, both the World Bank and the ADB used to force debtors to accept policy conditionalities attached to the financial assistance packages, such as the stabilization, liberalization and privatization of the domestic economy (Hecan, 2016; Raman, 2009). In addition, loan projects were required to minimize the environmental and social impacts and provide feasible debt repayment plans. From the Japanese point of view, if the AIIB has lower loan conditions, it will harm not only the competitiveness of the ADB's loans but also the implementation of Bretton Woods arrangements in the region.

Japan's official suspicion regarding the bank was echoed by the US. In a joint press conference, US President Barack Obama shared Prime Minister Abe's concern that

> To create such an enormous financial institution . . . fair governance is necessary . . . It's not only about the lenders, but the borrowing nations. . . . [V]arious infrastructure projects may not be sustainable. It may have too much of a burden on the environment. If this is the case, this will be . . . very negative . . . [R]igorous review is very important. . . . Japan and the United States should cooperate, and we need to continue dialogue with China.
>
> (Obama, 2015)

Even two years after the bank's establishment, Tokyo's distrust of the bank's governance continues. When asked again why Japan refused to join the AIIB in mid-2017, Abe reiterated that "there remains the issue of whether impartial governance can be established . . . there is the issue of sustainability of debt servicing on the part of the borrowing countries and whether the societal and environmental impacts are duly considered" (Chandran & Fujita, 2017). Finance Minister Aso criticized the AIIB more harshly, saying, "If the borrower doesn't make a good plan to pay the money back, and faces a situation similar to getting caught up with a loan shark, then they could lose everything" (*The Mainichi*, 2017).

While questioning the governance of the AIIB, Tokyo, together with Washington, made efforts to counter China's fast-rising financial presence in the region. In early 2019, the Japanese government urged the ADB to stop granting news loans to China because China's gross national income per capita reached US$8,690, which is at the upper end of what the ADB has set for prospective borrowers (Sakaguchi, 2019). In addition, the ADB expanded its lending scale by double-digits for two consecutive years after 2016 (see Table 4.14 in Chapter 4). Furthermore, the Japanese government set forth the "Quality Infrastructure Initiative" in response to China's quantity-driven overseas investment spree that might burden borrowers with loans they are incapable of repaying. In some cases, geopolitical contestations between China and its rivals harm the legitimacy and attractiveness of Chinese money and, therefore, inversely increase the reputation and legitimacy of Japan-led financial projects (Trinidad, 2019). Additionally, some have criticized China's loans as initially cheap but with a stupendous amount of maintenance costs down the line (Osaki, 2019). Admittedly, such criticism targets China's BRI projects more than the AIIB itself. However, if Japan cannot be reassured that the AIIB will not become a financial arm of the BRI, Tokyo is likely to continue its wait-and-see attitude regarding whether to engage with the AIIB.

In summary, Japan's decision to stay away from the AIIB stems more from the country's fear of the declining regional influence of the ADB and itself. Strategic concerns remained too high to ignore the pressure from the US. Tokyo's perception of and behavior toward the AIIB resemble those of Washington in many aspects. However, Tokyo's concern is different from Washington's concern about the power transition. Japan acts more like a junior partner of the US that tries to help the US preserve the Bretton Woods system and ensure that China's rise can be contained under US leadership. This system can best help Japan preserve its established regional influence. One should note, however, that although the Abe administration avoided the AIIB, the Japan-led ADB opened its arms to the AIIB. Both institutions have signed memorandums guiding their collaboration. They have jointly co-financed quite a few infrastructure projects. At present, competition and cooperation coexist in infrastructure financing from Japan and China.

Taiwan: sovereignty first

From an economic point of view, Taiwan is a developed state that enjoys a high level of domestic infrastructure. According to the Global Competitiveness Report 2016–2017, Taiwan's overall infrastructure performance was ranked 13 out 138 surveyed countries. Its overall global competitiveness index was ranked 14, which means that the country performs better than many Western developed countries (Schwab, 2016). Like the US and Japan, Taiwan does not require external loans for developing its domestic infrastructure. Taiwan's current national budget and independent financial policy are sufficient for sustaining continuous infrastructure development. As a result, unlike most developing countries in the region, Taiwan has no pressing need to ask for membership in the AIIB or subsequent project loans from the AIIB. In addition, according to Taiwan's official statistics about external investments in 2014, infrastructure-related industry accounted for only approximately 4.1% of the country's total investments. Based on economic power, Taiwan simply cannot quantitatively compete with major infrastructure investment exporting countries such as China and Japan (Chen, 2015).

Decades ago, however, Taiwan was a developing country desperate for financial assistance from abroad. In the 1970s and 1980s, governments across the Taiwan Strait were vying for legitimacy in representing China in major international organizations, including United Nations specialized agencies, the IMF and the World Bank (please refer to Chapter 1 for more discussion on this). The ADB was another battleground. When the ADB opened for business in December 1966, the Republic of China (Taiwan) represented China in the United Nations and the ADB. From 1968 to 1971, Taiwan received 15 ADB loans amounting to US$100.39 million. Since 1972, Taiwan stopped applying for loans and began to act as a main regional donor in the bank. Political rivalry in the international stage across the Taiwan Strait began to trump economic considerations. As Taiwan's UN membership was officially replaced by the People's Republic of China (PRC; China hereafter), its membership status in the ADB became another cross-strait political battleground. In 1983, China relayed its intention of obtaining ADB membership and ousting Taiwan. After years of negotiation, the ADB approved China's succession of the ROC membership in 1986. Although Taiwan stayed in the ADB, it was forced to change its name from the ROC to "Taipei, China," which was a degradation of Taiwan's sovereign status. After Hong Kong was returned to China, it joined the ADB under the name "Hong Kong, China." At the same time, under Taiwan's continuous protest against its status in the ADB, the bank also decided to change Taiwan's official name to "Taipei,China," deliberately omitting the blank space after the comma to reflect that Taiwan had a different relationship to China than Hong Kong did. By the end of 2018, Taiwan had 115,620 ADB shares, which amounted to 155,317 votes, or 1.168% of the voting power. The selection of a proper name for Taiwan's participation in international organizations has become a major point of contention on both sides of the Taiwan Strait.

The political dimension in Taiwan's case differs from those in the previous two cases. As Washington and Tokyo are concerned that the emergence of the AIIB may lead to the relative decline of their power and undermine their geopolitical objectives, Taiwan's middle power status means that the country is less concerned about the change in the power distribution than it is about the great powers in general. Although Taiwan's military capability and economic development outperform most countries around the world, it remains difficult to narrow the quickly expanding gap in material capabilities across the strait. China continues to expose itself as a military and diplomatic threat to Taiwan. In response, Taiwan cannot turn a blind eye to the possible ramifications that will follow the emergence of the AIIB.

When 21 prospective members gathered for the creation of the AIIB in October 2014, Taiwan was under the leadership of the second term of the Ma Ying-jeou (馬英九) administration, which was affiliated with Kuomintang (KMT, or Chinese Nationalist Party). Under Ma's leadership, the KMT, contrary to its main domestic political rival, the China-bashing Democratic Progressive Party (DPP), embraced a China-friendly policy that placed the Beijing-accepted "1992 Consensus" as the basis for cross-strait relations. Numerous economic agreements were concluded or were about to be concluded under Ma administration. As a result, the Ma government was keen to seek a proper space for participation in the AIIB. Soon after the first AIIB memorandum was signed in late 2014, Taiwan's premier asked the Ministry of Finance to devise a response strategy to cope with the emergence of the AIIB. On March 4, 2015, the ministry completed its first evaluation; on March 24, Taipei notified Washington of its intention to join the AIIB. Later, President Ma officially gave three reasons why Taiwan should join the AIIB: "Taiwan could serve as a peacemaker and humanitarian aid provider in the international community; taking part in the AIIB would be helpful to Taiwan's bids to be part of the Trans-Pacific Partnership and the Regional Comprehensive

Economic Partnership; working with China in its widely supported initiatives would benefit cross-strait relations" (Shih, 2015b). On March 26, Vincent Siew (蕭萬長), who was the vice president during Ma's first term, expressed Taiwan's intent to take part in the AIIB to Chinese President Xi Jinping during the Boao Forum (*Taipei Times*, 2015b).

The Ministry of Finance delivered a ten-page evaluation report to the Legislative Yuan on April 2, 2015. Criticized as hasty and perfunctory by legislators, the report nonetheless pointed out four potential benefits of joining the AIIB, which included (1) increasing Taiwan's participation and visibility in international affairs; (2) facilitating Taiwan's integration into the regional economy; (3) offering new directions for cross-strait economic and trade cooperation; and (4) increasing cross-national business opportunities. The ministry estimated that Taiwan could obtain US$355 million capital shares, which would constitute 3.28% of the voting power, which is higher than the country's voting power in the ADB. However, the government was also aware of the need to maintain the nation's reputation (Ministry of Finance, Taiwan, 2015). In addition, the government remained vigilant regarding the domestic political turmoil such a move might cause. As President Ma said, "Taiwan should actively take part instead of staying on the sidelines." On March 30, 2015, Minister Andrew Hsia (夏立言) from Taiwan's Mainland Affairs Council (MAC) added that the government would seek to join the bank as long as the bank clarified its organizational structure and regulations and allowed Taiwan to stand on "an equal footing and with mutual respect" (*Taipei Times*, 2015c). On March 31, 2015, Premier Mao Chi-kuo (毛治國) said that "Taiwan would rather not take part in China's proposed AIIB if it is not treated with dignity and equality" (Shih, 2015a). With a few reservations, the Ministry of Finance officially submitted a letter of intent to apply for a founding membership. Due to Taiwan's sovereignty dispute, the application went through the cross-strait communication channel between the MAC and the Taiwan Affairs Office of China's State Council instead being submitted to China's foreign ministry as the applications of other countries were. It had been suggested that Taiwan would not be considered a sovereign state but an economic region in the AIIB (Wu, 2015).

When asked to comment on Taiwan's application, China's Ministry of Foreign Affairs spokeswoman Hua Chunying (华春莹) said, "As for Taiwan joining the AIIB, we maintain that we should avoid the 'two Chinas' and 'one China, one Taiwan' situation." Apparently, the governments on both sides of the strait intended to facilitate Taiwan's membership but disagreed on Taiwan's membership name. According to the AIIB's Articles of Agreement, its regional membership is open to members of the Asian Development Bank classified as Asia and Oceania by the United Nations. Non-UN ADB members are allowed to become members by a special majority vote of the Board of Governors. Article 3 regarding AIIB membership also stipulates that applicants who are not sovereign or not responsible for the conduct of their international relations and their membership application shall be presented or agreed upon by the member of the bank responsible for the organization's international relations. China applied this rule to Taiwan's membership application. However, many Taiwanese people were unable to accept being treated as a non-sovereign state. Under such institutional circumstances, the Ma administration remained enthusiastic about joining the bank, but it stressed that Taiwan would not accept an AIIB membership under the name "Taipei, China" (which is used in the ADB). The minimally acceptable name was "Chinese Taipei".

The circumspect and conservative attitude revealed by the Ma government was a result of the Sunflower Student Movement, which happened from March to April of 2014, a year before Taiwan applied to join the AIIB. This massive domestic protest, mainly by students and civic groups, was brought about by an abrupt and cursory attempt by KMT legislators to pass a domestic ratification of the Cross-Strait Services Trade Agreement in the Legislative Yuan, which aimed to open service trade with China. The then opposition party, the DPP, accused the Ma government of failing to be transparent in its negotiations with China. As a result, the demonstration deepened Taiwan's grassroots distrust of China and the fear that greater economic dependency on China will ultimately backfire and endanger the island's national security (Hsieh, 2015). The year 2015 was Ma's last year in the government, which made him a lame-duck president. That, together with the political ramifications of the Sunflower Student Movement, meant that the government enjoyed little leeway in making China-related policies. The domestic political circumstances further complicated Ma's policy toward the AIIB.

In the grassroots society in Taiwan, people neither ignored the probable economic opportunities, nor strongly opposed joining the China-led international financial organization. In April 2015, according to a public poll conducted by a Taiwanese media company, TVBS, approximately 54% of respondents supported Taiwan's move to join the AIIB, while 28% did not. Even for those who supported the anti-China opposition party, the DPP, 39% supported the move to join the AIIB, while 49% did not (TVBS Poll Center, 2015). For some Taiwanese people, rejecting the AIIB meant a loss of economic opportunities. In another poll conducted at the same time by Taiwan Indicators Survey Research (台灣指標民調), 75.3% of the respondents expressed their support for joining the China-led international organization only if the sovereignty of Taiwan would not be impinged upon. In addition, 59.5% of people could not accept Taiwan's participation under the name of either "Taiwan, China" or "Taipei, China" (Taiwan Indicators Survey Research, 2015).

On April 13, 2015, China's Taiwan Affairs Office confirmed that Taiwan's request to become an AIIB founding member had been rejected. The office emphasized that Taiwan's application would be considered only "under an appropriate name." On the same day, the Taiwanese government, having reached a consensus between the executive and legislative branches, officially announced its failure to obtain AIIB membership. Commenting on joining the AIIB, Legislative Speaker of Taiwan Wang Jin-pyng (王金平) mentioned that the name had to at least be "Chinese Taipei" and that the Taiwanese government would not accept anything less. A presidential office spokesman also commented that "Taiwan would rather stay out of the AIIB unless it is treated with dignity and equality." Faced with the rejection, the Ma administration remained positive about the option of a future bid. President Ma stated that, according to the AIIB's Multilateral Interim Secretariat,

Taiwan could still become a member of the bank. However, the opposition parties criticized the Ma government's rushed application as a slap in the face by China. The decision was irresponsible and there was a lack of sufficient communication with the public. The application also signified Taiwan's self-degrading of its sovereignty. Many argued that Taiwan should ally with the US and Japan in their non-participation in the AIIB (*Taipei Times*, 2015a).

In 2016, the DPP presidential candidate, Tsai Ing-wen (蔡英文), won the election and assumed power in May. In April, the AIIB president, Jin Liqun, had mentioned that if Taiwan wanted to join the AIIB, it needed to follow the Hong Kong model and have China's Ministry of Finance apply on its behalf. By taking this route, Taiwan would be treated as a non-sovereign participant in the bank. In response, Taiwan's finance minister in the outgoing under Ma government, Chang Sheng-ford (張盛和), stated that Taiwan would not be applying for participation in the AIIB: "We cannot accept such a model . . . it hurts not only our national dignity, but also violates the principle of dignity." It was up to President-Elect Tsai Ing-wen to decide whether to apply for membership (Chung, 2016). Since her presidential inauguration, President Tsai has not publicly spoken even a word regarding the AIIB. One can find nothing about Tsai's remarks regarding the AIIB in Taiwan's Office of the President or the media. There are no visible debates about Taiwan's AIIB policy. The topic is almost absent from Taiwanese society.

In summary, contrary to the US and Japan, Taiwan, under the China-friendly Ma administration, worried less about the geopolitical effects of joining the AIIB. Instead, the government tried to join the bank as a founding member for fear of losing out on opportunities in regional businesses and economic integration. However, both the government and the majority of Taiwanese people refused to participate at the expense of their country's sovereignty and dignity. China insisted that Taiwan's application and subsequent participation must be in accordance with China's policy, which would clearly harm the sovereign status of Taiwan. Due to this unsolved political disagreement and the growing suspicion of China in Taiwanese society, the Ma administration failed in its AIIB application and did not revive it before Ma stepped down. His successor, President Tsai, has further distanced her administration from the AIIB. The AIIB issue is apparently a high strategic concern in regard to Taiwan's national survival.

Conclusion

China's active overseas financial adventures have surely motivated many regional and non-regional members to participate in its regional initiative. The AIIB has received a great deal of welcome in developing countries in the region, even if such countries have varying levels of concern about the existence of an assertive China. However, for those developed countries that have considered the benefits of joining the AIIB to be more ambiguous, strategic concerns trump the economic benefits and thus keep those countries away from the AIIB. Strategic concerns are the highest among China's traditional power rivals in the region, such as the US and Japan, as well as those that are militarily threatened by China, such as Taiwan.

The US and Japan fear that endorsing the AIIB will further boost China's comprehensive power capability in the region and the AIIB's legitimacy and visibility at the expense of their relative power and regional influence. They also worry that the emergence of the AIIB will dilute the importance of the World Bank and the ADB, which are under their control. The established liberal order under the Bretton Woods system may be sacrificed. Taiwan, which shares some of this apprehension, once tried to join the bank but ultimately gave up the application due to the direct and urgent threat to its sovereignty. For Taiwan, joining the bank would risk the gradual degradation of the country's sovereignty. Although China had actively invited participation to acquire expertise and experience and further boost the bank's international legitimacy, the AIIB has not yet reassured these potential member countries of the hidden political ramifications of involvement. Although the AIIB currently appears to be compliant with best practices and free of apparent political ambitions, it remains to be seen how long it will continue on its current path. If the AIIB continues to integrate into and cooperate with established institutions, allow a greater level of representation, isolate itself from the BRI and provide appropriate participation options, the strategic concerns will decline in the non-member countries, and their applications for membership can subsequently be anticipated.

8 Conclusion

Crouching tiger, hidden dragon

Ang Lee's movie, *Crouching Tiger, Hidden Dragon*, may provide an appropriate metaphor for the China-led AIIB. In this martial arts film, the hidden dragon, Jen Yu, is emerging as an expert swordswoman. Having grown up in an aristocratic family that abides by traditional Chinese etiquette, she has an unstoppable desire to escape from the shackles of tradition and lead a life of adventure. Jen is quiet on the outside but inside she is ambitious and yearns for freedom and excitement. As she gets more deeply involved in her sophisticated circle, she finally frees herself of her inner shackles only to get her hands dirty. Although she is emotionally contented, Jen's recklessness and willfulness cause the death of Li Mu Bai, the legendary Wudong swordsman with whom she has fallen in love. In the end, Jen jumps to her death off a cliff, probably because she realizes that she will never be rid of the constraints of traditional society.

The AIIB resembles that hidden dragon, possessing the inner potential to exercise power and influence but on the surface acting with self-restraint. Under Beijing's leadership, the bank has accepted the established international financial arrangements. The bank's popularity on other continents, especially Europe, has satisfied China's desire for enhanced international status. Positive recognition from the international community will make China less likely to direct the bank away from its current course. If this continues, the AIIB is unlikely to become an instrument in the service of China's geopolitical ambitions. At present, China and the AIIB appear to have reached an equilibrium; whether China's latent ambitions will reawaken in the future remains to be seen. With rapid changes in world affairs and the geopolitical situation, it is too early to tell whether the AIIB will stay on its present track as it confronts more external stimuli and difficult challenges. The dragon may not be shackled forever, especially when it becomes even stronger and aspires to having the world revolve around itself.

The conclusions I draw below are a synthesis of my findings in previous chapters. First, I demonstrate how the AIIB reflects the power transition phenomenon, meaning that the bank has the potential to become a revisionist instrument. Second, I show that the AIIB has, on the outside, appeared to be obedient. Finally, I contrast the AIIB and the BRI and speculate whether the AIIB will one day turn into a BRI-like financial vehicle.

Inner ambition

On the basis of data presented in previous chapters, the Asia-Pacific power transition hypothesis appears to hold true. Although, militarily, there remains a huge gap between China and the US, this gap is shrinking. Economically and financially, China has caught up with and even surpassed the US in several dimensions and is becoming a regional economic hegemon. Without its alliance with the US, Japan will not be able to compete with China. These circumstances fuel China's ambition to protect its interests and to achieve the recognition it believes it deserves given its current status. However, within the international financial system, Beijing has struggled for global recognition of its powerful status. Before 2014, China was dissatisfied with its failure to gain more influence within the Bretton Woods system and frustrated at its low global sovereign credit rating and failure to have its currency included in the IMF's Special Drawing Right (SDR). During this power transition period, China's own perception of its financial power has outstripped that of the international community. This status discrepancy, which is discussed in Chapter 3, was the source of China's dissatisfaction with the current system, and in this book, I argue that it was an factor influencing the establishment of the AIIB through which China is striving to flex its financial muscle. When the idea of the AIIB was first mooted, it looked as though the bank would be an instrument for maximizing Chinese power and would serve China's own strategic interests. Once the IMF gave China a larger voting share and included the renminbi in the SDR and once European countries started to join the AIIB in defiance of political pressure from Washington, the AIIB became a more inclusive bank.

Initially, the AIIB attracted a lot of countries that were dissatisfied with the power structure within the Bretton Woods system. Quantitative evidence presented in Chapter 3 demonstrates that countries that are underrepresented in the World Bank are more likely to join the AIIB. In these circumstances, the bank has the potential to develop into a club for "avengers" under the leadership of "Captain" China. Beijing can certainly capitalize on global discontent with the Bretton Woods system. The institutional design of the AIIB would allow China to flex its muscles if it wanted to. China retains more than 25% of voting power, which enables Beijing to veto any important institutional changes. The AIIB's non-resident board design concentrates power in the hands of the bank's president, who for the time being is a Chinese national. The evidence I present in Chapter 4 suggests that, most of the time, the board is united in support of the president's recommendations. These arrangements have the potential to allow control of the AIIB by the Chinese Communist Party in the future. There is a higher level of disagreement among members of the ADB and the World Bank. For example, at an ADB board meeting in February 2019, Bangladesh and Malaysia opposed inviting Israel to attend the 52nd meeting of the board of governors as an observer, while the United States opposed giving the Russian Federation observer status and strongly supported the participation of Iceland, Israel, Kuwait, Niue and a number of international organizations as observers (Asian Development Bank,

2019c). Opposition or abstention on proposals occurs more frequently in the ADB than it does in the AIIB, demonstrating that there are more checks and balances in the Bretton Woods institutions. This suggests that the AIIB has the potential to be manipulated by its dominant member.

Washington and Tokyo, which are at the helm of the World Bank and the ADB, respectively, have so far refused to join the AIIB. Although many European powers became founding members of the AIIB, some European countries have hesitated for strategic reasons. Although both Washington and Tokyo have refrained from using realist-oriented rhetoric to explain their decisions not to join, both countries are concerned not only with the growth of China's relative power and influence but also with the possible negative impact of the AIIB on the ADB and the World Bank. The AIIB might be used to fulfill China's geopolitical ambitions. In Chapter 5, the case of the Pacific Island countries most clearly shows the AIIB's geopolitical potential. For those countries, severing diplomatic relations with Taiwan is a condition for acquiring AIIB membership. Chapter 7 focuses on the political relationship between the two sides of the Taiwan Strait in connection with Taiwan's possible membership.

Confronted with competition, the ADB has engaged more actively than the World Bank. Not only has it increased its commitments, the Japanese government has also come up with more aid and investment that emphasizes the quality of the programs, in contrast to China's quantity-oriented and sometimes exploitative programs. Australia, although it was an AIIB founding member, was alarmed by China's intensive economic and financial engagement with the Pacific Island countries, which Canberra considers to be strategically important. Disquiet in the US and Japan was also manifested in their reactions to China's loans from the ADB and the World Bank. Neither Washington nor Tokyo believe that China should qualify for funding from these two sources given its economic power. For example, during a meeting of the ADB in January 2020, the US opposed China's loan application for the Anhui Huangshan Xin'an River Ecological Protection and Green Development Project (Asian Development Bank, 2020). The US had opposed another Chinese application, this time for the Yunnan Lincang Border Economic Cooperation Zone Development Project, in February 2019 (Asian Development Bank, 2019a), as well as another two green energy projects proposed by China in December the previous year (Asian Development Bank, 2019b). US opposition to Chinese applications for ADB funding is much higher than it is for applications from other members. Although these projects were ultimately approved, Washington's opposition reflects its concerns about China's growing financial power.

Briefly, the timing of its establishment and the institutional design of the AIIB further support the power transition hypothesis. The unsatisfactory strategic circumstances in which China found itself in the early 2010s prompted it to create an international financial institution which it could control. Comparing the shape of the AIIB with that of its regional counterparts leads us to conclude that the bank is a revisionist instrument. Nonetheless, it is also important to assess whether it behaves like one.

Outward obedience

Is the AIIB behaving in line with its revisionist configuration? Based on the evidence presented in previous chapters, the answer is no, at least so far. The AIIB does not appear to be challenging the established international financial arrangements. Although China is the only member with veto power, the AIIB Charter, as well as its policies and regulations, are largely borrowed from the existing IFIs, which signals that the AIIB is trying to mirror its competitors. It is reasonable for the AIIB to be a follower as it is still a rookie in the league. In addition, although its president, Jin Liqun, is a Chinese national, its other senior officers are either from Western countries or from regional competitors, such as India or Russia. Since there is no resident board, they bear greater responsibility for shaping the bank's trajectory. The AIIB's current configuration demonstrates that it is a multilateral bank that includes more non-regional members (soon to be more than 50% of the total) than the ADB. Middle-income African countries are looking forward to the bank's further expansion and are keen to benefit from a higher level of participation (Prinsloo, 2019). The countries of Latin America and the Caribbean are also being encouraged to apply for membership (Mendez, 2019). From a regional base, the AIIB is evolving into an international bank.

In the eyes of Natalie Lichtenstein, a former World Bank lawyer who was the AIIB's inaugural general counsel and chief counsel for its negotiations, the AIIB's policies are comparable to those of other similar institutions, although they differ in some respects, such as the non-resident board, streamlined decision-making and uniquely detailed oversight arrangements (Lichtenstein, 2019). As I show in Chapter 4, a large proportion of AIIB projects are co-financed with other IFIs, whose policies concerning financing, environmental and social safeguards, procurement and anti-corruption are accepted by the AIIB. The AIIB is also seeking to collaborate with other IFIs around the world. As a result, the AIIB has maintained a triple A or equivalent credit rating from Moody's, Fitch, and Standard and Poor's (S&P). All of this suggests that where the AIIB's internal management is concerned, it has adopted established best practice. At present, the AIIB is allowing itself to be shaped and influenced by the existing international financial system.

In the most hotly debated area of social and environmental safeguards, the evidence presented in Chapter 4 suggests that the AIIB has only moderately deviated from the policies of its Bretton Woods counterparts. If one compares AIIB projects with those of China's Belt and Road (BRI), the former appear to be way more compliant than the latter. The BRI has been the target of criticism for its debt-for-equity swaps, but the AIIB has so far steered clear of such exploitative practices. It has also rejected loan applications for infrastructure projects that have adverse environmental or social impacts. However, one cannot ignore the fact that the AIIB's proportion of Category C projects (having minimal or no adverse impacts) remains too low and in this respect it has not shown any improvement. Besides, the BRI, which is funded by China's policy banks, may become another effective financial vehicle for those projects denied funding by the AIIB. It is by no means certain how long and how well the AIIB will remain obedient and keep itself separate from the BRI.

Although the AIIB appears to be compliant, Lichtenstein (2019, p. 485) points out that "shifts in international relations and geopolitics will have an impact on AIIB's members, and may in turn influence their ability and willingness to contribute to and benefit from AIIB. Institutional governance and leadership have been another source of uncertainty." It is imperative to ascertain whether the AIIB has become another IFI that sometimes acts geopolitically. Evidence in Chapter 3 suggests that countries may have joined the bank for political reasons due to their dissatisfaction with the current system, and that they are seeking more equal representation in the AIIB. However, according to the findings presented in this book, their representation in the AIIB does not differ much from that in the other IFIs. The evidence also suggests that international or domestic political factors played an insignificant role in each country's decision to join the bank, nor did such factors influence each country's voting power in the bank or the total AIIB commitments it received. Factors such as whether the country is an authoritarian regime or whether its foreign policy perspective is similar to China's do not significantly affect its interaction with the AIIB either.

Pakistan, Jordan, Japan, Kuwait, Vietnam, South Korea, Malaysia, Kazakhstan and Indonesia have all, at one time or another, represented the Asia-Pacific region as non-permanent members of the United Nations Security Council (UNSC), and these countries have been proved to be more likely to receive a greater number of World Bank projects and IMF loans with fewer strings attached (Dreher, Sturm, & Vreeland, 2009, 2015). By the end of 2019, only Pakistan, Indonesia and Kazakhstan had projects approved by the AIIB. The effect of geopolitics should be the strongest in the case of Kazakhstan, since it has an abundance of natural resources. However, my case study shows that geopolitical factors play only a minor role in its interaction with the AIIB. The loans received by Indonesia are due to Jakarta's active pursuit of external financial resources rather than geopolitical factors. Pakistan, as China's military ally, might expect to be favored by the AIIB for political reasons. But, if that is the case, how can we explain why China's main regional rival, India, has so far received the largest volume of loans, accounting for about 25% of total AIIB commitments. The case of India demonstrates that even China's main geopolitical rival chooses to see the AIIB as it exists today as multilateral, consultative, open, transparent and compliant with recognized international norms. Quantitative and qualitative evidence suggests that, so far, geopolitical factors play an insignificant role in directing the bank's policies.

In terms of competition, the evidence suggests that the arrival on the scene of the AIIB has not made much difference. In the bank's first four years, AIIB lending has grown substantially each year, but comparatively speaking, the bank's contribution to regional funding is no more than moderate; it still falls short of what is needed for infrastructure development. Confronted with the emergence of the AIIB, the ADB has responded more actively than the World Bank, which has decreased its engagement in the Asia-Pacific region. In the case of the ADB, no systematic effect is found that can explain any increase or decrease in ADB commitments to countries which have received loans from the AIIB. The evidence in relation to the World Bank, however, suggests that although it has made more commitments to AIIB members in general, the level of growth in these commitments is significantly lower for AIIB members than for non-members. This suggests that the World Bank's competition with the AIIB is more conservative than that of the ADB. The arrival of the AIIB and the retreat of the World Bank cancel each other out, so there has only been a limited increase in funds available for investment in regional infrastructure. In addition, there is no evidence to suggest that the AIIB is causing other IFIs to lower their standards when making financial commitments. This is evident in the case of India, which might have had an incentive to pit the ADB against the AIIB to obtain loans for coal-fired energy projects. But ADB-financed projects in India, as well as in Indonesia, have not shown any deterioration in terms of environmental and social impacts. The AIIB may have unintentionally facilitated improvements and reforms in the other IFIs. The IMF voting quota reform was implemented with Washington's consent right after the establishment of the AIIB in mid-2015. The ADB and its lead country, Japan, started to emphasize the high quality and standard of its funded projects.

Unlike the ADB and the World Bank, the AIIB promised to exclude policy conditions from its loan decisions, and so far, there is no sign of any neoliberal policy conditions being applied to AIIB loans. In terms of loans, the AIIB does not seem to be any harsher or more lenient than other providers. For instance, in an approved co-financed "Natural Gas Infrastructure and Efficiency Improvement" project for Bangladesh, both the AIIB and the ADB issued LIBOR-based loans with a 25-year term that included a grace period of 5 years at the bank's standard interest rate for sovereign-backed loans. In this case, the level of the AIIB's funding was only 36% of the ADB's level. In a project co-financed with the World Bank – the "Karachi Water and Sewerage Services Improvement Project" in Pakistan, both banks committed US$40 million. While the World Bank's term to maturity was 25 years with a grace period of 6 years, the AIIB's term was 30 years with a grace period of 5.5 years. So far, the average term to maturity of all AIIB projects is 23.1 years with a grace period of 5.8 years. All are sovereign-backed LIBOR-based loans, which do not look very different from those offered by other IFIs.

To summarize, the AIIB at age four has neither substantially deviated from international best practice, nor has it shown any intention of doing so. In addition, the bank has not shown signs of seeking to serve China's geopolitical or strategic purposes. As the bank has evolved, it has drawn in more members from different continents and adopted similar policies and regulations to those of its partners around the world. Although China remains dominant in the AIIB, its power will be checked by the influence of the growing number of members and the bank's own regulations. If China one day wants to manipulate the AIIB in its favor, it will have to make a concerted effort to mobilize support from other members.

The BRI and the future of the AIIB

The above analysis indicates that although the AIIB's institutional design makes it vulnerable to domination by China, there is little evidence that the bank is behaving as Beijing's geopolitical instrument. Another question that arises is the AIIB's relationship with the BRI, Beijing's grand new global strategy. The BRI is configured to solve China's domestic, economic and geopolitical challenges (Clarke, 2017). Both the BRI and the AIIB were proposed by Xi Jinping in late 2013, raising suspicions that the two initiatives would support and complement each other. However, as the AIIB has evolved into a multilateral and transparent institution, the BRI has become opaque and problematic. The AIIB's president, Jin Liqun, was probably right when he said that "the AIIB was not created to finance One Belt, One Road" (Wei, 2016). The case of India, which I discuss in Chapter 5, also reveals the lack of coordination between China's two grand plans. Although a thorough study of the BRI is beyond the scope of this book, a rapid overview will help us flag up a few differences between the AIIB and the BRI.

First, the AIIB and the BRI have different funding sources. While the AIIB's capital is subscribed by both regional and non-regional members, most of the BRI's projects are bankrolled by China's policy banks, such as the China Development Bank, the Agricultural Development Bank and the Export-Import Bank of China, as well as huge commercial banks, such as the China Construction Bank. In addition, the BRI mostly involves large Chinese multinational corporations (MNCs). For these reasons, the BRI is more likely to be exposed to Chinese domestic politics and more susceptible to control by the Chinese Communist Party.

Second, the scope of investment of the two initiatives is quite different. So far, the AIIB has concentrated on projects in regional member states while the BRI projects have a more global scope. For example, according to data from the China Global Investment Tracker (CGIT), maintained by the American Enterprise Institute and the Heritage Foundation, from 2013 to 2019, about 21.7% of BRI investments went to Sub-Saharan Africa. The difference in the amount of investment is even bigger than the difference in regional distribution. By the end of 2019, total BRI investments were estimated at US$730 billion while the AIIB had only committed US$11.7 billion.

Third, AIIB projects are implemented and monitored by a multilateral institution that involves members from all over the world and other international organizations. The bank's policies and directives, as well as details of the projects, are available on the AIIB's website just as they are for other IFIs. Most BRI projects, in contrast, are bilateral contracts between the destination country and China. No information is made available to outsiders. If a BRI project is located in a country with a poor governance record, corruption is likely to occur.

Fourth, there is evidence to suggest that BRI projects could easily leave their recipients indebted to China, and they may be forced to hand over strategic assets in order to clear their debts (Kliman et al., 2019; Parker & Chefitz, 2018; Rajah, Dayant, & Pryke, 2019). No such problems have arisen with AIIB projects so far.

Based on these differences, this book argues that the AIIB and the BRI are not complementary. They have developed into two independent institutions different not only in nature but also in practice. The BRI is more likely to become an instrument for furthering China's geopolitical ambitions. The initial evidence suggests that it is more likely to be shaped by political factors.

First, while the largest beneficiary of the AIIB is India, its main regional rival, Pakistan, which is one of China's few military allies in the region, has received the largest volume of BRI investments, an estimated US$46 billion. This is partly thanks to China's commitment to the flagship BRI project, the "China-Pakistan Economic Corridor," which will facilitate China's strategic deployment in the region. Second, while the AIIB has so far refrained from bankrolling coal-fired energy projects, there are, according to CGIT data, 68 coal-related projects being developed under the auspices of the BRI worth US$54 billion. Not surprisingly, Pakistan is the largest beneficiary, with 12 of these projects totaling US$11.5. Coal-fired projects in other Southeast and South Asian countries are also being funded handsomely by the BRI. This is clear evidence that the BRI has not shied away from investing in controversial and sensitive sectors.

Third, Figure 8.1 uses CGIT data to show how BRI investments are concentrated in countries that are politically closer to China. To make it easier to observe the association, I standardize each country's total BRI investments and its foreign policy distance from China. The plot suggests the existence of a negative association, which implies that those countries with a similar perception of global affairs to China (smaller foreign policy distance) are more likely to secure more BRI investments.

Finally, I adopt the same quantitative strategy as I did in the previous chapter and try to locate the association shown in Figure 8.1 by controlling for other political and economic factors. Model 1 of Table 8.1 lists the factors with a significant relationship to total amounts of BRI investments, while Model 2 lists

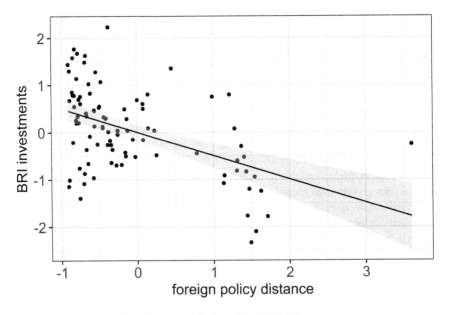

Figure 8.1 Foreign policy distance vs. Belt and Road Initiative

Table 8.1 Political economy of the Belt and Road Initiative

	(1)	(2)
	BRI all	BRI Construction
GDP (log)	0.533***	0.548***
	(0.109)	(0.0923)
Democracy	0.0114	−0.0126
	(0.0202)	(0.0200)
Infrastructure level	−0.149	−0.576
	(0.434)	(0.384)
Economic risk	−0.00297	−0.00647
	(0.0126)	(0.0118)
Foreign policy distance	−0.906***	−0.799***
	(0.315)	(0.247)
Geographical distance (1,000km)	−0.0274	−0.0321
	(0.0333)	(0.0369)
UN Security Council	0.314	0.160
	(0.235)	(0.250)
N	89	84
Adjusted R-Square	0.339	0.356

total amounts of BRI investments related to the construction sector. The results of regression models show that foreign policy difference is indeed negatively associated with BRI investments even when we control for other factors. In other words, BRI investment decisions are based more on whether a country "speaks the same language" as China and less on whether that country really needs the infrastructure project or on the level of investment risk. Political factors are harder to detect in the case of the AIIB.

When Xi Jinping first proposed the idea of a China-led investment bank, many observers predicted that the bank would behave like the BRI. So far, this has not happened, but is the AIIB likely to move in that direction in the future? The answer is probably yes. The institutional design of the AIIB allows it to be turned into an instrument of Beijing's geopolitical ambitions. Although the current configuration makes it difficult for China to manipulate the AIIB, this book suggests that the chance exists. The question is, when will this happen, and how soon will this hidden dragon start to display its power and influence and use the AIIB in the service of its geopolitical ambitions? The answer may lie in whether changes in international relations and geopolitics will influence China's perception of its status in the international financial system. Should China's level of satisfaction improve, the AIIB will likely stay as it is. However, if China's dissatisfaction intensifies, it will be more likely to turn the bank into a revisionist tool. The most pessimistic scenario in this era of power transition is that nothing is impossible.

Bibliography

Abbott, Kenneth W., & Snidal, Duncan. (1998). Why States Act Through Formal International Organizations. *Journal of Conflict Resolution*, 42(1), 3–32.

Abdi, Bilal. (2018, October 22). India's Crude Oil Import Bill to Peak at Record $125 Billion in Current Fiscal: Oil Ministry. *The Economic Times*. Retrieved from https://energy.economictimes.indiatimes.com/news/oil-and-gas/indias-crude-oil-import-bill-to-peak-at-record-125-billion-in-current-fiscal-oil-ministry/66319124

Advancing US Economic Interests in Asia, Committee on Foreign Affairs, US House of Representatives, 114th Sess (2015).

Agrawal, Pradeep. (2015). Infrastructure in India: Challenges and the Way Ahead. *IEG Working Paper* (350), 1–30.

Aldayarov, Mirlan, Dobozi, Istvan, & Nikolakakis, Thomas. (2017). *Stuck in Transition: Reform Experiences and Challenges Ahead in the Kazakhstan Power Sector*. Washington DC: The World Bank.

Allcott, Hunt, Collard-Wexler, Allan, & O'Connell, Stephen D. (2016). How Do Electricity Shortages Affect Industry? Evidence from India. *American Economic Review*, 106(3), 587–624.

Allison, Graham T. (2018). *Destined for War: Can America and China Escape Thucydides's Trap?* London, UK: Scribe Publications.

Ambrosio, Thomas. (2008). Catching the 'Shanghai Spirit': How the Shanghai Cooperation Organization Promotes Authoritarian Norms in Central Asia. *Europe-Asia Studies*, 60(8), 1321–1344.

American Cultural Center, Bucharest, Romania. (2006). In Celebration of 125 Years of US and Romanian Diplomatic Relations. *The DISAM Journal*, 28(3), 15–26.

American Journal of International Law. (2017). After Lengthy Delay, Congress Approves IMF Governance Reforms that Empower Emerging Market and Developing Countries. *American Journal of International Law*, 110(2), 368–374.

Anderlini, Jamil. (2016, April 22). Lunch with the FT: Jin Liqun. *Financial Times*. Retrieved from https://www.ft.com/content/0564ce1e-06e3-11e6-a70d-4e39ac32c284

Anderlini, Jamil, & Giles, Chris. (2011, April 1). G20 Fails to Ease Tension over Monetary Reform. *Financial Times*, p. 8.

Andersen, Thomas Barnebeck, Hansen, Henrik, & Markussen, Thomas. (2006). US Politics and World Bank IDA-Lending. *Journal of Development Studies*, 42(5), 772–794.

Aneja, Atul. (2015, June 30). 50 Nations in, AIIB Takes Shape. *The Hindu*. Retrieved from https://www.thehindu.com/news/national/india-signs-articles-that-determine-each-countrys-share-in-asian-infrastructure-investment-bank/article7368050.ece

Ashford, Nicholas. (1976, July 15). Chinese Hand Over Tanzam Railway and Western Critics Have to Eat Their Words. *The Times*, p. 6.

Asia Times. (2017, July 20). China's AIIB Gathers Three Highest Global Credit Ratings. *Asia Times*. Retrieved from https://asiatimes.com/2017/07/chinas-aiib-gathers-three-highest-global-credit-ratings/

Asian Development Bank. (2019a). Minutes of the Meeting of the Board of Directors of the Asian Development Bank Held at 10:00 A.M. on 10 December 2018. Retrieved from https://www.adb.org/sites/default/files/institutional-document/486686/m33-18-10dec18.pdf

Asian Development Bank. (2019b). Minutes of the Meeting of the Board of Directors of the Asian Development Bank Held at 10:00 A.M. on 13 December 2018. Retrieved from https://www.adb.org/sites/default/files/institutional-document/486696/m34-18-13dec18.pdf

Asian Development Bank. (2019c). Minutes of the Meeting of the Board of Directors of the Asian Development Bank Held at 10:00 A.M. on 19 February 2019. Retrieved from https://www.adb.org/sites/default/files/institutional-document/487671/m1-19-19feb19.pdf

Asian Development Bank. (2020). Minutes of the Meeting of the Board of Directors of the Asian Development Bank Held at 10:00 A.M. on 14 January 2020. Retrieved from https://www.adb.org/sites/default/files/institutional-document/561711/m21-20-31jan2020.pdf

Asian Development Bank Institute. (2009). *Infrastructure for a Seamless Asia*. Tokyo, Japan: Asian Development Bank Institute.

Asian Infrastructure Investment Bank. (2015). President-Designate Jin Meets President Joko Widodo of Indonesia. Retrieved from https://www.aiib.org/en/news-events/news/2015/President-designate-Jin-meets-President-Joko-Widodo-of-Indonesia.html

Asian Infrastructure Investment Bank. (2016). President-Designate Jin Meets Indian Prime Minister H.E. Narendra Modi and Other Government Leaders. Retrieved from https://www.aiib.org/en/news-events/news/2016/President-designate-Jin-meets-Indian-Prime-Minister-H-E-Narendra-Modi-and-other-government-leaders.html

Asian Infrastructure Investment Bank. (2017a). AIIB Says No to Doing Business with Corrupt Bidders. Retrieved from https://www.aiib.org/en/news-events/news/2017/AIIB-Says-No-to-Doing-Business-with-Corrupt-Bidders.html

Asian Infrastructure Investment Bank. (2017b). AIIB Supports UN Anti-Corruption Day with Week of Events. Retrieved from https://www.aiib.org/en/news-events/news/2017/AIIB-Supports-UN-Anti-Corruption-Day-with-Week-of-Events.html

Asian Infrastructure Investment Bank. (2017c). The Basel Committee on Banking Supervision Assigns Eligible AIIB Liabilities a 0% Risk Weighting. Retrieved from https://www.aiib.org/en/news-events/news/2017/The-Basel-Committee-on-Banking-Supervision-assigns-eligible-AIIB-liabilities-a-0-risk-weighting.html

Babson, Bradley. (2015, May 26). Could the New Asian Infrastructure Investment Bank Change the Dynamics of Economic Engagement with North Korea? *38 North*. Retrieved from https://www.38north.org/2015/05/bbabson052515/

Bailey, Martin. (1975). Tanzania and China. *African Affairs*, 74(294), 39–50.

Bailey, Michael A., Strezhnev, Anton, & Voeten, Erik. (2017). Estimating Dynamic State Preferences from United Nations Voting Data. *Journal of Conflict Resolution*, 61(2), 430–456.

Balachandran, Niruban. (2017). The US Should Join the Asian Infrastructure Investment Bank. *Asia Pacific Bulletin* (397). Retrieved from https://www.eastwestcenter.org/system/tdf/private/apb397.pdf?file=1&type=node&id=36284

Banila, Nicoleta. (2017, May 15). Romania Becoming Asian Infrastructure Investment Bank Member. *SeeNews*. Retrieved from https://seenews.com/news/romania-becoming-asian-infrastructure-investment-bank-member-finmin-568719

Banks, Martin. (2015, November 17). Interview: Belgian Defense Minister Steven Vandeput. *Defense News*. Retrieved from https://www.defensenews.com/interviews/2015/11/17/interview-belgian-defense-minister-steven-vandeput/

Beckley, Michael. (2017). The Emerging Military Balance in East Asia: How China's Neighbors Can Check Chinese Naval Expansion. *International Security*, 42(2), 78–119.

Beeson, Mark, & Xu, Shaomin. (2019). China's Evolving Role in Global Governance. In Ka Zeng (Ed.), *Handbook on the International Political Economy of China* (pp. 345–360). Cheltenham, UK: Edward Elgar Publishing.

Belt & Road News. (2019, March 1). AIIB Report: India Joining the Belt & Road After 2019 Elections. Retrieved from https://www.beltandroad.news/2019/03/01/aiib-report-india-joining-the-belt-road-after-2019-elections/

Bendix, Aria. (2019, August 28). Indonesia is Spending $33 Billion to Move Its Capital from a Sinking City to an Island Where Forests Have Been Burning. *Business Insider*. Retrieved from https://www.businessinsider.com/indonesia-capital-move-jakarta-borneo-environmental-concerns-2019-8

Berkofsky, Axel. (2019, December 4). China and the EU: "Strategic Partners" No More. *Issue Brief*, Stockholm, Sweden: Institute for Security & Development Policy. Retrieved from https://isdp.eu/content/uploads/2019/12/China-and-the-EU-04.12.19.pdf

Bermingham, Finbarr. (2015, September 23). Xi Jinping Reiterates US Invitation to AIIB. *Global Trade Review*. Retrieved from https://www.gtreview.com/news/asia/xi-jinping-reiterates-us-invitation-to-aiib/

Bernovici, Anca. (2016, August 25). Romania Wants to Become Member of the Asian Infrastructure Investment Bank. *The Romania Journal*. Retrieved from https://www.romaniajournal.ro/business/news/romania-wants-to-become-member-of-the-asian-infrastructure-investment-bank/

Besliu, Raluca. (2014, March 4). Romania: Chinese are Coming! *YaleGlobal Online*. Retrieved from https://yaleglobal.yale.edu/content/romania-chinese-are-coming

Biswas, Rajiv. (2015). Reshaping the Financial Architecture for Development Finance: The New Development Banks. *LSE Global South Unit Working Paper Series* (2).

Black, Ian, & MacAskill, Ewen. (2003, June 13). US Threatens NATO Boycott Over Belgian War Crimes Law. *The Guardian*. Retrieved from https://www.theguardian.com/world/2003/jun/13/nato.warcrimes

Blustein, Paul. (1999, June 22). World Bank to Vote on Controversial Loan to China. *Washington Post*, p. E03.

Brauchli, Marcus W., Guenther, Robert, & Hunt, Christopher. (1989, June 22). Japanese and Western Banks Put Their Lending to China on Hold. *Wall Street Journal*.

Breuning, Marijke. (2016). Contesting Belgium's Role in Development Cooperation. In Cristian Cantir & Juliet Kaarbo (Eds.), *Domestic Role Contestation, Foreign Policy, and International Relations* (pp. 73–88). Abingdon, UK: Routledge.

Brummitt, Chris, & Amin, Haslinda. (2016, February 11). Jokowi Leans on China, Central Bank to Revive Indonesia GDP. *Bloomberg*. Retrieved from https://www.bloomberg.com/news/articles/2016-02-11/jokowi-seeks-china-funds-rate-cuts-to-meet-indonesia-gdp-target

Calderón, César, & Servén, Luis. (2004). The Effects of Infrastructure Development on Growth and Income Distribution. *World Bank Policy Research Working Paper* (3400). Washington, DC: The World Bank. Retrieved from https://openknowledge.worldbank.org/handle/10986/14136

Callaghan, Mike, & Hubbard, Paul. (2016). The Asian Infrastructure Investment Bank: Multilateralism on the Silk Road. *China Economic Journal*, 9(2), 116–139.

Cassidy, Emily, & Hamzah, Hidayah. (2019, October 1). 5 Maps Show How Moving Indonesia's Capital Could Impact the Environment. *TheCityFix*. Retrieved from https://thecityfix.com/blog/5-maps-show-moving-indonesias-capital-impact-environment-emily-cassidy-hidayah-hamzah/

Cavanough, Edward. (2019, December 7). When China Came Calling: Inside the Solomon Islands Switch. *The Guardian*. Retrieved from https://www.theguardian.com/world/2019/dec/08/when-china-came-calling-inside-the-solomon-islands-switch

Cave, Damien. (2019, October 16). China is Leasing an Entire Pacific Island. Its Residents are Shocked. *New York Times*. Retrieved from https://www.nytimes.com/2019/10/16/world/australia/china-tulagi-solomon-islands-pacific.html

Chakravorti, Bhaskar. (2015). China's New Development Bank is a Wake-Up Call for Washington. *Harvard Business Review*. Retrieved from https://hbr.org/2015/04/chinas-new-development-bank-is-a-wake-up-call-for-washington

Chan, Lai-Ha. (2017). Soft Balancing Against the US 'Pivot to Asia': China's Geostrategic Rationale for Establishing the Asian Infrastructure Investment Bank. *Australian Journal of International Affairs*, 71(6), 568–590.

Chandran, Nyshka, & Fujita, Akiko. (2017, May 17). Seven Takeaways from CNBC's Interview with Japan's PM. *CNBC*. Retrieved from https://www.cnbc.com/2017/05/17/japanese-prime-minister-shinzo-abe-seven-takeaways-from-cnbcs-interview.html

Chang, Jae-soon. (2014, July 8). US Official Expresses Strong Skepticism About China's Push for New Development Bank. *Yonhap News Agency*. Retrieved from https://en.yna.co.kr/view/AEN20140708000351315

Chaudhury, Dipanjan Roy. (2016, February 18). India May Seek Asian Infrastructure Investment Bank Funding for PM Narendra Modi's Pet Projects. *The Economic Times*.

Chen, Ian Tsung-yen. (2014). Balance of Payments and Power: Assessing China's Global and Regional Interdependence Relationship. *International Relations of the Asia-Pacific*, 14(2), 271–302.

Chen, Ian Tsung-yen. (2015). *Opportunities and Challenges of Taiwan's Participation in the AIIB*. Unpublished Paper. Taipei, Taiwan.

Chen, Ian Tsung-yen. (2016). Is China a Challenger? The Predicament of China's Reformist Initiatives in the Asian Infrastructure Investment Bank. *Mainland China Studies*, 59(3), 83–109.

Chen, Ian Tsung-yen. (2018). European Participation in the Asian Infrastructure Investment Bank: Making Strategic Choice and Seeking Economic Opportunities. *Asia Europe Journal*, 16(4), 297–315.

Chen, Ian Tsung-yen. (2020). China's Status Deficit and the Debut of the Asian Infrastructure Investment Bank. *The Pacific Review*, 33(5), 697–727.

Cheng, Allen T. (2017, April 24). Asian Development Bank: A Force of Stability. *Institutional Investor*. Retrieved from https://www.institutionalinvestor.com/article/b1505p76sfj6x6/asian-development-bank-a-force-of-stability

Chin, Gregory T. (2016). Asian Infrastructure Investment Bank: Governance Innovation and Prospects. *Global Governance: A Review of Multilateralism and International Organizations*, 22(1), 11–25.

Chin, Gregory, & Helleiner, Eric. (2008). China as a Creditor: A Rising Financial Power? *Journal of International Affairs*, 62(1), 87–102.

China Central Television. (2000). Haoshi weishime youren fandui [Why Would People Object Good Things?]. *Chaidamu Kaifa Yanjiu* (3), 9–12.

China Daily. (2004, May 4). Germany Adheres to 'One China' Policy. Retrieved from https://www.chinadaily.com.cn/english/doc/2004-05/04/content_328169.htm

Chow, Daniel C. K. (2016). Why China Established the Asia Infrastructure Investment Bank. *Vanderbilt Journal of Transnational Law*, 49(5), 1255–1298.

Christensen, Thomas J. (1999). China, the US-Japan Alliance, and the Security Dilemma in East Asia. *International Security*, 23(4), 49–80.

Christianson, Giulia, Lee, Allison, Larsen, Gaia, & Green, Ashley. (2017). *Financing the Energy Transition: Are World Bank, IFC, and ADB Energy Supply Investments Supporting a Low-Carbon Future?* Retrieved from Washington, DC: https://www.wri.org/publication/financing-the-energy-transition

Chung, Lawrence. (2016, April 12). Taiwan Says it Will Not Join Beijing-Led AIIB After Rejecting Condition that 'Violates Dignity'. *South China Morning Post*. Retrieved from https://www.scmp.com/news/china/policies-politics/article/1935492/taiwan-says-it-will-not-join-beijing-led-aiib-after

Clarke, Michael. (2017). The Belt and Road Initiative: China's New Grand Strategy? *Asia Policy* (24), 71–79.

Cook, Malcolm. (2015). China's Power Status Change: East Asian Challenges for Xi Jinping's Foreign Policy. *China Quarterly of International Strategic Studies*, 1(1), 105–131.

Council of the European Union. (2016). *EU Strategy on China*. Brussels, Belgium. Retrieved from https://eeas.europa.eu/sites/eeas/files/council_conclusions_eu_strategy_on_china.pdf

Cuomo, Joe. (1989, April 26). Chinese Dissident Advocates Divestment. *Wall Street Journal*.

Dai, Yi, & Li, Yankang. (2015). Yazhou jichu sheshi touzi yinhang de guoji zhengzhi jingjixue fenxi [An International Political Economic Analysis of Asian Infrastructure Investment Bank]. *Shehui zhuyi yanjiu [Socialism Studies]* (3), 168–172.

Das, Khanindra Ch. (2017). The Making of One Belt, One Road and Dilemmas in South Asia. *China Report*, 53(2), 1–18.

Dave, Bhavna, & Kobayashi, Yuka. (2018). China's Silk Road Economic Belt Initiative in Central Asia: Economic and Security Implications. *Asia Europe Journal*, 16(3), 267–281.

Davis, Bob. (2011, May 17). Asia Set for Larger Role at IMF. *Wall Street Journal*.

Davis, Bob, & Sahu, Prasanta. (2014, October 23). China's Plans for Development Bank Fall Short. *Wall Street Journal*.

DeGhett, Torie Rose. (2015, October 7). Romania is Starting to Freak Out About Russian Designs on Transnistria. *VICE News*. Retrieved from https://news.vice.com/article/romania-is-starting-to-freak-out-about-russian-designs-on-transnistria

De Jonge, Alice. (2017). Perspectives on the Emerging Role of the Asian Infrastructure Investment Bank. *International Affairs*, 93(5), 1061–1084.

Deng, Yong. (2008). *China's Struggle for Status: The Realignment of International Relations*. Cambridge, MA: Cambridge University Press.

Der Spiegel. (2004, December 6). German Papers: Chinese Horse Trading: Weapons Embargo for a Security Council Seat. Retrieved from https://www.spiegel.de/international/german-papers-chinese-horse-trading-weapons-embargo-for-a-security-council-seat-a-331224.html

Desai, Raj M., & Vreeland, James Raymond. (2015, April 6). How to Stop Worrying and Love the Asian Infrastructure Investment Bank. *Washington Post*. Retrieved from https://www.washingtonpost.com/blogs/monkey-cage/wp/2015/04/06/how-to-stop-worrying-and-love-the-asian-infrastructure-investment-bank/

Deschouwer, Kris. (2012). *The Politics of Belgium: Governing a Divided Society*. London, UK: Palgrave Macmillan.

Diela, Tabita. (2016, January 14). Indonesia Eyeing Strategic Positions in AIIB: Finance Minister. *Jakarta Globe*. Retrieved from https://jakartaglobe.id/context/indonesia-eyeing-strategic-positions-aiib-finance-minister/

Dittmer, Lowell. (1981). The Strategic Triangle: An Elementary Game-Theoretical Analysis. *World Politics*, 33(4), 485–515.

Donnan, Shawn. (2015, December 17). US Congress Moves Closer to Approving Long-Stalled IMF Reforms. *Financial Times*. Retrieved from https://www.ft.com/content/bee64f68-a412-11e5-873f-68411a84f346

Dreher, Axel, Sturm, Jan-Egbert, & Vreeland, James Raymond. (2009). Development Aid and International Politics: Does Membership on the UN Security Council Influence World Bank Decisions? *Journal of Development Economics*, 88(1), 1–18.

Dreher, Axel, Fuchs, Andreas, & Nunnenkamp, Peter. (2013). New Donors. *International Interactions*, 39(3), 402–415.

Dreher, Axel, Fuchs, Andreas, Parks, Bradley, Strange, Austin M., & Tierney, Michael J. (2015). *Apples and Dragon Fruits: The Determinants of Aid and Other Forms of State Financing from China to Africa* AidData Working Paper (15). Williamsburg, VA: AidData at William & Mary.

Dreher, Axel, Sturm, Jan-Egbert, & Vreeland, James Raymond. (2015). Politics and IMF Conditionality. *Journal of Conflict Resolution*, 59(1), 120–148.

Dreher, Axel, Fuchs, Andreas, Parks, Bradley, Strange, Austin M., & Tierney, Michael J. (2017). *Aid, China, and Growth: Evidence from a New Global Development Finance Dataset* (AidData Working Paper #46). Williamsburg, VA: AidData.

Dwinanda, Reiny. (2018, March 12). Jokowi Thanks AIIB for Funding Infrastructure Projects. *REPUBLIKA*. Retrieved from https://www.republika.co.id/berita/en/national-politics/18/03/12/p5hfsb414-jokowi-thanks-aiib-for-funding-infrastructure-projects

Dyer, Geoff, & Parker, George. (2015, March 12). US Attacks UK's 'Constant Accommodation' with China. *Financial Times*. Retrieved from http://on.ft.com/1Mw9WbN

Earl, Greg. (2019). Economic Diplomacy: Indonesian Trade, ADB v BRI and Chinese Money. *The Interpreter*. Retrieved from https://www.lowyinstitute.org/the-interpreter/economic-diplomacy-indonesian-trade-adb-v-bri-and-chinese-money

Earl, Greg, & Murray, Lisa. (2015, March 21). Can China Run the World. *The Australian Financial Review*, p. 20.

The Economic Times. (2014, October 24). India, 20 Others Set up Asian Infrastructure Investment Bank. Retrieved from https://economictimes.indiatimes.com/news/international/business/india-20-others-set-up-asian-infrastructure-investment-bank/articleshow/44922254.cms

The Economist. (2010, February 1). The EU and Arms for China.

Engel, Susan. (2018, November 21). If There's One Thing Pacific Nations don't Need, it's Yet Another Infrastructure Investment Bank. *The Conversation*. Retrieved from https://theconversation.com/if-theres-one-thing-pacific-nations-dont-need-its-yet-another-infrastructure-investment-bank-107198

Etzioni, Amitai. (2016). The Asian Infrastructure Investment Bank: A Case Study of Multifaceted Containment. *Asian Perspective*, 40(2), 173–196.

European Commission. (2019). *Joint Communication to the European Parliament, the European Council and the Council: EU-China-A Strategic Outlook*. Retrieved from https://ec.europa.eu/commission/sites/beta-political/files/communication-eu-china-a-strategic-outlook.pdf

Evans, Peter, & Finnemore, Martha. (2001). Organizational Reform and the Expansion of the South's Voice at the Fund. Retrieved from https://unctad.org/en/docs/pogdsmd pbg24d15.en.pdf

Fackler, Martin. (2015, March 31). Japan, Sticking with US, Says it won't Join China-Led Bank. *New York Times*. Retrieved from https://nyti.ms/1MurkRA

Fails, Matthew D., & Woo, Byungwon. (2015). Unpacking Autocracy: Political Regimes and IMF Program Participation. *International Interactions*, 41(1), 110–132.

Falkenberg, Kai. (2011, November 16). First Responder. *Forbes*. Retrieved from https://www.forbes.com/forbes/2011/1205/feature-passions-health-care-reform-jim-yong-kim-falkenberg.html#2b9458a35027

Fallon, Theresa. (2015). The New Silk Road: Xi Jinping's Grand Strategy for Eurasia. *American Foreign Policy Interests*, 37(3), 140–147.

Farnsworth, Clyde H. (1983, December 6). China Bars US Bidding Project. *New York Times*, p. D2.

Farnsworth, Clyde H. (1990, February 9). China Wins Two Loans Backed by US *New York Times*, p. A3.

The Federal Governemnt of Germany. (2014, March 28). Joint Declaration Between Germany and China. *The Press and Information Office*. Retrieved from https://www.bundesregierung.de/Content/EN/Pressemitteilungen/BPA/2014/2014-03-28-china-declaration.html

Federal Ministry of Finance, Germany. (2015). German Cabinet Adopts Legislation to Join Asian Infrastructure Investment Bank. Retrieved from https://www.bundesfinanz ministerium.de/Content/EN/Pressemitteilungen/2015/2015-09-02-legislation-to-join-aiib.html

Federal Ministry of Finance, Germany. (2019). *Asian Infrastructure Investment Bank Achieves Major Milestones in Its First Three Years*. Berlin, Germany. Retrieved from https://www.bundesfinanzministerium.de/Content/EN/Standardartikel/Topics/Financial_markets/Articles/2019-04-03-AIIB-milestones.html

Feigenbaum, Evan A. (2011). Why America No Longer Gets Asia. *The Washington Quarterly*, 34(2), 25–43.

Feigenbaum, Evan A. (2017). China and the World: Dealing with a Reluctant Power. *Foreign Affairs*, 96(1), 33–40.

Feng, Bree. (2014, November 27). Indonesia Formally Pledges to Join China-Sponsored Regional Bank. *New York Times*. Retrieved from https://nyti.ms/1tlNmrk

Feng, Hao. (2017, May 12). China's Belt and Road Initiative Still Pushing Coal. *China-dialogue*. Retrieved from https://www.chinadialogue.net/article/show/single/en/9785-China-s-Belt-and-Road-Initiative-still-pushing-coal

Feng, Zhongping, & Huang, Jing. (2014). China's Strategic Partnership Diplomacy: Engaging with a Changing World. *European Strategic Partnerships Observatory* (Working Paper 8), 1–19. Retrieved from https://www.egmontinstitute.be/content/uploads/2014/06/WP-ESPO-8-JUNE-2014.pdf?type=pdf

Ferdinand, Peter. (2016). Westward Ho – The China Dream and 'One Belt, One Road': Chinese Foreign Policy Under Xi Jinping. *International Affairs*, 92(4), 941–957.

Fiji Sun. (2016, June 28). Moves for Fiji to Become Full Member of Asian Infrastructure Investment Bank. *Fiji Sun*. Retrieved from https://fijisun.com.fj/2016/06/28/moves-for-fiji-to-become-full-member-of-asian-infrastructure-investment-bank/

The Financial Express. (2012, May 26). Why BRICS Proposes an Alternative to the World Bank.

Financial Times. (2015, November 17). The Renminbi Receives a Symbolic Seal of Approval. *Financial Times*, p. 10.

Flanders News. (2015, October 1). US Ambassor Calls on Belgium to Invest More in Defence. *Flanders News.* Retrieved from http://deredactie.be/cm/vrtnieuws.english/News/1.2457471

Fleck, Robert K., & Kilby, Christopher. (2006). World Bank Independence: A Model and Statistical Analysis of US Influence. *Review of Development Economics*, 10(2), 224–240.

Foot, Rosemary. (2017). Power Transitions and Great Power Management: Three Decades of China – Japan – US Relations. *The Pacific Review*, 30(6), 829–842.

Francis, David R. (1982, September 8). US Delays, but World Bank Funds Likely to Continue. *Christian Science Monitor.*

Fried, Stephanie. (2015). Concerns About the AIIB Exclusion List and a Comparison with the ADB Prohibited Investment List, IFC Project Exclusion List, and Investments Prohibited Under World Bank Safeguards. *Ulu Foundaion.* Retrieved from https://goo.gl/DjHvW5

Fu, Jing. (2015, April 10). Belgium's Mixed Signals to China. *China Daily Europe.* Retrieved from http://europe.chinadaily.com.cn/epaper/2015-04/10/content_20043373.htm

The Future of the Multilateral Development Banks Subcommittee on Monetary Policy and Trade of the Committee on Financial Services 114th Sess (2015).

Gabusi, Giuseppe. (2017). "Crossing the River by Feeling the Gold": The Asian Infrastructure Investment Bank and the Financial Support to the Belt and Road Initiative. *China & World Economy*, 25(5), 23–45.

Gallup. (2015). The US-Global Leadership Report: What People Worldwide Think of US Leadership. Retrieved from https://www.meridian.org/wp-content/uploads/2015/07/US_Global_Leadership_Report_05_15_2015.pdf

Garlick, Jeremy. (2017). If You Can't Beat'em, Join'em: Shaping India's Response to China's 'Belt and Road'Gambit. *China Report*, 53(2), 143–157.

Garlick, Jeremy. (2018). Deconstructing the China – Pakistan Economic Corridor: Pipe Dreams Versus Geopolitical Realities. *Journal of Contemporary China*, 27(112), 519–533.

Gibler, Douglas M. (2009). *International Military Alliances, 1648–2008.* Washington, DC: CQ Press.

Gill, Indermit S., & Pugatch, Todd (Eds.). (2005). *At the Frontlines of Development: Reflections from the World Bank.* Washington, DC: The World Bank.

Gilpin, Robert. (1981). *War and Change in World Politics.* Cambridge, MA: Cambridge University Press.

Global Times. (2014, March 29). China, Germany Establish Comprehensive Strategic Partnership. *Global Times.* Retrieved from https://www.globaltimes.cn/content/851501.shtml

Goh, Brenda. (2014, October 24). Three Major Nations Absent as China Launches W. Bank Rival in Asia. *Reuters.* Retrieved from https://www.reuters.com/article/china-aiib-three-major-nations-absent-as-china-launches-w-bank-rival-in-asia-idINKCN0ID09520141024

GRAIN. (2019, February 18). The Belt and Road Initiative: Chinese Agribusiness Going Global. *GRAIN.* Retrieved from https://www.grain.org/en/article/6133-the-belt-and-road-initiative-chinese-agribusiness-going-global

Greenfield, Charlotte. (2019, May 22). Vanuatu to Seek More Belt and Road Assistance from Beijing: PM. *Reuters.* Retrieved from https://www.reuters.com/article/us-pacific-china-vanuatu/vanuatu-to-seek-more-belt-and-road-assistance-from-beijing-pm-idUSKCN1SS0R7

Hamanaka, Shintaro. (2016). Insights to Great Powers' Desire to Establish Institutions: Comparison of ADB, AMF, AMRO and AIIB. *Global Policy*, 7(2), 288–292.

He, Kai. (2008). Institutional Balancing and International Relations Theory: Economic Interdependence and Balance of Power Strategies in Southeast Asia. *European Journal of International Relations*, 14(3), 489–518.

He, Alex. (2016). *The Dragon's Footprints: China in the Global Economic Governance System Under the G20 Framework*. Waterloo, Ontario: Centre for International Governance Innovation.

He, Kai, & Feng, Huiyun. (2019). Leadership Transition and Global Governance: Role Conception, Institutional Balancing, and the AIIB. *The Chinese Journal of International Politics*, 12(2), 153–178.

Hecan, Mehmet. (2016). Dynamics of Institutional Proliferation in Financing for Development: The Birth of the AIIB. *Development*, 59(1–2), 158–166.

Henry, M. Paulson, Jr. (2015). *Dealing with China: An Insider Unmasks the new Economic Superpower* (1st ed.). New York, NY: Twelve.

Herlijanto, Johannes. (2017, December 4). Public Perceptions of China in Indonesia: The Indonesia National Survey. *Perspective* (89). Singapore: ISEAS-Yusof Ishak Institute. Retrieved from https://www.iseas.edu.sg/images/pdf/ISEAS_Perspective_2017_89.pdf

Heydarian, Richard Javad. (2015, April 8). China's Plan to Obliterate American Supremacy. *The National Interest*. Retrieved from https://nationalinterest.org/feature/chinas-plan-obliterate-american-supremacy-12577

Higgins, Andrew, & Sangermarch, David E. (2015, March 17). 3 European Powers Say They Will Join China-Led Bank. *New York Times*. Retrieved from http://nyti.ms/18WEHrs

Hirsch, Thomas, Bartosch, Sophie, Anqi, Yao, Hongyu, Guo, Menshova, Yulia, Padhi, Ajita Tiwari, & Shamsuddoha, Md. (2019). *Aligning the Asian Infrastructure Investment Bank (AIIB) with the Paris Agreement and the SDGs: Challenges and Opportunities*. Bonn, Germany: Germanwatch. Retrieved from https://www.germanwatch.org/en/16354

Hornby, Lucy, & Smyth, Jamie. (2018, November 15). China-Australia Rivalry Heats Up Over Pacific Islands. *Financial Times*. Retrieved from https://www.ft.com/content/6a2e1e2c-e7f5-11e8-8a85-04b8afea6ea3

Horridge, Mark, Yusuf, Arief A., Ginting, Edimon, & Aji, Priasto. (2016). Improving Indonesia's Domestic Connectivity: An Inter-Regional CGE Analysis. *ADB Papers on Indonesia* (17). Metro Manila, Philippines: Asian Development Bank. Retrieved from https://www.adb.org/sites/default/files/publication/217206/ino-paper-17-2016.pdf

Horsefield, J. Keith, & De Vries, Margaret Garritsen. (1969). *The International Monetary Fund, 1945–1965; Twenty Years of International Monetary Cooperation*. Washington, DC: International Monetary Fund.

Howes, Stephen, Davies, Robin, & Betteridge, Ashlee. (2013, April 27). Asian Development Bank Defies G20. *East Asia Forum*. Retrieved from https://www.eastasiaforum.org/2013/04/27/asian-development-bank-defies-g20/

Hsieh, John Fuh-sheng. (2015). Taiwan in 2014: A Besieged President Amid Political Turmoil. *Asian Survey*, 55(1), 142–147.

Huang, Zhiyong, Tan, Chunzhi, & Lei, Xiaohua. (2013). Choujian yazhou jichu sheshi touzi yinhang de jiben silu ji duice [Ideas and Countermeasures for the Establishment of the Asian Infrastructure Investment Bank]. *Dongnanya zongheng [Around Southeast Asia]* (10), 3–9.

Ikenberry, G. John, & Lim, Darren J. (2017). *China's Emerging Institutional Statecraft: The Asian Infrastructure Investment Bank and the Prospects for Counter-Hegemony.* Washington, DC: Brookings. Retrieved from https://www.brookings.edu/wp-content/uploads/2017/04/chinas-emerging-institutional-statecraft.pdf

Interfax. (2016, Jun 28). Kazakh Economy Minister Appointed Governor Representing Kazakhstan to Asian Infrastructure Investment Bank. *Interfax: Central Asia & Caucasus Business Weekly.* Aurora, CO: Interfax America, Inc.

International Bank for Reconstruction and Development. (2019). Minutes of Meeting of the Executive Directors of the Bank and IDA Held in the Board Room on Thursday, June 24, 1999 at 10:11 a.m. Retrieved from https://www.adb.org/sites/default/files/institutional-document/486696/m34-18-13dec18.pdf

International Monetary Fund. (2010). IMF Executive Board Approves Major Overhaul of Quotas and Governance. (10/418). Retrieved from https://www.imf.org/external/np/sec/pr/2010/pr10418.htm

Ito, Takatoshi. (2015). *The Future of the Asian Infrastructure Investment Bank: Concerns for Transparency and Governance.* New York, NY: Center on Japanese Economy and Business, Columbia University. Retrieved from https://academiccommons.columbia.edu/doi/10.7916/D86M3GFV/download

Iwanek, Krzysztof. (2019, September 6). Fully Invested: India Remains the China-Led AIIB's Biggest Borrower. *The Diplomat.* Retrieved from https://thediplomat.com/2019/09/fully-invested-india-remains-the-china-led-aiibs-biggest-borrower/

Jacob, Jabin T. (2017). China's Belt and Road Initiative: Perspectives from India. *China & World Economy*, 25(5), 78–100.

Jacobson, Harold Karan, & Oksenberg, Michel. (1990). *China's Participation in the IMF, the World Bank, and GATT: Toward a Global Economic Order.* Ann Arbor, Michigan: University of Michigan Press.

Jaishankar, Subrahmanyam. (2015, March 2). *Speech by Foreign Secretary at Raisina Dialogue in New Delhi.* Retrieved from https://mea.gov.in/Speeches-Statements.htm?dtl/26433/Speech_by_Foreign_Secretary_at_Raisina_Dialogue_in_New_Delhi_March_2_2015

The Japan Times. (2015, April 16). Germany's Merkel Urged Japan to Join AIIB: Sources. Retrieved from https://www.japantimes.co.jp/news/2015/04/16/business/germanys-merkel-urged-japan-join-aiib-sources

Jin, Liqun. (1997). Jin liqun buzhang zhuli de jianghua [Remarks from the Assistant Minister, Jin Liqun]. *Caizheng yanjiu [Public Finance Research]* (1), 7–9.

Kajimoto, Tetsushi. (2015, March 20). Japan Split on Joining AIIB Bank, Caught Between US, China. *Reuters*, p. 1. Retrieved from https://www.reuters.com/article/us-asia-aiib-japan-idUSKBN0MG07Y20150320

Kang, David C. (2003). Getting Asia Wrong: The Need for New Analytical Frameworks. *International Security*, 27(4), 57–85.

Kastner, Scott L., & Saunders, Phillip C. (2012). Is China a Status Quo or Revisionist State? Leadership Travel as an Empirical Indicator of Foreign Policy Priorities. *International Studies Quarterly*, 56(1), 163–177.

Kastner, Scott L., Pearson, Margaret M., & Rector, Chad. (2018). *China's Strategic Multilateralism: Investing in Global Governance.* Cambridge, MA: Cambridge University Press.

Katada, Saori. (2016). At the Crossroads: The TPP, AIIB, and Japan's Foreign Economic Strategy. *AsiaPacific Issues* (125). Retrieved from https://www.eastwestcenter.org/system/tdf/private/api125.pdf?file=1&type=node&id=35659

Katzenstein, Peter, & Sil, Rudra. (2008). Eclectic Theorizing in the Study and Practice of International Relations. In Christian Reus-Smit & Duncan Snidal (Eds.), *The Oxford Handbook of International Relations* (pp. 109–130). New York, NY: Oxford University Press.

Kaufmann, Daniel, Kraay, Aart, & Mastruzzi, Massimo. (2010). *The Worldwide Governance Indicators: Methodology and Analytical Issues* (Policy Research Working Paper 5430). Retrieved from https://openknowledge.worldbank.org/handle/10986/3913

Kaya, Ayse, & Woo, Byungwon. (2018). *China and the Asian Infrastructure Investment Bank: The Influence-Legitimacy Tradeoff*. Paper presented at the The 11th Annual Conference on The Political Economy of International Organizations, Madison, Wisconsin.

Kazinform. (2017, October 30). Law on Kazakhstan's Membership in Int'l Financial Organizations Amended. *Kazinform*. Retrieved from http://lenta.inform.kz/en/law-on-kazakhstan-s-membership-in-int-l-financial-organizations-amended_a3080270

Kembayev, Zhenis. (2018). Development of China – Kazakhstan Cooperation. *Problems of Post-Communism*. doi:10.1080/10758216.2018.1545590

Keohane, Robert O. (1984). *After Hegemony: Cooperation and Discord in the World Political Economy*. Princeton, N.J.: Princeton University Press.

Keohane, Robert O., & Martin, Lisa L. (1995). The Promise of Institutionalist Theory. *International Security*, 20(1), 39–51.

Kilby, Christopher. (2006). Donor Influence in Multilateral Development Banks: The Case of the Asian Development Bank. *The Review of International Organizations*, 1(2), 173–195.

Kilby, Christopher. (2009). The Political Economy of Conditionality: An Empirical Analysis of World Bank Loan Disbursements. *Journal of Development Economics*, 89(1), 51–61.

Kim, Dong Jung. (2020). Unfaithful Allies? US Security Clients in China-Led International Institutions. *International Relations of the Asia-Pacific*, 20(1), 61–90.

Kim, Jisan. (2016). Regulating Economic Development: Environmental and Social Standards of the AIIB and the IFC. *Harvard Journal of International Law*. Retrieved from https://harvardilj.org/2016/04/regulating-economic-development-environmental-and-social-standards-of-the-aiib-and-the-ifc/

Kim, Woosang. (1991). Alliance Transitions and Great Power War. *American Journal of Political Science*, 35(4), 833–850.

Kliman, Daniel, Doshi, Rush, Lee, Kristine, & Cooper, Zack. (2019). *Grading China's Belt and Road*. Washington, DC: Center for a New American Security. Retrieved from https://www.cnas.org/publications/reports/beltandroad

Knoerich, Jan, & Urdinez, Francisco. (2019). Contesting Contested Multilateralism: Why the West Joined the Rest in Founding the Asian Infrastructure Investment Bank. *The Chinese Journal of International Politics*, 12(3), 333–370.

Koh, Gui Qing. (2015, September 2). Exclusive: China's AIIB to Offer Loans with Fewer Strings Attached – Sources. *Reuters*. Retrieved from https://www.reuters.com/article/us-aiib-china-loans/exclusive-chinas-aiib-to-offer-loans-with-fewer-strings-attached-sources-idUSKCN0R14UB20150901

Koremenos, Barbara, Lipson, Charles, & Snidal, Duncan. (2001). The Rational Design of International Institutions. *International Organization*, 55(4), 761–799.

Kumar, Manoj, & Munroe, Tony. (2014, November 6). For India, China-Backed Lender May Be Answer to Coal Investment. *Reuters*. Retrieved from https://www.reuters.com/article/us-india-aiib-insight/for-india-china-backed-lender-may-be-answer-to-coal-investment-idUSKBN0IP2S020141106

Kundnani, Hans, & Parello-Plesner, Jonas. (2012). China and Germany: Why the Emerging Special Relationship Matters for Europe. *ECFR Policy Briefs* (ECFR/55). Berlin, Germany: European Council on Foreign Relations. Retrieved from https://www.files. ethz.ch/isn/173460/ECFR55_CHINA_GERMANY_BRIEF_AW.pdf

Kynge, James. (2017, May 4). AIIB Chief Unveils Aim to Rival Lenders Such as ADB and World Bank. *Financial Times*. Retrieved from https://www.ft.com/content/3a938ee4-0288-11e7-aa5b-6bb07f5c8e12

LaForgia, Rebecca. (2017). Listening to China's Multilateral Voice for the First Time: Analysing the Asian Infrastructure Investment Bank for Soft Power Opportunities and Risks in the Narrative of 'Lean, Clean and Green'. *Journal of Contemporary China*, 26(107), 633–649.

Lam, Peng Er. (2014). China's Asian Infrastructure Investment Bank: East Asian Responses. *East Asian Policy*, 6(4), 127–135.

Lane, Max. (2015, August 18). The Politics of Widodo's Prioritisation of Accelerated Infrastructure Construction. *Perspective* (43). Singapore: ISEAS-Yusof Ishak Institute. Retrieved from https://iseas.edu.sg/images/pdf/ISEAS_Perspective_2015_43.pdf

Lardy, Nicholas R. (1999). China and the International Financial System. In Elizabeth Economy & Michel Oksenberg (Eds.), *China Joins the World: Progress and Prospects* (pp. 206–230). New York, NY: Council on Foreign Relations Press.

Larsen, Gaia, & Gilbert, Sean. (2016, March 4). Asian Infrastructure Investment Bank Releases New Environmental and Social Standards. How Do They Stack up? *World Resources Institute*. Retrieved from https://www.wri.org/blog/2016/03/asian-infrastructure-investment-bank-releases-new-environmental-and-social-standards

Larson, Deborah Welch, & Shevchenko, Alexei. (2014). Managing Rising Powers: The Role of Status Concerns. In Deborah Welch Larson, T. V. Paul, & William C. Wohlforth (Eds.), *Status in World Politics* (pp. 33–57). Cambridge, MA.: Cambridge University Press.

Lederman, Daniel, Loayza, Norman V., & Soares, Rodrigo R. (2005). Accountability and Corruption: Political Institutions Matter. *Economics & Politics*, 17(1), 1–35.

Li, Tania M. (2011). Rendering Society Technical: Government Through Community and the Ethnographic Turn at the World Bank in Indonesia. In David Mosse (Ed.), *Adventures in Aidland: The Anthropology of Professionals in International Development* (pp. 57–80). Oxford, UK: Berghahn.

Li, Xiang. (2016, June 6). AIIB Will Have 100 Countries as Members by Year-End, Says the Bank's President Jin Liqun. *The Telegraph*. Retrieved from https://www.telegraph. co.uk/sponsored/business/12210676/asian-infrastructure-investment-bank-growth.html

Liao, Rebecca. (2015, July 27). Out of the Bretton Woods: How the AIIB is Different. *Foreign Affairs*. Retrieved from https://www.foreignaffairs.com/articles/asia/2015-07-27/out-bretton-woods

Liao, Janet Xuanli. (2019). China's Energy Diplomacy Towards Central Asia and the Implications on its "Belt and Road Initiative". *The Pacific Review*, 1–33. doi:10.1080/09512748.2019.1705882

Liao, Jessica C., & Dang, Ngoc-Tram. (2020). The Nexus of Security and Economic Hedging: Vietnam's Strategic Response to Japan – China Infrastructure Financing Competition. *The Pacific Review*, 33(3–4), 669–696.

Lichtenstein, Natalie. (2019). AIIB at Three: A Comparative and Institutional Perspective. *Global Policy*, 10(4), 582–586.

Lim, Daniel Yew Mao, & Vreeland, James Raymond. (2013). Regional Organizations and International Politics: Japanese Influence Over the Asian Development Bank and the UN Security Council. *World Politics*, 65(1), 34–72.

Lin, Leo. (2019). A State Visit by Kazakhstan's President Demonstrates China's Increasing Influence in Central Asia. *China Brief*, 19(20), 10–15.

Lipscy, Phillip Y. (2015a). Explaining Institutional Change: Policy Areas, Outside Options, and the Bretton Woods Institutions. *American Journal of Political Science*, 59(2), 341–356.

Lipscy, Phillip Y. (2015b, May 7). Who's Afraid of the AIIB?: Why the US Should Support China's Asian Infrastructure Investment Bank. *Foreign Affairs*. Retrieved from https://www.foreignaffairs.com/articles/china/2015-05-07/whos-afraid-aiib

Liu, Lei. (2007). Yige zhanzai yazhou jinrong langjian shang de zhongguoren [The Chinese National Who Surfs the Sea of Finance in Asia]. *Zhongguo jinrongjia [China Financialyst]* (8), 5–15.

Long, Jing. (2014). Relations between China and CEE Countries: Development, Challenges and Recommendations. *China International Studies* (5), 44–60.

Lowy Institute. (2019). *Lowy Institute Asia Power Index 2019*. Sydney, Australia: Lowy Institute. Retrieved from https://power.lowyinstitute.org/downloads/Lowy-Institute-Asia-Power-Index-2019-Pocket-Book.pdf

Lyons, Kate. (2019, August 27). Why is Indonesia Moving its Capital City? Everything You Need to Know. *The Guardian*. Retrieved from https://www.theguardian.com/world/2019/aug/27/why-is-indonesia-moving-its-capital-city-everything-you-need-to-know

Lyons, Kate. (2020, January 7). 'On Right Side of History': Xi Jinping Praises Kiribati for Switch to China. *The Guardian*. Retrieved from https://www.theguardian.com/world/2020/jan/07/china-xi-jinping-praises-kiribati-for-switch-taiwan

Magnier, Mark. (2015, June 08). How China Plans to Run AIIB: Leaner, with Veto. *Wall Street Journal*.

Maher, Richard. (2016). The Elusive EU – China Strategic Partnership. *International Affairs*, 92(4), 959–976.

The Mainichi. (2017, November 30). Deputy PM Aso Doubts AIIB 'Knowhow,' 'Waiting to See' China-Backed Bank's Results. *The Mainichi*. Retrieved from https://mainichi.jp/english/articles/20171130/p2a/00m/0na/010000c

Malan, Franck A. (2018). Does Being an IMF Executive Board Member (Re)Pay? An Examination of IMF Loans and Repayments. *The World Economy*, 41(10), 2669–2690.

Malkin, Anton, & Momani, Bessma. (2016). An Effective Asian Infrastructure Investment Bank: A Bottom Up Approach. *Global Policy*, 7(4), 521–530.

Malpass, David. (2018). *Statement of Under Secretary David Malpass Before the US House Financial Services Subcommittee on Monetary Policy and Trade*. Washington, DC: US Department of the Treasury. Retrieved from https://home.treasury.gov/news/press-releases/sm572

Marshall, Monty G., Gurr, Ted Robert, & Jaggers, Keith. (2014). *Polity™ IV Project: Political Regime Characteristics and Transitions, 1800–2013*. Vienna, Virginia, The Center for Systemic Peace

Martin, Lisa L. (1992). Interests, Power, and Multilateralism. *International Organization*, 46(4), 765–792.

Mayeda, Andrew. (2015, December 19). Congress Approves IMF Change in Favor of Emerging Markets. *Bloomberg*. Retrieved from https://www.bloomberg.com/news/articles/2015-12-18/congress-approves-imf-changes-giving-emerging-markets-more-sway

McCawley, Peter. (2017). *Banking on the Future of Asia and the Pacific: 50 Years of the Asian Development Bank*. Metro Manila, Philippines: Asian Development Bank.

McDonald, Ian. (1972, February 17). Mr Nixon Goes to Peking as Apostle of New Era. *The Times*, p. 6.

Mearsheimer, John J. (1994). The False Promise of International Institutions. *International Security*, 19(3), 5–49.

Mendel, Toby, & Summers, Elizabeth. (2016). *Comments on the Public Information Interim Policy of the Asian Infrastructure Investment Bank*. Halifax, Nova Scotia: Centre for Law and Democracy. Retrieved from https://www.law-democracy.org/live/wp-content/uploads/2016/12/AIIB-Note-on-Interim-Policy.pdf

Mendez, Alvaro. (2019). Latin America and the AIIB: Interests and Viewpoints. *Global Policy*, 10(4), 639–644.

Mietzner, Marcus. (2015). Indonesia in 2014: Jokowi and the Repolarization of Post-Soeharto Politics. *Southeast Asian Affairs*, 117–138.

Ministry of Finance, Taiwan. (2015). *Report on the Benefits and Risk Assessment Regarding Taiwan's Application for Joining the AIIB*. Ministry of Finance, Taiwan: Taipei, Taiwan.

Ministry of Foreign Affairs, Romania. (2016). *Romania's Accession to the Asian Infrastructure Investment Bank*. Bucharest, Romania. Retrieved from https://www.mae.ro/en/node/41791

Möller, Kay. (1996). Germany and China: A Continental Temptation. *The China Quarterly*, 147, 706–725.

Molokovitch, Anatoli. (2019). *Logistics and Transport Competitiveness in Kazakhstan*. Geneva, Switzerland: The United Nations Economic Commission for Europe.

Mukhtarov, Daniyar. (2014, May 5). China Interested in Energy Cooperation with Kazakhstan. *McClatchy-Tribune Business News*.

Muna, Fauzul. (2018, July 25). Indonesia's Logistics Performance Remains Poor. *The Insider Stories*. Retrieved from https://theinsiderstories.com/indonesias-logistics-performance-remains-poor/

Nakamichi, Takashi. (2013, February 27). Japan Gears Up for ADB Presidential Race. *Wall Street Journal*.

Nanwani, Suresh. (2019). Belt and Road Initiative: Responses from Japan and India – Bilateralism, Multilateralism and Collaborations. *Global Policy*, 10(2), 284–289.

Naughton, Barry. (2007). *The Chinese Economy: Transitions and Growth*. Cambridge, MA: MIT Press.

Nelson, Stephen C. (2014). Playing Favorites: How Shared Beliefs Shape the IMF's Lending Decisions. *International Organization*, 68(2), 297–328.

New York Times. (1971, January 29). Tanzania-Zambia Railway: A Bridge to China? p. 65.

New York Times News Service. (1989, October 2). World Bank Refuses to Lift Loan Ban on China. *Chicago Tribune*, p. 4.

Nikkei. (2015, June 24). Yan Xuetong: Zhongmei niandi huoyou yanzhong chongtu [Yan Xuetong: There Might Be Serious Sino-US Conflict in the End of the Year]. *Rijing Zhongwenwang [NIKKEI Chinese]*. Retrieved from http://zh.cn.nikkei.com/column viewpoint/viewpoint/14919-20150624.html?start=1

Nikkei Asian Review. (2015, March 31). Japan Puts off Decision. Retrieved from https://asia.nikkei.com/Economy/Japan-puts-off-decision

Obama, Barack. (2015). *Remarks by President Obama and Prime Minister Abe of Japan in Joint Press Conference*. Washington DC: The White House. Retrieved from https://obamawhitehouse.archives.gov/the-press-office/2015/04/28/remarks-president-obama-and-prime-minister-abe-japan-joint-press-confere

OECD. (2017). Reforming Kazakhstan: Progress, Challenges and Opportunities. Retrieved from https://www.oecd.org/eurasia/countries/OECD-Eurasia-Reforming-Kazakhstan-EN.pdf

Oehler-Şincai, Iulia Monica. (2016). Determinants, Goals and Different Approaches of the 16+1 Strategic Cooperation Framework. *Global Economic Observer*, 4(2), 74–85.

O'Neill, Jim. (2011). Building Better Global Economic BRICs. *Global Economics Paper* (66). New York, NY: Goldman Sachs. Retrieved from https://www.goldmansachs.com/insights/archive/archive-pdfs/build-better-brics.pdf

O'Neill, Jim. (2015). *UK Signs Founding Articles of Agreement of the Asian Infrastructure Investment Bank*. London, UK. Retrieved from https://www.gov.uk/government/news/uk-signs-founding-articles-of-agreement-of-the-asian-infrastructure-investment-bank

Ong, David M. (2017). The Asian Infrastructure Investment Bank: Bringing 'Asian Values' to Global Economic Governance? *Journal of International Economic Law*, 20(3), 535–560.

Organski, A. F. K. (1968). *World Politics* (2nd ed.). New York, NY: Knopf.

Osaki, Tomohiro. (2019, June 25). In Blow to China, Japan's 'Quality Infrastructure' to Get Endorsement at Osaka G20. *The Japan Times*. Retrieved from https://www.japantimes.co.jp/news/2019/06/25/business/economy-business/blow-china-japans-quality-infrastructure-get-endorsement-osaka-g20/#.Xj6cB2gzaCg

Otto, Ben. (2015, April 10). China-Led Bank to Focus on Big-Ticket Projects, Indonesia Says. *The Wall Street Journal*. Retrieved from https://www.wsj.com/articles/china-led-aiib-to-focus-on-big-ticket-projects-indonesia-says-1428647276

Paelinck, Gianni. (2015, June 24). België kandidaat-lid Aziatische investeringsbank (Belgium Becomes a Candidate in AIIB). *Deredactie.Be*. Retrieved from http://deredactie.be/cm/vrtnieuws/economie/1.2375052

Page, Jeremy. (2014, November 9). China Sees Itself at Center of New Asian Order. *The Wall Street Journal*. Retrieved from https://www.wsj.com/articles/chinas-new-trade-routes-center-it-on-geopolitical-map-1415559290?tesla=y

Palma, Stefania. (2019, December 1). Indonesia Eyes China-Backed AIIB to Fund New Capital City. *Financial Times*. Retrieved from https://www.ft.com/content/868ab026-10e9-11ea-a7e6-62bf4f9e548a

Panda, Ankit. (2015, March 28). South Korea Joins the AIIB. *The Diplomat*. Retrieved from https://thediplomat.com/2015/03/south-korea-joins-the-aiib/

Panda, Ankit. (2018, March 19). If India won't Put up with the Belt and Road, Why is it the Largest Recipient of AIIB Funds? *The Diplomat*. Retrieved from https://thediplomat.com/2018/03/if-india-wont-put-up-with-the-belt-and-road-why-is-it-the-largest-recipient-of-aiib-funds/

Pang, Dongmei. (2014, July 1). Yatouhang jiangcheng zhengfujian xingzhi duobian kaifa yinheng [The AIIB Will Become Intergovernmental Multilateral Development Bank]. *Jinrong shibao [Financial News]*, p. 005.

Parameswaran, Prashanth. (2019, July 9). Where is Indonesia on China's Belt and Road Initiative? *The Diplomat*. Retrieved from https://thediplomat.com/2019/07/where-is-indonesia-on-chinas-belt-and-road-initiative/

Parker, Sam, & Chefitz, Gabrielle. (2018). *Debtbook Diplomacy: China's Strategic Leveraging of its Newfound Economic Influence and the Consequences for US Foreign Policy*. Cambridge, MA: Belfer Center for Science and International Affairs, Harvard Kennedy School. Retrieved from https://www.belfercenter.org/publication/debtbook-diplomacy

Peceny, Mark, Beer, Caroline C., & Sanchez-Terry, Shannon. (2002). Dictatorial Peace? *American Political Science Review*, 96(1), 15–26.

Peng, Zhongzhou, & Tok, Sow Keat. (2016). The AIIB and China's Normative Power in International Financial Governance Structure. *Chinese Political Science Review*, 1(4), 736–753.

People's Daily. (2004, June 14). China, Romania Pledge to Work for Full-Range Partnership Relations. Retrieved from http://en.people.cn/200406/14/eng20040614_146237.html

People's Daily. (2013, March 21). Xi Jinping da jinzhuan guojia jizhe wen [Xi Jinping Answers Questions from BRICS Countries' Reporters]. Retrieved from http://cpc.people.com.cn/BIG5/n/2013/0321/c64094-20862471.html

Perlez, Jane. (2006, September 18). China Competes with West in Aid to its Neighbors. *New York Times*, p. A1.

Perlez, Jane. (2014, October 10). US Opposing China's Answer to World Bank. *New York Times*, p. A1.

Perlez, Jane. (2015, December 5). Beijing's Rival to World Bank Moves Forward Without US *New York Times*, p. A1.

Perlez, Jane, & Cochrane, Joe. (2013, October 8). Obama's Absence Leaves China as Dominant Force at Asia-Pacific Meeting. *New York Times*, p. A8.

Popescu, Liliana, & Brînză, Andreea. (2018). Romania-China Relations: Political and Economic Challenges in the BRI Era. *Romanian Journal of European Affairs*, 18(2), 20–38.

Prinsloo, Cyril. (2019). AIIB Membership for African Countries: Drawcards and Drawbacks. *Global Policy*, 10(4), 625–630.

Rajah, Roland, Dayant, Alexandre, & Pryke, Jonathan. (2019). *Ocean of Debt? Belt and Road and Debt Diplomacy in the Pacific*. Sydney, Australia: Lowy Institute. Retrieved from https://www.lowyinstitute.org/publications/ocean-debt-belt-and-road-and-debt-diplomacy-pacific

Rajasingham, Sanjivi. (2017). *7 Priorities for Infrastructure Investment in the Pacific*. Metro Manila, Philippines: Asian Development Bank. Retrieved from https://blogs.adb.org/blog/7-priorities-infrastructure-investment-pacific

Raman, K. Ravi. (2009). Asian Development Bank, Policy Conditionalities and the Social Democratic Governance: Kerala Model Under Pressure? *Review of International Political cal Economy*, 16(2), 284–308.

Reisen, Helmut. (2015). Will the AIIB and the NDB Help Reform Multilateral Development Banking? *Global Policy*, 6(3), 297–304.

Ren, Xiao. (2016). China as an Institution-Builder: The Case of the AIIB. *The Pacific Review*, 29(3), 435–442.

Renard, Thomas. (2015a). The Asian Infrastructure Investment Bank (AIIB): China's New Multilateralism and the Erosion of the West. *EGMONT Secutiry Policy Brief* (63). Retrieved from http://aei.pitt.edu/64789/1/SPB63-Renard.pdf

Renard, Thomas. (2015b). To Join or Not to Join: The AIIB and the EU's Dilemma. *EGMONT: Royal Institute for International Relations*. Retrieved from https://www.egmontinstitute.be/publication_article/to-join-or-not-to-join-the-aiib-and-the-eus-dilemma/

Renshon, Jonathan. (2017). *Fighting for Status: Hierarchy and Conflict in World Politics*. Princeton, New Jersey: Princeton University Press.

Rodina, Mihaela. (2016). US Missile Shield Begins Operations in Romania to Russian Anger. *Defense News*. Retrieved from https://www.defensenews.com/story/defense/international/europe/2016/05/12/us-missile-shield-begins-operations-romania-russian-anger/84275982/

Rolland, Nadège. (2017). China's "Belt and Road Initiative": Underwhelming or Game-Changer? *The Washington Quarterly*, 40(1), 127–142.

Rosenzweig, Joshua. (2016, June 24). The AIIB and Human Rights. *The Diplomat.* Retrieved from https://thediplomat.com/2016/06/the-aiib-and-human-rights/

Rosser, Andrew, & Tubilewicz, Czeslaw. (2016). Emerging Donors and New Contests Over Aid Policy in Pacific Asia. *The Pacific Review*, 29(1), 5–19.

Rowley, Anthony. (2014, November 14). Leading Development Banks Wary of New EM Entrants. *The Business Times.* Retrieved from https://www.businesstimes.com.sg/banking-finance/leading-development-banks-wary-of-new-em-entrants

Rust, Susanne. (2019, December 31). They Came Here After the US Irradiated Their Islands. Now They Face an Uncertain Future. *Los Angeles Times.* Retrieved from https://www.latimes.com/world-nation/story/2019-12-31/marshall-islands-uncertain-future-us-marshallese-spokane

Sachdeva, Gulshan. (2018). Indian Perceptions of the Chinese Belt and Road Initiative. *International Studies*, 55(4), 285–296.

Sakaguchi, Yukihiro. (2019, April 17). Japan Pushes Asian Development Bank to End China Loans. *Nikkei Asian Review.* Retrieved from https://asia.nikkei.com/Politics/International-relations/Japan-pushes-Asian-Development-Bank-to-end-China-loans

Sanders, Gerard J. (2017). The Asian Infrastructure Investment Bank and the Belt and Road Initiative: Complementarities and Contrasts. *Chinese Journal of International Law*, 16(2), 367–371.

Sanger, David E. (1999, June 25). China to Get World Bank Loan Despite US Objections. *New York Times*, p. A12.

Schiefelbein, Mark. (2016, December 6). Civil Society Analysis Finds AIIB Access to Information Policy Needs Improvement. *Reuters.* Retrieved from https://www.bankinformationcenter.org/asian-infrastructure-bank-access-to-information-policy-weak/

Schwab, Klaus (Ed.). (2015). *The Global Competitiveness Report 2015–2016.* Geneva, Switzerland: World Economic Forum.

Schwab, Klaus (Ed.). (2016). *The Global Competitiveness Report 2016–2017.* Geneva, Switzerland: World Economic Forum.

Scissors, Derek. (2020). China's Global Investment in 2019: Going out Goes Small. *AEI Reports.* Retrieved from https://www.aei.org/wp-content/uploads/2020/01/Chinas-global-investment-in-2019-1.pdf

Scobell, Andrew. (2012). Learning to Rise Peacefully? China and the Security Dilemma. *Journal of Contemporary China*, 21(76), 713–721.

Sehrawat, Vivek. (2019). Reforming the World Bank to Transform India. *NUJS Law Review*, 10(4), 643–668.

Shah, Rishi, & Sikarwar, Deepshikha. (2011, April 29). India Unlikely to Support China's Renminbi as IMF Reserve Currency. *The Economic Times.* Retrieved from https://economictimes.indiatimes.com/news/economy/policy/india-unlikely-to-support-chinas-renminbi-as-imf-reserve-currency/articleshow/8113220.cms

Shambaugh, David. (2005). The New Strategic Triangle: US and European Reactions to China's Rise. *The Washington Quarterly*, 28(3), 5–25.

Shih, Hsiu-chuan. (2015a, April 1). Equality Necessary for AIIB Bid: Mao. *Taipei Times*, p. 1.

Shih, Hsiu-chuan. (2015b, March 28). Siew to Voice Taiwan's Interest in AIIB. *Taipei Times*, p. 1.

Simoes, Alexander James Gaspar, & Hidalgo, César A. (2011). *The Economic Complexity Observatory: An Analytical Tool for Understanding the Dynamics of Economic Development.* Paper presented at the Workshops at the Twenty-Fifth AAAI Conference on Artificial Intelligence.

Simonov, Eugene. (2016). Silk Road Project Suspended Over Threats to Lake Baikal. *Chinadialogue*. Retrieved from https://www.chinadialogue.net/article/show/single/en/9040-Silk-Road-project-suspended-over-threats-to-Lake-Baikal

Singer, J. David, Bremer, Stuart, & Stuckey, John. (1972). Capability Distribution, Uncertainty, and Major Power War, 1820–1965. In Bruce Russett (Ed.), *Peace, War, and Numbers* (pp. 19–48). Beverly Hills: Sage.

Snyder, Glenn H. (1997). *Alliance Politics*. Ithaca, NY: Cornell University Press.

Snyder, Jack L. (2004). One World: Rival Theories. *Foreign Policy* (145), 53–62.

Snyder, Francis. (2009). *The European Union and China, 1949–2008*. Portland, OR: Hart Publishing.

Sobolewski, Matthias, & Lange, Jason. (2015, March 17). US Urges Allies to Think Twice Before Joining China-Led Bank. *Reuters*. Retrieved from https://www.reuters.com/article/us-europe-asia-bank-idUSKBN0MD0B320150317

Stacey, Kiran, Mundy, Simon, & Feng, Emily. (2018, March 18). India Benefits from AIIB Loans Despite China Tensions. *Financial Times*. Retrieved from https://www.ft.com/content/da2258f6-2752-11e8-b27e-cc62a39d57a0

Stanciu, Ancuṭa. (2015, August 10). Romania's Option to Join the Asian Infrastructure Investment Bank in the Process of Being Reviewed. *Bursa (Romania)*. Retrieved from https://www.bursa.ro/romanias-option-to-join-the-asian-infrastructure-investment-bank-in-the-process-of-being-reviewed-276032&s=english_section&articol=276032.html

Standish, Reid. (2019a). China's Central Asian Plans are Unnerving Moscow. *Foreign Policy*. Retrieved from https://foreignpolicy.com/2019/12/23/china-russia-central-asia-competition/

Standish, Reid. (2019b). China's Path Forward is Getting Bumpy. *The Atlantic*. Retrieved from https://www.theatlantic.com/international/archive/2019/10/china-belt-road-initiative-problems-kazakhstan/597853/

Stanzel, Angela. (2017, April 21). *A German View of the Asian Infrastructure Investment Bank*. Berlin, Germany: European Council on Foreign Relations. Retrieved from https://www.ecfr.eu/article/commentary_a_german_view_of_the_aiib_7275

Steinmeier, Frank-Walter. (2016). Germany's New Global Role. *Foreign Affairs*, 95(4), 106–113.

Stiglitz, Joseph E. (2002). *Globalization and its Discontents* (1st ed.). New York: W. W. Norton.

Stone, Randall W. (2011). *Controlling Institutions: International Organizations and the Global Economy*. Cambridge, MA: Cambridge University Press.

The Straits Times. (2014). China-Backed Infrastructure Bank Draws Questions from Existing Players. Retrieved from https://www.straitstimes.com/business/banking/china-backed-infrastructure-bank-draws-questions-from-existing-players

Sun, Yun. (2015). China and the Changing Asian Infrastructure Bank. In *PacNet* (p. 43). Honolulu, Hawaii: Pacific Forum CSIS.

Suokas, Janne. (2016, June 3). Romania Seeks to Join Asian Infrastructure Investment Bank. *GBTIMES*. Retrieved from http://gbtimes.com/business/romania-seeks-join-asian-infrastructure-investment-bank

Suryadinata, Leo. (2016, April 26). Did the Natuna Incident Shake Indonesia-China Relations? *Perspective* (19). Singapore: ISEAS-Yusof Ishak Institute. Retrieved from https://www.iseas.edu.sg/images/pdf/ISEAS_Perspective_2016_19.pdf

Sutter, Robert G. (2008). *Chinese Foreign Relations: Power and Policy Since the Cold War*. Lanham, Maryland: Rowman & Littlefield.

Suzuki, Shogo. (2008). Seeking 'Legitimate' Great Power Status in Post-Cold War International Society: China's and Japan's Participation in UNPKO. *International Relations*, 22(1), 45–63.

Swaine, Michael D. (2015). Chinese Views and Commentary on the 'One Belt, One Road'Initiative. *China Leadership Monitor* (47). Retrieved from https://www.hoover.org/sites/default/files/research/docs/clm47ms.pdf

Szabo, Stephen F. (2009). Can Berlin and Washington Agree on Russia? *The Washington Quarterly*, 32(4), 23–41.

Taipei Times. (2015a, April 14). China Rejects Taiwan's AIIB Application, p. 1.

Taipei Times. (2015b, March 29). Siew Delivers Message to Xi as Boao Forum Opens, p. 1.

Taipei Times. (2015c, March 31). Taiwan Will Consider Joining AIIB: Hsia, p. 1.

Taiwan Indicators Survey Research. (2015). *News Release: Surevy on Taiwan Mood Barometer Survey, the AIIB and Cross-Strait Relations*. Taipei, Taiwan. Retrieved from https://www.tisr.com.tw/wp-content/uploads/2012/06/TISR_TMBS_201504_1.pdf

Tang, Siew Mun, Thuzar, Moe, Ha, Hoang Thi, Chalermpalanupap, Termsak, Thao, Pham Thi Phuong, & Qian, Anuthida Saelaow. (2019). *The State of Southeast Asia: 2019 Survey Report*. Singapore: ISEAS-Yusof Ishak Institute.

Tarrant, Bill. (2016, November 10). US Should Have Joined China-Led Infrastructure Bank: Trump Adviser. *Reuters*. Retrieved from https://www.reuters.com/article/us-usa-election-china-infrastructure-idUSKBN13519P

Taylor, Paul, & James, William. (2015, March 22). How Europe and US Stumbled into Spat Over China-Led Bank. *Reuters*. Retrieved from https://www.reuters.com/article/us-china-bank-europe-insight-idUSKBN0MI0ER20150322

Teng, Pei-ju. (2019, September 20). Kiribati Switches Recognition to China, Taiwan Loses Second Pacific Ally in One Week. *Taiwan News*. Retrieved from https://www.taiwannews.com.tw/en/news/3780704

Thacker, Strom C. (1999). The High Politics of IMF Lending. *World Politics*, 52(1), 38–75.

Thomas, Andrea, & Hutzler, Charles. (2015, March 17). Germany, France, Italy to Join China-Backed Development Bank. *Wall Street Journal*. Retrieved from https://www.wsj.com/articles/germany-france-italy-to-join-china-backed-development-bank-1426597078

Transparency International. (2014). *Corruption Perceptions Index 2014: Clean Growth at Risk*. Retrieved from https://www.transparency.org/cpi2014/press

Trinidad, Dennis. (2019). Strategic Foreign Aid Competition: Japanese and Chinese Assistance in the Philippine Infrastructure Sector. *Asian Affairs: An American Review*, 46(4), 89–122.

TVBS Poll Center. (2015). *Poll on Chi-Xi Meeting and the AIIB*. Taipei, Taiwan. Retrieved from https://cc.tvbs.com.tw/portal/file/poll_center/2017/20170602/20150423093338536.pdf

Udland, Myles. (2015, April 15). Hank Paulson: 'That's Bulls – T'. *Business Insider*. Retrieved from https://www.businessinsider.com/hank-paulson-on-asian-infrastructure-investment-bank-2015-4

The US Rebalance in East Asia: Budget Priorities for FY 2016. US House of Representatives, 114th Sess (2015, April 23). Retrieved from https://docs.house.gov/meetings/FA/FA05/20150423/103369/HHRG-114-FA05-Transcript-20150423.pdf

Valero, Jorge. (2018, June 26). Asian Investment Bank: 'We Could Invest in the EU'. *Fondation EURACTIV*. Retrieved from https://www.euractiv.com/section/eu-china/interview/asian-investment-bank-we-could-invest-in-the-eu/

Varrall, Merriden. (2016). Domestic Actors and Agendas in Chinese Aid Policy. *The Pacific Review*, 29(1), 21–44.

Vestergaard, Jakob, & Wade, Robert H. (2013). Protecting Power: How Western States Retain the Dominant Voice in the World Bank's Governance. *World Development*, 46, 153–164.

Vestergaard, Jakob, & Wade, Robert H. (2015). Still in the Woods: Gridlock in the IMF and the World Bank Puts Multilateralism at Risk. *Global Policy*, 6(1), 1–12.

Vieira, Vinícius Rodrigues. (2018). Who Joins Counter-Hegemonic IGOs? Early and Late Members of the China-Led Asian Infrastructure Investment Bank. *Research & Politics*, 5(2), 1–7.

Voeten, Erik, Strezhnev, Anton, & Bailey, Michael. (2016). *United Nations General Assembly Voting Data* (Publication no. hdl/1902.1/12379). Harvard Dataverse. http://hdl.handle.net/1902.1/12379

Vogl, Frank. (1980a, May 12). China Poised to Join World Bank in Move for Modern Economy. *The Times*, p. 6.

Vogl, Frank. (1980b, July 15). World Bank: The Problems Facing Mr McNamara's Successor. *The Times*, p. 6.

Volgy, Thomas J., Corbetta, Renato, Grant, Keith A., & Baird, Ryan G. (2011). Major Power Status in International Politics. In *Major Powers and the Quest for Status in International Politics* (pp. 1–26). London, UK: Palgrave Macmillan.

Wade, Robert Hunter. (2002). US Hegemony and the World Bank: The Fight Over People and Ideas. *Review of International Political Economy*, 9(2), 215–243.

Wall Street Journal. (1984, March 1). World Bank Sets Limit on Combined Amount of China, India Loans.

Wan, Ming. (2016). *The Asian Infrastructure Investment Bank: The Construction of Power and the Struggle for the East Asian International Order*. London, UK: Palgrave Macmillan.

Wang, Yu. (2018). The Political Economy of Joining the AIIB. *The Chinese Journal of International Politics*, 11(2), 105–130.

Wang, Xiaoguang. (2020). Leadership-Building Dilemmas in Emerging Powers' Economic Diplomacy: Russia's Energy Diplomacy and China's OBOR. *Asia Europe Journal*, 18(1), 117–138.

Watts, Jake Maxwell. (2015, September 19). Up to 20 Countries Waiting to Join China-Led AIIB, President-Designate Says; Jin Liqun Says Bank won't Favor Chinese Companies and Will Invest in Projects like Railroads and Power. *Wall Street Journal*.

Watts, Jonathan. (2019, April 25). Belt and Road Summit Puts Spotlight on Chinese Coal Funding. *The Guardian*. Retrieved from https://www.theguardian.com/world/2019/apr/25/belt-and-road-summit-puts-spotlight-on-chinese-coal-funding

Weatherbee, Donald E. (2017). Indonesia and China: The Bumpy Path to a Wary Partnership. In Lowell Dittmer & Chow Bing Ngeow (Eds.), *Southeast Asia and China: A Contest in Mutual Socialization* (pp. 131–159). Singapore: World Scientific.

Weaver, Catherine. (2015). The Rise of China: Continuity or Change in the Global Governance of Development? *Ethics & International Affairs*, 29(4), 419–431.

Wechsler, Pat. (1989, June 27). World Bank Delays China Loans Move Follows Bush Bid to Hold up Funds. *Newsday*, p. 47.

Wei, Lingling. (2016, January 22). China-Led Development Bank AIIB Will Be Lean, Clean and Green, Says its President. *Wall Street Journal*. Retrieved from https://www.wsj.com/articles/china-led-development-bank-will-be-lean-clean-and-green-says-head-1453479933

Wei, Lingling, & Davis, Bob. (2015, March 23). China Forgoes Veto Power at New Bank to Win Key European Nations' Support. *Wall Street Journal*. Retrieved from http://on.wsj.com/28SCSBv

Werner, Suzanne. (2000). The Effects of Political Similarity on the Onset of Militarized Disputes, 1816–1985. *Political Research Quarterly*, 53(2), 343–374.

White House Office of Trade and Manufacturing Policy. (2018). How China's Economic Aggression Threatens the Technologies and Intellectual Property of the US and the World. Retrieved from https://www.whitehouse.gov/wp-content/uploads/2018/06/FINAL-China-Technology-Report-6.18.18-PDF.pdf

Wihtol, Robert. (2014a). Whither Multilateral Development Finance? *ADBI Working Paper Series* (491). Tokyo, Japan: Asian Development Bank Institute. Retrieved from https://www.adbi.org/files/2014.07.21.wp491.whither.multilateral.dev.finance.pdf

Wihtol, Robert. (2015). Beijing's Challenge to the Global Financial Architecture. *Georgetown Journal of Asian Studies*, 2(1), 7–15.

Wilson, Jeffrey D. (2017). The Evolution of China's Asian Infrastructure Investment Bank: From a Revisionist to Status-Seeking Agenda. *International Relations of the Asia-Pacific*, 19(1), 147–176.

Witte, Michelle. (2015, May 12). China, Kazakhstan Agree to Align Development Strategies. *The Astana Times*. Retrieved from https://astanatimes.com/2015/05/china-kazakhstan-agree-to-align-development-strategies/

Wolf, Martin. (2010, March 16). China and Germany Unite to Impose Global Deflation. *Financial Times*. Retrieved from http://on.ft.com/1WgwhQm

Wolf, Charles, Jr. (2015). China's Foreign Aid Offensive. *The Weekly Standard*, 20(41), 17–18.

Wong, John, & Lye, Liang Fook. (2014). Reviving the Ancient Silk Road: China's New Diplomatic Initiative. *East Asian Policy*, 6(3), 5–15.

Woods, Ngaire. (2000). The Challenge of Good Governance for the IMF and the World Bank Themselves. *World Development*, 28(5), 823–841.

The World Bank. (2014). Statement by the Heads of the Multilateral Development Banks and the IMF on Infrastructure. Retrieved from https://www.worldbank.org/en/news/press-release/2014/11/13/statement-heads-multilateral-development-banks-imf-infrastructure

Wu, Linjun. (2015). AIIB, OBOR and Taiwan's AIIB Bid. *Prospect Journal* (14), 1–26.

Wu, Xiaohui. (2017). Friendly Competition for Co-Progressive Development: The Asian Infrastructure Investment Bank vs. the Bretton Woods Institutions. *Chinese Journal of International Law*, 16(1), 41–76.

Wu, Chien-Huei. (2018). Global Economic Governance in the Wake of Asian Infrastructure Investment Bank: Is China Remaking Bretton Woods? *Journal of World Investment and Trade*, 19(3), 542–569.

Xing, Yuqing. (2016). The Asian Infrastructure Investment Bank and China's Role in Regional Economic Governance. *East Asian Policy*, 8(2), 25–36.

Xinhua. (2010, July 12). China Unveils 1st Sovereign Credit Rating Report. *China Daily*. Retrieved from https://www.chinadaily.com.cn/china/2010-07/12/content_10092373.htm

Xinhua. (2014, March 7). Wheels in Motion for New Asian Investment Bank. *China Daily*. Retrieved from https://www.chinadaily.com.cn/business/2014-03/07/content_17331602.htm

Xu, Jiajun, & Carey, Richard. (2015). China's Development Finance: Ambition, Impact and Transparency. *IDS Policy Briefing* (92). Retrieved from http://opendocs.ids.ac.uk/opendocs/bitstream/123456789/5996/1/P92_AGID353_ChinaDevFinance_Online.pdf

Yang, Hai. (2016). The Asian Infrastructure Investment Bank and Status-Seeking: China's Foray into Global Economic Governance. *Chinese Political Science Review*, 1(4), 754–778.

Yao, Kevin. (2013, December 2). China's Dagong Sees Lower US Rating, No China Local Debt Default. *Reuters*. Retrieved from https://www.reuters.com/article/us-china-dagong/chinas-dagong-sees-lower-u-s-rating-no-china-local-debt-default-idUSBRE9B102 K20131202

Yao, Shujie, Zhang, Fan, Wang, Pan, & Luo, Dan. (2017). Location Determinants of China's Outward Foreign Direct Investment. *China & World Economy*, 25(6), 1–27.

Zakaria, Fareed. (2014, November 14). China's Growing Clout. *The Washington Post*. Retrieved from https://www.washingtonpost.com/opinions/fareed-zakaria-chinas-growing-clout/2014/11/13/fe0481f6-6b74-11e4-a31c-77759fc1eacc_story.html

Zedillo, Ernesto. (2009). *Re-Powering the World Bank for the 21st Century: Report of the High Level Commission on Modernization of World Bank Group Governance*. Washington DC: World Bank Group.

Zeng, Jinhua. (2015, March 26). Zhongfang xunqiu huo fangqi yipiao foujuequan shi weimingti [It is a Pseudo Proposition that China Seeks or Abandons the Veto Power]. *Jingji ribao [Economic Daily]*, p. 007.

Zha, Daojiong. (2015). China's Economic Diplomacy: Focusing on the Asia-Pacific Region. *China Quarterly of International Strategic Studies*, 1(1), 85–104.

Zheng, Yangpeng. (2016, January 26). Promise of a Clean, Lean and Green Institution. *The Telegraph*. Retrieved from https://www.telegraph.co.uk/sponsored/china-watch/business/12115196/promise-of-a-clean-lean-and-green-institution.html

Zheng, Jianghua, & Pan, Geping. (2017, May 7). Interview: Belgium Eyes Tapping into China's Belt and Road Initiative: Deputy PM. *Xinhua*. Retrieved from https://www.xinhuanet.com//english/2017-05/07/c_136262962.htm

Zhumabayeva, Kamila. (2016). Nazarbayev Signs Asian Infrastructure Investment Bank Ratification into Law. *The Astana Times*. Retrieved from https://astanatimes.com/2016/02/nazarbayev-signs-asian-infrastructure-investment-bank-ratification-into-law/

Zi, Han. (2009). Yahang shouren zhongguoji fuhangzhang jin liqun [ADB's First Chinese Vice President: Jin Liqun]. *Zhonghua ernu [China Profiles]* (3), 73–75.

Zweig, David. (2002). *Internationalizing China: Domestic Interests and Global Linkages*. Ithaca, New York: Cornell University Press.

Index

Note: Page numbers in *italics* indicate a figure and page numbers in **bold** indicate a table on the corresponding page.

Printed in the United States
By Bookmasters